Beyond the masks

Psychology has had a number of things to say about black and colonised peoples. *Beyond the Masks* is a book which seeks to go beyond Franz Fanon's concept of black identity as a 'white mask', placing race and gender at the centre of our understanding of identity.

Amina Mama argues that rather than simply internalising what psychological theory and dominant culture have to say about them, black women invoke collective history in a continuous struggle to counteract the racism and sexism of their cultural milieu and so to develop new subjectivities. The contradictions imposed on individuals by an oppressive social order inspire personal struggles that generate a new self-awareness and lead to social change.

Colonial and racist psychological discourses on 'the African' and 'the Negro' are located in the history of slavery and colonialism, demonstrating the complex interplay between psychological science and dominant interests. To overcome this hegemony, Amina Mama re-theorises subjectivity as a continuous creative and dynamic response to the mechanisms of domination and subjugation. Through a study of the changing consciousness of a number of black women, she uses the racialised and gendered aspects of identity as the base for a radically different conceptualisation of subjectivity itself.

Beyond the Masks is an exciting book which, using the insights of contemporary social theory, investigates the history of racist psychology and then theorises the dynamics of black femininity. It will appeal to a wide and diverse audience, including all those involved with gender politics and ethnic identity.

Amina Mama is an academic who works with a range of African and European institutions. She holds a doctorate in psychology and teaches feminist studies and gender and development studies. Her earlier book *The Hidden Struggle* (1989) was the first published study of woman abuse in Britain's black communities. Married to Somali novelist Nuruddin Farah, she has a daughter and currently resides in Kaduna.

Critical Psychology
Series editors

John Broughton
Columbia University, New York

David Ingleby
University of Utrecht

Valerie Walkerdine
Goldsmith's College, London

Since the 1960s there has been widespread disaffection with traditional approaches in psychology and talk of a 'crisis' has been endemic. At the same time, psychology has encountered influential contemporary movements such as feminism, neo-Marxism, post-structuralism and post-modernism. In this climate, various forms of 'critical psychology' have developed vigorously.

Unfortunately, such work – drawing as it does on unfamiliar intellectual traditions – is often difficult to assimilate. The aim of the Critical Psychology series is to make this exciting new body of work readily accessible to students and teachers of psychology, as well as presenting the more psychological aspects of this work to a wider social scientific audience. Specially commissioned works from leading critical writers will demonstrate the relevance of their new approaches to a wide range of current social issues.

Beyond the masks

Race, gender and subjectivity

Amina Mama

London and New York

First published 1995
by Routledge
11 New Fetter Lane, London EC4P 4EE

Simultaneously published in the USA and Canada
by Routledge
29 West 35th Street, New York, NY 10001

Typeset in Times Ten by Florencetype Ltd,
Stoodleigh, Devon

Printed and bound in England by Biddles Ltd,
Guildford and King's Lynn

British Library Cataloguing in Publication Data
A catalogue record for this book is available from the
British Library

Library of Congress Cataloguing in Publication Data
A catalogue record for this book has been requested

ISBN 0–415–03543–0 (hbk)
ISBN 0–415–03544–9 (pbk)

For Abyan and Nuruddin, with boundless love

Contents

Acknowledgements

To all the women with whom I talked and upon whose accounts my theorising relies: my thanks. Also I continue to be indebted to my parents, my brothers, and to all the friends who helped in a variety of ways when I first wrote the thesis on which this revised version is based. My gratitude to Wendy Hollway who, as my supervisor, assisted in giving shape to my ideas; and to Valerie Walkerdine who not only suggested that I turn it into a book but, believing steadfastly in my intellectual capacities, patiently waited for several years until I finished it. More specific thanks to Yaba Badoe, Charmaine Pereira, Patricia Mohammed and Kum-Kum Bhavani for their constructive remarks on earlier versions of several chapters, to Cecil Gutzmore of the Garvey-Rodney Archive, and to Pat Haward for support during the copy-editing and correcting stage. Finally I thank my husband for his perseverance and the tender support he gave me until both the book and our daughter were delivered into the world, within a week of each other. Needless to say, no one else can be credited with any weakness or inaccuracies in the text; for those I alone am responsible.

The author wishes to acknowledge permission to use the following: illustrations 1 and 2 (pp. 22 and 42) are taken from John Gabriel Stedman, *Narrative of a Five Year Expedition Against the Revolted Negroes of Surinam* (London: J. Johnson, 1796, 2 vols.); Illustration 3 (p. 92) is by permission of the Collection Photothèque du Musée de l'Homme, Paris; Illustration 4 (p. 110) is by permission of Garvey-Rodney; Illustration 5 (p. 144) is by permission of Armet Francis.

Amina Mama

Chapter 1

Introduction

Beyond the Masks is a study that explores the construction of subjectivity and puts forward a theoretical account of the processes through which subjectivities are constituted. This is undertaken through a two-fold study of black subjectivity. The first three chapters of this book are devoted to the deconstruction of the black subject construed by scientific psychology, while the remainder is devoted to developing a theoretical approach to the construction of particular post-colonial black subjectivities.

I start by examining how the western academic establishment, particularly within the discipline of psychology, has historically construed the black subject in ways that have stereotyped and derogated black people, and so upheld white supremacist regimes. I argue that the reliance of both mainstream (white-dominated) and black psychology[1] on the post-Enlightenment philosophical assumption of the human subject as a rational, unitary and fixed entity is responsible for the narrow and simplified constructions of 'the Negro' and 'the Black'. The subject of colonial and white-dominated psychological discourses concerning the African and the Negro are deconstructed, revealed to be not an objective scientific truth but rather a product of wider social conditions and the unequal power relations that have characterised white supremacist discourse and practice. I then examine the newer theorisations of identity developed by contemporary black American psychologists: theorisations that I argue have done much to redress psychological racism but that have been limited by their remaining within the empiricist paradigm.

I then set out to develop a different approach to the study and theorisation of historically racialised identities, using conceptual tools drawn from recent advances in post-structuralist and psychodynamic theory. I use the concept of subjectivity instead of the psychological terms 'identity' and 'self' to indicate my rejection of the dualistic notion of psychological and social spheres as essentially separate territories: one internal and one external to the person. Instead I regard both as being continuously constituted and changing, as being locked in a recursive relationship of mutually advancing production and change. Subjectivity is conceptualised throughout this study but for introductory purposes it is worth stating that my use of the term follows the authors of *Changing the Subject*, a leading text in post-structuralist psychology. Here subjectivity is used to refer to 'individuality and self-awareness – the condition of being a subject' (Henriques *et al.* 1984: 3). Weedon has succinctly located the concept and its usage as follows:

> The terms *subject* and *subjectivity* are central to post-structuralist theory and they mark a crucial break with humanist conceptions of the individual which are still central to western philosophy and political and social organisation. 'Subjectivity' is used to refer to the conscious and unconscious thoughts and emotions of the individual, her sense of herself and her ways of understanding her relation to the world. . . . (P)ost-structuralism proposes a subjectivity which is precarious, contradictory and in process, constantly being constituted in discourse each time we think or speak.
>
> (Weedon 1987: 32–3)

I investigate the production of subjectivity through a case study of how contemporary black women construct their own subjectivities in the particular social context of 1980s and 1990s Britain, and the role played by the contradictions of race and gender experienced in the course of their personal development. My approach looks at the historical and social material they draw on, and how they creatively transform and yet remain influenced by some of the discourses that have historically positioned black women living in Western Europe. Through my exploration of the subjectivities of a number of black women, I develop and apply a theorisation of subjectivity that does not assume a unitary, static subject at its core but instead conceptualises subjectivity as multiple, dynamic and continuously produced in the course of social relations that are themselves changing and at times contradictory.

I take the epistemological position that all knowledge is socially situated. Therefore there is no such thing as value-free social theory, and the goal of intellectual rigour can best be served not by claiming objectivity and ignoring the values underpinning one's intellectual work but rather by acknowledging the commitments, motivations and conditions that are likely to have played a part in its production. It is in keeping with this position that I now highlight some of the social and theoretical changes that have influenced this work.

BLACK POLITICS, BLACK FEMINISM

The arena of struggle that has been most central to the production of this work has been that of the black political struggles being waged outside but later carried into the academies and institutions of governance, in the years immediately prior to the Labour Party winning control of the Greater London Council.

Involvement in the black women's movement greatly heightened my awareness of the fact that questions of identity were central to the black radical and black women's politics of both the late 1970s and early 1980s. Having arrived in London in 1979, and trying to make sense of the racial and sexual dynamics of the community in which I found myself in the area of South London where I lived, I joined the black women's group nearest to my rented room in central Brixton, known at that time simply as the 'Black Women's Group' (BWG).

Brixton Black Women's Group (BBWG), as it later became known, was one of the first to be set up, established as it was in 1973 by women who had been involved in the Black Power movement organisations that mushroomed across London in the late 1960s and early 1970s. Women angered by the suppression of gender issues within the black movement had begun to hold caucus meetings at the beginning of the 1970s, before deciding to form an autonomous organisation to address the concerns of black women. Subsequently these were joined by women who felt alienated by the reluctance of the women's liberation movement (WLM) to address the realities of racism both within and beyond their ranks. Black women's groups subsequently formed in other parts of London and all over Britain. In addition to these community-based groups, many of the African women living in Britain were active through national organisations – the ZANU Women's League, the Eritrean and Ethiopian Women's Study Groups, the Black Women's Alliance of South Africa, and others.

After an initial meeting held in February 1978, a national umbrella organisation known as the Organisation for Women of Africa and African descent (OWAAD) was formed with the aim of prioritising African and Afro-Caribbean women's issues. The central committee of OWAAD produced a newsletter *FOWAAD!* and brought the various emerging local black women's organisations together at annual conferences. At the local level, black women organised political campaigns and cultural activities and serviced their communities through the establishment of women's centres, advice lines and refuges for women facing abuse. In the course of all these activities, a great many underwent a process of self-discovery and change, developing their identities in various ways, some of which are detailed in Chapters 4 to 8. At the collective level, political awareness was developed, both through campaigning work and through study and consciousness-raising activities. For example, the BBWG articulated its position as being one of black feminism as early as 1981, as is documented in a position statement published in the collective's newsletter *Speak Out*:

> The status of black women places us at the intersection of all forms of subjugation in society – racial oppression, sexual oppression and

economic exploitation. This means that we are a natural part of many different struggles – both as black people and as women . . . It is in the context of an understanding of our oppression based on sex, race and class, and the recognition of our struggle being part and parcel of the greater struggle for the liberation of all our people from all forms of oppression, that black feminism is defined for us.

(BBWG 1981)

The early history of the black women's movement and its active participation in the wider antiracist and anti-sexist struggles has been outlined elsewhere (see BBWG 1984a, Bryan *et al.* 1985, Williams 1993). What has not been fully explored is the way in which issues of identity were continuously problematic terrain within a black women's movement committed to the ideal of unity, yet faced with the reality of cultural and political diversity within its ranks. This diversity undermined the bold political proclamations of black unity and the ideal of a united, autonomous black feminist movement, and must be counted among the factors that contributed to the demise of OWAAD in 1983, only five years after its formation:

The task of uniting so many diverse and differing elements, particularly in the absence of a fundamental grounding and appreciation of the concrete experiences of each particular grouping, proved too much.

(BBWG statement, 1984b)

In the same statement, various sources of this difficulty are detailed. First among these was the problematic nature of realising the proclaimed commitment to the unity of African and Afro-Caribbean interests, when these disparate groups of women knew so little about each other and were loaded with historical prejudices and presumptions about each other. After all, until the later development of Black Studies, people of African and Caribbean descent derived whatever limited knowledge they had about each other from the same colonial and racist education systems as everyone else in the West. Asserting the 'objective reality' of unity did not automatically forge an alliance out of the very diverse subjective realities and political priorities that characterised Britain's black communities.

Within its first year the organisation began to focus on the realities of life in Britain where, by this time, approximately half of the non-white population were of Asian extraction. Before the end of 1978, OWAAD changed its name from the Organisation for Women of Africa and African Descent to become the Organisation for Women of African and Asian Descent, adopting a commitment to the unity of Afro–Caribbean and Asian women as one of its central tenets. With this shift in focus came other changes. During the annual national conferences held in 1978–82 for example, OWAAD reflected the concerns of its constituent groups in focusing more on British antiracist and feminist concerns than on anti-imperialist and African national liberation struggles. While this may have made a great deal of sense politically, it failed to ameliorate the difficulties emanating from the cultural and historical diversity of the membership. There was heightened attention to specific histories and a growing interest in exploring cultural roots, so that while political commonality was being asserted, differences in identity were being discovered. The political assertion of black unity and sisterhood was accompanied by a construction of the black woman as a unitary identity category.[2]

The inner-city disturbances of April and July 1981 overtook the black women's movement before a more thorough exploration of these and other contradictions could be undertaken. When these were followed up by mass arrests and intense community defence, members of the largest group within OWAAD, the BBWG, devoted much of its energy to the Brixton Defence Campaign: to picketing courts and police stations, to campaigning against the Scarman Inquiry,[3] and to supporting men as well as women who had been subjected to the oppressive policing and the legal injustices that preceded and followed the disturbances.

These were also the early years of municipal socialism, with the Greater London Council making resources available at community level. This led to a preoccupation with the practical activities of establishing and managing projects for black women, rather than with political activism and campaigning work. With few exceptions, many activist groups can be said to have become increasingly 'projectised', that is to say, drawn into the management of funded welfare projects, during this period. One consequence of becoming a funded project was that activists became volunteers; they had less time for intellectual and political activities as community servicing and the bureaucratic tasks that result from becoming accountable to funders took over.

By 1982, the weakened state of OWAAD, the exhaustion of a central committee that was no longer united and the increased concentration of constituent groups on local community concerns rather than national or international politics, led to the inevitable decline of the organisation. With hindsight one can see that the historical importance of the black women's movement lay in the way in which it created a new discursive space within which a great many black women were able to share and explore their identities and develop their political awareness through a collective process. In Britain at least, black feminism was first articulated within this movement.[4] Long after OWAAD itself had ceased to exist, the proliferation of new cultural forms and articulations of identity has continued in the black communities and subsequently in the wider society.

Many of the difficulties that this fledgling movement encountered were about the relationship between identity and politics, the contradictions between one's subjectivity and one's professed position. The influential feminist slogan 'the personal is the political' was generally taken as meaning that the one was the same as the other and therefore, that if one had the correct political analysis, all else would fall into place. History has demonstrated that nothing could be further from the truth. Adopting political rhetoric and symbolism, however earnestly, does not unproblematically lead to personal change.

The late 1970s and early 1980s were a period of intense engagement with class, race and gender issues. Similar processes were occurring in the antiracist struggles of ethnic minorities across Europe. These newly articulated post-colonial identities were dynamic and changing, and forced a more general reconsideration of European identities. The relationships between race and nationality were soon to be reappraised in many countries (see for example Gilroy 1987). The new black identities in particular were forged in the cauldrons of new forms of repression and resistance. In Britain it was an era of political campaigns against heavy-handed policing and the repeated deaths of young blacks in custody, of protests against immigration harassment at ports of entry and through the notorious workplace fishing raids. Community groups also organised campaigns against racism in the education system, in housing, in the health and welfare services and on the job market. Within the various community organisations, people sought to redefine themselves, to articulate what it meant to be black in Britain and to demand their rights as British citizens. Within these struggles, black people also sought to redefine themselves and their cultures positively, as proud and assertive rather than as inferior and pathological. Political change was seen as a lived reality, with personal and cultural change as an integral aspect of wider social transformation towards a racially equal society.

Assertions of black identity in the early 1980s were the psychological and cultural aspects of the post-colonial metropolitan struggle against racism and white supremacy, a struggle carried out not only on the battle-field of liberation struggles in Africa but in the imperial heartlands – in the inner cities in the belly of the beast.[5] More than this, the articulation of black identities was about changing into a different kind of human being – about changing one's consciousness of one's position in the world, about constructing new subjectivities and rejecting the disempowering legacies of centuries.

The changes within London's black communities were part of my own growing political awareness during the 1980s, and have influenced the direction and subject matter of this study, as well as forming part of its contents. The analysis and theory of subjectivity put forward in the later chapters is based on studying that ongoing process of cultural and individual change, change that was happening simultaneously within individuals and at the collective, social level.

FEMINIST STARTING POINTS

The other major influence on *Beyond the Masks* has been the emergence
and development of feminist theory and research throughout the 1970s and
1980s, and the particular engagement that has taken place between black
and mainstream feminism. At the most general level, a commitment to
women's liberation was as central to this research as the anti-imperialist
and antiracist commitments I have already discussed. At the intellectual
level, this meant a commitment to developing an approach that would not
reproduce either the racial or the gender divisions of existing knowledge
about my subject group.

I chose to base the entire project on black women's experience, not
just because I was positioned as a black woman and a feminist myself but
also because this seemed a good way to begin to redress the race and
gender inequalities being perpetuated in existing social theory, and in
work on identity and subjectivity in particular. It is therefore a black-
woman-centred piece of work. My early literature searches showed that
black women have been neglected as much by black psychologists as by
feminists. The historical material discussed in the first three chapters
therefore reveals the first sin of omission. The absence of black women
from consideration illustrates the more general marginalisation of disempowered groups within knowledge production. It is after the first three
chapters, where we leave pre-existing discourses behind and come to
develop an alternative theory of subjectivity, that black women can take
the centre stage.[6]

Feminist commitments influenced the theoretical and methodological
approach that I adopted in the early 1980s in a number of other ways
worth mentioning at the outset. The last decade has seen enormous developments in feminist theory and methodology. Some of these developments
echo the approach that I took in the initial thesis and some differ from
it in important ways. My 1982 starting points are therefore discussed here
alongside a consideration of those theoretical and methodological developments within feminist theory that have the most relevance to anyone
researching or thinking about subjectivity. While I define methodology
to include both theory and method, and would insist that the two are
intimately related, here my focus is on feminist politics and the feminist
theoretical approaches derived from feminist politics. The practical steps
of the research method that I derived from both black and feminist
political and theoretical commitments are detailed in Chapter 4, where
my own theorising on subjectivity begins.

Feminist theory has always been derived from feminist politics. Feminist
perspectives on the world imply new ways of understanding it, of making
sense of women's experience of conflict, contradiction and oppression.
Feminist scholarship has sought ways of conceptualising male power,

femininity, masculinity, sexuality and subjectivity. It has consistently emphasised the importance of women's experience in developing both politics and theory. At the level of politics this has meant forging a politics of the personal through a collective articulation of women's experience. It has meant defining women as a social group – a group that is oppressed by patriarchy and that faces the task of identifying its own concerns and struggling for liberation. The 1970s slogan 'the personal is political' provided a rallying call for women to come together to share their experiences and discover that many of the most problematic aspects of their personal lives were characteristic of other women's lives, and that these were not the product of individual circumstances or personal failings but of a social set-up that was oppressive to women. Chris Weedon puts it this way:

> Most feminists assume an integral relationship between theory and practice. Starting from the politics of the personal, in which women's subjectivities and experiences of everyday life become the site of the redefinition of patriarchal meanings and values and of resistance to them, feminism generates new theoretical perspectives from which the dominant can be criticized and new possibilities envisaged.
>
> (Weedon 1987: 6)

Before long, women's organisations across the globe had yielded a plethora of feminist world-views, and with these have emerged a multitude of feminist theories.

Feminist theory has particularly sought to challenge men's domination of the academies and the processes of knowledge production. Feminists have argued that this male domination has affected the kinds of knowledge produced, making it androcentric and incomplete. A main element of this critique has pointed to the gender assumptions underpinning social theory and the patriarchal character of these assumptions.

Feminist intellectuals have highlighted the neglect and omission of women from consideration in theory, pointing out that the theories that have claimed to address humanity have been inapplicable to women. Feminist philosophers have drawn attention to the fact that the unitary rational subject at the heart of social theories articulated and developed by 'man the scientist' has been man. Although social theory has claimed to be objective, it has been imbued with male assumptions. In other words, universalist claims have been made about knowledge that has been particular and partial. Feminist theory has therefore challenged the universalism of existing social theory and its grandiosity. As an aside, it is worth mentioning here that feminist theorists have not been alone in rejecting the possibility of grand theories of the social world, since many others have also argued that theory is always historically and culturally specific, grounded in social reality (Glaser and Strauss 1967). This is also a central tenet of postmodernism. Nor have all feminists rejected grand theory; a great many have come up with grand theories of their own, premised on a unitary female subject instead of a male one.

The objectivity claims of male scientists have been rejected as fallacious, with many arguing that no theory is value-free. Male scientists and theorists have been accused of assuming that they have a 'God's eye view' on the social world, whereas in fact they are inevitably part of it:

> (O)bjectivity turns out to be about particular and specific embodiment and definitely not about the false vision promising transcendence of all limits and responsibility.
>
> (Haraway 1989: 582)

Beyond this most general level, there have been a great many different suggestions.

Some have rejected the notions of theory and rationality altogether, dismissing them as characteristically masculine ways of thinking, masculine devices which have been used to oppress women (e.g. Daly 1979, Griffin 1984). Some have argued that we need different methodologies and concepts, that, in Audre Lorde's words, the master's tools cannot be used to dismantle the master's house (Lorde 1984). As a corollary to this, such thinkers have argued that there is an essentially different, feminine way of thinking and communicating that must be released and developed if women are to liberate themselves from patriarchy. Some have even gone so far as to reject the whole idea of theory as a male device that has been used against women, arguing that women's experience constitutes the best basis for generating knowledge, and that there is no need for any theory to mediate between experience and knowledge (Stanley and Wise 1983).

More theoretically inclined feminist thinkers have opted not to throw the baby out with the bath water. Instead they have redefined the whole idea of science and objectivity. This school of thought is transformative in that it changes the whole idea of knowledge, taking it away from the notion of disembodied or value-free truth and arguing that knowledge production can be enhanced and greater objectivity can be achieved if we recognise that knowledge cannot be absolute and universal. Haraway expresses this in the following terms:

> Feminist objectivity is about limited location and situated knowledge, not about transcendence and splitting of object and subject. It allows us to become answerable for what we learn how to see.
>
> (Haraway 1989: 583)

Early feminist theory, like early feminist politics, assumed the existence of woman as a category with common, definable interests and goals. The female subject at the heart of early feminist discourse was the archetypal

Other featured in the writings of de Beauvoir, Firestone, Greer, Millet, a unified subject that stood counterpoised to, and was oppressed by, man. Society was monolithically patriarchal and a single movement united around the common interests of the woman subject would succeed in liberating women from male domination and oppression. Mainstream feminism in the 1970s was stridently optimistic, confident that womankind, strong and united around a common cause, would challenge and overcome male domination. Feminist theorists across the social sciences wrote in universalist terms that, while polemically powerful and politically influential, assumed a unitary notion of womanhood and women's oppression, whether they wrote about psychology or the economy (for example, Barrett 1980, Chodorow 1978, Gilligan 1982, Mitchell 1974).

By the 1980s, however, it was clear on several fronts that things were not going to be that simple. Even within itself, feminism was not a single approach to women's liberation but a range of different political and theoretical perspectives, each with different and sometimes competing ways of viewing the world and women's oppression and what strategies would best overcome this. Within feminist scholarship it soon also became apparent that there was no single feminist epistemology or methodology, as had been assumed in early texts on feminist research (such as that by Stanley and Wise 1983). Feminist discourse in general was not as unitary as had previously been thought and, as a corollary to this, the female subject assumed to lie at its heart turned out not to be representative of all women. There had already been major debates between socialist, liberal and radical feminists, and between heterosexual and lesbian feminists. Now the contradictions between white and black feminists surfaced.

I have already noted that black feminist politics emerged to redress the inadequacies of the pre-existing black and women's movements, both of which insisted on prioritising either race or gender and so occluding the experiences and interests of those who felt both simultaneously and felt themselves to be a part of all these struggles – black women. For white feminists, as for black men, the discontents of black women were potentially divisive. Both sought to exercise their hegemony over black women and both were primarily concerned with preserving the unity and focus that their political discourse appeared to depend on. White women, having defined themselves as victims of male oppression, at first found it inconceivable that they could also be accused of being oppressive to others. Their initial reactions to the attempts of black women to challenge the evident hegemony of the white majority were often highly defensive and at times antagonistic. Some continued to ignore the whole issue of race, seeing it as something for black women to sort out, and many continued to have difficulty with admitting that feminists could be racist.[7]

Yet it was now patently clear that black women's subjective experience and political interests were not identical with those that had been articulated as women's concerns by the dominant white majority within the Women's Liberation Movement (WLM). Sometimes these interests were common interests but very often black and white women not only had different interests but antithetical ones. At the beginning of the 1980s, Carby (1982) was able to detail some of these differences. While white women were campaigning for abortion rights, many black women were being sterilised without their consent and having their fertility curtailed through the use of injectible contraceptives. Although many black women also needed the right to abortion, they also wanted to be in a position to bear and raise healthy children. This challenge to the prevailing call for abortion rights resounded on both sides of the Atlantic and eventually led to the terms of the debate shifting, so that it became an international feminist struggle for 'reproductive rights' that would address the need for women to have freedom of choice and control over all aspects of their reproductive capacity (see Davis 1981: 202–21).

In a similar vein, while white housewives were fighting for the right to work, black women were suffering from chronic overwork, in exploitative and under-remunerated jobs, often as the sole breadwinners in their households (Mama 1984). The debate over women and work and the terms of the domestic labour debate have been completely transformed by the different situations of black women, and by working women from all over the developing and developed world.

Problems also arose over the ways in which the white WLM conceptualised sexuality, particularly with the focus on pornography and male violence as lying at the root of women's oppression. Racist discourses had already cast black men as violent rapists, and black women were concerned to challenge this depiction. Black women were only too well aware of their own sexual exploitation but at the same time found it necessary to challenge the way in which racist discourses cast black men as the archetypal violators of women. Black women had difficulty with the thesis that violence was essentially masculine, knowing as they did that black men were themselves frequently subjected to sexual abuse and humiliation, even though they were commonly portrayed as hypersexual studs. Across the Atlantic, African-American women were drawing attention to the history of lynching and castration of black men, and the participation of white women as well as white men in the construction of the black man as a sexually violent beast (Davis 1981, 1990). Also in the field of sexuality, radical feminist proclamations that 'feminism is the theory, lesbianism is the practice' alienated the many black women who were more concerned with improving relations between themselves and black men than with coming out as lesbians. Black women therefore set out to create a non-racist space in which to address the very real problems in gender relations and the abuse and sexual exploitation of black women by men.[8]

In international forums, women from Africa, Asia, Latin America and the Caribbean were challenging the domination of the scene by white western women, challenging such domination as imperialistic, and articulating their own concerns in no uncertain terms. The notion of feminism as something that more advanced western women had and could impart to their 'underprivileged sisters' as an exercise in global sisterhood was roundly challenged during the United Nations Decade for Women, and subsequently by studies which have documented the long history of women's resistance to male domination in many so-called underdeveloped parts of the world; a plethora of studies have debunked the notion of feminism as an exclusively white, western product (see Jayawardena 1986). In the early 1980s I coined the term 'imperial feminism' to indicate the much denied historical participation of white women in the colonial and racial domination of black people, even in the course of the struggle for their own liberation as women, and to isolate the more imperialistic elements within the international women's movement (a usage taken up by Amos and Parmar 1984).

At the epistemological level, overcoming the assumption of the white, western female subject at the heart of feminist theory has not been a simple affair. Mohanty (1988), writing as a non-western feminist, pointed out that the speaking subject of feminist epistemology is still invariably a western woman and that as a result of this, non-western women are homogenised into a single category, as 'Third World women', who are once again spoken about rather than speaking. She highlights the consequences of this for feminist scholarship:

> Western feminists alone become the true 'subjects' of this counter-history. Third World women, on the other hand, never rise above the debilitating generality of their 'object' status.
>
> (Mohanty 1988: 80)

Some feminist thinkers have responded to the critiques of non-western feminists by advocating that feminist thought should emanate from the least powerful groups of women, given that it is now possible to speak of a feminist élite. Greater objectivity is then not only a question of acknowledging the situational and positioned character of knowledge but also one of reversing the status quo in order to see the world from the viewpoint of the most oppressed. Such a view confers epistemic privilege on those who are disempowered and marginalised in our societies (Haraway 1988, Harding 1991).[9]

Narayan (1989) ascribed the 'epistemic advantage' of non-western women to the fact that they often inhabit more than one context simultaneously, in a way that members of dominant groups cannot readily achieve. Epistemic advantage is a result of the historical inequality that has imposed the western world-view on non-western people, while the reverse has not occurred. She goes on to point out that multiplicity of experience does not necessarily mean that one decided to inhabit two contexts critically. More often, people faced with this situation suppress one aspect in order to live more comfortably in one or other, since the two are often incompatible. Alternatively they may dichotomise their lives, so that they are 'western' in some spheres of activity and 'traditional' in others. For those who do choose to inhabit two worlds critically, Narayan injects a cautionary note, pointing out that there is often the price of a sense of unbelonging or alienation from both, a sense which can be more or less transient, or which can become overwhelming and disempowering.

In this study I take the view that multiplicity rather than duality characterises metropolitan life and that most people inhabit not one but several contexts simultaneously, so that this has become a normal state of affairs in a post-colonial world. This is a world in which no context is as fixed or static as is assumed by the manichean and dualistic colonial frameworks that counterpoise West and non-West. Instead, cultural and social conditions are undergoing constant change and exchange. In this context it becomes necessary to use multiplicity of vision in intellectual work – to concretise it in research practice and theory-building.

By the early 1990s the notion of woman as a unitary category was no longer holding sway among activists, and contemporary feminist theory (for example, Butler 1990, Nicholson 1990, Weedon 1987) now constantly interrogates the unitarist and ethnocentric premises of earlier feminism. This was not just a result of black and non-western feminist interventions but also an influence of post-structuralist thought. Here too the notion of a unitary subject at the heart of western philosophy was being challenged. The set of dualistic oppositions – of men and women, of black and white, of western and non-western – was also recognised as inadequate in the post-colonial world in which there are black Europeans, white Africans and all manner of cultural, racial and philosophical combinations.

My own experiences as a feminist raised and educated as both African and European, as both black and white, and with intimate connections to a good many other places and peoples besides these has always made a nonsense of all these dualisms. Throughout this work I view the histori-cally produced category 'black women' with the eyes of an insider and an outsider, seeing multiplicity and differences between and within individ-uals and the struggle to construct coherences and commonalities out of a potentially infinite set of possibilities.

To sum up this discussion, we can say that feminists have argued unan-imously for the importance and validity of subjective experience and for women's experience in particular to be taken seriously in social analysis and theory. In so doing they have challenged the dualistic opposition of objective to subjective and the notion of the unitary, universal subject. For feminist theorists, greater attention to subjective factors in research processes is a way of ensuring greater objectivity. When the researched people are members of an already oppressed group – as black and colonised people and women are – then this objectification has acted to perpetuate existing power relations and definitions of reality, and with these the subjection of the oppressed. Feminist and anti-imperialist theorists have therefore insisted that subordinated groups be empowered to articulate their realities and become subjects rather than objects in knowledge–production processes. In the process, the dualistic framework which counterposes black and white, western and non-western, masculine and feminine, has also proved to be inadequate to the complexities of post-colonial realities. Starting from women's lives has come to mean starting from all women's lives, insisting on the multiplicity of women and rejecting absolutism and foundationalist theories in favour of seeking and revealing new knowledges and truths.

This book is about the centrality of historical and individual experience in the construction of subjectivity. None the less, I do not take the view that it is enough simply to describe experience. The specific experiences of the research participants are not the experiences of all women and, for this reason alone, the general processes through which subjectivities are constituted need to be theorised, if this work is to have relevance to anyone other than the actual participants. In other words, I share the view that:

> (I)t is not enough to refer unproblematically to experience ... we need a theory of the relationship between experience, social power and resistance. ... Theory must be able to address women's experience by showing where it comes from and how it relates to material social practices and the power relations which structure them.
>
> (Weedon 1987: 8)

At one level to theorise is to generalise. I set out to make some generalisations about the processes through which individuals and social groups become subjects, and about the resources that black people utilise in overcoming racist discourses, individually and collectively. I set out to generate theory because of my conviction that describing and sharing experience, however enriching and important this may be, will not be enough to transform our oppressive social relations.

NOTES

1 Black psychology is used to mean psychology conducted by black psychologists in Europe and North America. Black psychologists distinguish black psychology from white-dominated mainstream psychology, and have generally been concerned with developing a black-centred perspective, with addressing the

needs and concerns of black communities, and with being antiracist in their approach (see Chapter 3).

2 This unitary identity category is evident in *The Heart of the Race: Black Women's Lives in Britain*. The three authors use the term 'we' throughout the narrative, to designate the collective identity of black women. However, the fact is that they are specifically speaking as the 'Afro-Caribbean' subset of black women who have their historical roots in the Caribbean (Bryan *et al.* 1985).

3 The Scarman Inquiry was the official investigation into the possible causes of the Brixton disturbances, led by Lord Scarman, and viewed by many members of the local community as an attempt to whitewash the police brutality and racial injustices which were seen to be the real causes.

4 It should be said here that not all black women accepted the appellation 'feminist', some preferring Alice Walker's term 'womanist', and not all those involved wanted to be referred to as 'black', some preferring the American term 'women of colour'.

5 James and Harris (eds) 1993 provide another useful collection covering this period in Britain.

6 In terms of structure of this book, Chapters 2 and 3 could just as well have examined psychological discourses on women, but for the fact that a number of feminist critiques and a growing number of volumes on feminist psychology are already available, whereas very little work has been done on psychology's construction of black and colonised people. The feminist works are as race-blind and ethnocentric as studies of the colonised and the black subject have been gender-blind and androcentric.

7 Barret and MacIntosh's (1985) response to the special issue of *Feminist Review* devoted to black feminism illustrates the reaction of many to the charge of racism within feminism. They reject the possibility of feminists being racist, choosing instead to discuss and acknowledge 'ethnocentrism' within the western women's movement.

8 Black women have been quick to challenge racism against black men, but as Michel Wallace (1979) observed, black men have often not challenged the racist myth of the black woman as a castrating matriarch. Although she addresses the African-American experience, black men on both sides of the Atlantic reacted to her work on this subject with enormous hostility.

9 Harding takes this position to its logical conclusion when she comes to examine the situation of members of dominant groups who wish to contribute to the production of liberatory knowledge. She concludes her book by advocating that they reinvent themselves as Other. This she explains as meaning that they should uncover and utilise the repressed aspects of themselves in their endeavours.

Chapter 2

Enslaving the soul of the Other

INTRODUCTION

In this chapter we shall take a critical look at the way in which the African has been construed as a subject in the context of African–European relations, as these have emerged during the period of transatlantic slavery and colonialism. The focus will be on the role played by the emergent western sciences of the mind – psychology and psychiatry – in propagating particular ideas about the black peoples whom the Europeans encountered on the African continent. The picture is not a simple one, for the relations that developed between Africans and Europeans not only varied widely, but also changed dramatically in the course of the seventeenth to twentieth centuries, whether one is considering the changes in trading and economic relations, political relations or social and psychological relations.[1]

It is worth pointing out that enslavement and colonisation did not only materially exploit and politically subordinate African resources and ways of life but at the same time transformed and subjected Africans to the imaginings and caprices of imperial culture and psychology. Colonisation was carried out by an expansionist regime that owed its success to both military and mercantile power, which it ruthlessly deployed in the practice of trade, conquest and enslavement. So it was that the imperial powers were able to assert, maintain and reproduce white supremacy across the globe. White supremacy can thus be conceptualised as a set of discourses and practices that subjugated non-European people and cast them in the position of subjected Others, while it advanced the interests of European nations. The set of knowledges and ideas about Africans devised by Europeans in the context of imperialism has been termed 'Africanist discourses' (see, for example, Miller 1986).

It is useful to distinguish these from 'pan-Africanist' ideas, namely the set of ideas developed by diasporan and continental Africans, often in response to western Africanist discourses. One main difference between the two is that while Africanist discourses have as their subject the objectified African as 'Other', pan-Africanist discourse has the African subject at its centre and is articulated by Africans. This is not to deny that they have often had overlapping ideas but the fact is that pan-Africanism in its various guises has developed in reaction to imperialism and racism, and has sought fundamentally to challenge western domination, including the construction of African subjects as the objectified Other of the European imagination.[2] In this chapter I will argue that ideas about the minds of Africans, and about the sanity and insanity of both Africans and Europeans, have been integral to the subordination of the enslaved and the colonised.

Some of the earliest notions about Africans have been documented by Miller (1986) in a detailed text aptly titled *Blank Darkness*, in which he addresses the French tradition of Africanist discourse. The sources of French notions of Africa and Africans are traced back as far as Homer, for whom Ethiopia was a remote place found at the extremes of the universe, a place of people who had discovered the gods and where the arts of banqueting, worship and sacrifice were practised. This idealisation is subsequently elaborated by both Herodotus and Diodorus, who describe not only people of great nobility but also more savage and monstrous tribes of 'dog-eared' and 'headless' men, some of whom were said to sport eyes in their chests. Miller observes the fantastic and strangely repetitive character of these fantasies, noting the persistent ambivalence which characterised the ancient Greek portrayals of Africans, portrayals which both ennobled and dehumanised black people.

Many centuries later, in 1677, a Dutchman was to report sighting a black man with a tail one foot long. This apparently fanciful notion was to be repeated by a number of others, all of whose reports propagated the fifteenth-century theme of Africa as a place full of non-human monsters, idolatry, barbarism and unbridled sexuality. Portrayals of Abyssinian kings too appear to have been highly mythological, reflecting ambivalent and contradictory responses to this capital of early Christendom. Figures such as the Christian king Prester John and his son Zaga-Christ became rich sources of fictions that were so intertwined with fact that truth and falsity became indistinguishable. Miller notes that even the tombstone of Zaga-Christ reflects this uncertainty, for upon it are carved the words:

> Here lies the king of Ethiopia
> The original or the copy.
>
> (Miller 1986: 38)

The constant theme that Miller identifies is that of nullity; Africa was a blank canvas on to which the fantasies of the Europeans might easily be inscribed, whether they reiterated the Homeric dream or the nightmares of Herodotus (Miller 1986).

A similar polarisation of Africanist thinking is evident in the eighteenth- and nineteenth-century writings of the European scientists, philosophers and poets. Jean-Jacques Rousseau's portrayal of 'primitive' people as existing in a state of nobility and freedom of spirit, unburdened by the exigencies and stresses of civilisation, represented the idealisation of 'primitive' life, a romanticisation that developed into the 'noble savage' idea and which was echoed in the writings of Voltaire and, later, the poetry of Baudelaire, and in Bougainville's depictions of Tahitian 'natives'.[3] Miller notes that for Baudelaire, 'Le beau est toujours bizarre' (the beautiful is always bizarre), and in the world of aesthetics, the French arrogated to themselves the central role of crafting the artistic raw material supplied by the uncivilised world, or as he puts it, 'The Barbarian is thus explicitly seen as the raw material in the economy of beauty' (Miller 1986: 93). Within this myth, the difference of the primitive was lauded and exoticised, and there were no pretensions to equality.

The opposing mythology with which Hobbes is often credited is that of pre-European Africa as a timeless place in which there was no art, letters or social organisation but instead only fear, danger and violent death. The French scholar Gobineau, who produced what is now seen by many as the master text of nineteenth-century European racism, *L'essai sur l'inégalité des races humaines*, shared Baudelaire's view of Africa as a source of the arts, but without any of Baudelaire's subtlety. For Gobineau this was a way of saying that Africans were completely devoid of intelligence. He regarded black people as being unable to think in any reflective manner and endowed them with an 'imagination' that he saw as being rooted in their blood. Art, in this scheme of things, was the antithesis of intellect, a thoughtless activity requiring only the reflection of sensuality. For Gobineau and his followers, Africans lacked the sophisticated linguistic skills, the scientific and political faculties of the Europeans, and were sentimental, affectionate and best suited to dancing, dressing up and singing. As such, and in keeping with the prevailing ideas concerning the inferiority of women, they were identified as the females in the human family.

During this period we can discern two schools of opinion, one exemplified by Hume, the other by Rousseau. The first is a wholly negative portrayal of the savage as a subhuman and tormented creature, worthy only of pity or contempt. This is a pathological construction, of the Negro as a degraded variant of the species. The second is the 'noble savage school' which utilises the African as a vehicle for that particularly European Judaeo-Christian nostalgia for an imaginary 'lost innocence' which intensified during the Enlightenment and the Industrial Revolution. Whereas both schools focus on racial differences, they differ on some key questions. On the question of madness, for example, Bougainville and Rousseau assumed that 'primitives' could not suffer from insanity, living as they did in joyous and unrepressed harmony with their environment, whereas for the others they were inherently mentally defective, a more pernicious notion which was to persist into twentieth-century psychiatry.

The remainder of this chapter will consider the recursive relationship between these competing and contradictory depictions of the African and the practices of slavery and colonialism.

PSYCHOLOGY CONSTRUCTS THE SLAVE IN THE NEW WORLD

Until the eighteenth century, America was a slave society, which placed Africans in complete subordination to the white 'master race', a subordination that was upheld by one of the most brutal regimes of punishment and coercion in human history. The white masters expected their slaves to accept the order they had created and imposed, not least because the penalties for resistance were so extremely harsh. None the less, while a great many lived out their fate as slaves, the appearance of outbreaks of resistance led whites to speculate on the possible sources of such un-believable recalcitrance; recalcitrance that persisted despite the use of an arsenal of repressive techniques (including the regular use of castration, flogging, amputation and summary execution). One version of the history of psychiatry has it that it was the sheer persistence of slave resistance that led the mental scientists of the time therefore to conclude that resis-tance itself must be the result of mental disease, an ailment of the brain that they named *drapetomania*, the main symptom of which was an incur-able urge to run away. Similarly, an ailment termed *dysesthesia Aethiopica* only affected slaves, causing those smitten by it to cease being faithful and happy-go-lucky, and to begin to slight their work and raise distur-bances with their overseers (Thomas and Sillen 1974).

It is clear that the invention of such slave-specific ailments served to naturalise slavery as the normal and happy state for blacks and to pathologise the behaviour of those who resisted and refused to resign themselves to their enslaved status. The alternative reading of slave 'symptomatology' as behaviour that was in fact generated by the brutality of the system was not in vogue at the time.[4] *Drapetomania* made more sense within the world-view of the slave holders. As they were significantly outnumbered by their slaves in many areas, it must also have performed the psychological assistance of soothing white fears of insurrection.

Examples such as these furnish us with some of the most transparent coincidences between scientific discourse and the racist *zeitgeist* of the wider society, with science rationalising social practices (in this case the cruel repression of slaves) and so consolidating a particular regime. Not only was white supremacy reaffirmed and sustained but black resistance to it was rendered pathological. This account differs from conspiracy theory in so far as it looks at the micro-mechanics of repression as it was reproduced from day to day.

For a great many years to come, psychological theories, both academic and lay, were to construct 'the Negro' in ways which concentrated on the malaise and pathology of the mind of the black man, thus deflecting attention from the injustices of racism.[5] The practices that accompanied and enforced slavery, and the apparent imperfections of the system, generated new quandaries and new needs for answers and explanations. Mental health scientists were among the assortment of phrenologists, biologists, geneticists and physical anthropologists who obliged by coming up with new truth-claims which constructed 'the Negro' according to their own desire and design. Not only was the Negro slave considered to be intellectually and morally inferior to the white man, he was also thought to be prone to particular pathologies. At that time, mental illness was conceptualised mainly in terms of moral degeneracy, so Negroes were expected to exhibit more lurid forms of mental disturbance.

Insane slaves were for the most part dealt with by their owners, presumably to avoid the cost of sending them to the mental hospitals that were being established in the late eighteenth and early nineteenth centuries. The only hospital to accept black people at all appears to have been the Eastern State Hospital established in Williamsburg, Virginia, in 1774; it was the only one which did not specifically exclude Negroes. The majority of asylums did not at that time accept black people at all and most of those black people unfortunate enough to be designated as insane were locked away in gaols and poorhouses, a practice as widespread in the northern states of the Union as in the slave-holding South (Prudhomme and Musto 1973).

The importation of slaves was outlawed in 1788 and over the ensuing eighty years the practice of keeping slaves was to become a major site of contestation, during which the American Civil War would take place. The final proclamation of the emancipation of all remaining slaves was not issued until 1863.

In 1869, shortly after the end of the Civil War, Central State hospital was established in Virginia, and here an old brickhouse was converted to accommodate Negroes, making it the first provision intended for black people. Little wonder then that it was immediately filled with unfortunate individuals who had until then been held in the local prisons and gaolhouses (Prudhomme and Musto 1973). All manner of arguments about black mental health appear during the nineteenth and early twentieth centuries, providing further examples of the relationship between science and maintenance of domination. During the mid-nineteenth century, when the battle over emancipation was still raging, racial differences were not just of academic interest to the scientific establishment. On the other side of the Atlantic, Gobineau produced his treatise on racial difference, and influential medical journals everywhere began to present catalogues of evidence that differences in skin pigmentation were accompanied by differences in brain size, musculature, nerves, membranes, sexual organs.

Numerous dissections were performed on the bodies of Africans, in order to draw comparisons between black people and apes, between criminals and 'lower races' and the mentally subnormal. Physicians argued that treating the diseases of the Negro required special expertise.[6] Negro inferiority was obsessively asserted again and again, with all the weight of the new scientific measurements and calibrations, with all the diagnostic powers of psychiatrists and doctors specialising in the pathologies that were said to blight the Negro.

Given that statistics were just coming into vogue as a new means of ascertaining the truth, the new techniques were deployed to demonstrate scientifically the pathological inferiority of black people. To the great discomfort of the establishment, however, early statistical surveys showed Indians and Negroes to have much *lower* rates of mental illness than white Americans. Theories of mental health had until that time concentrated on moral and religious factors in insanity, a framework which assumed that there would be *higher* rates of insanity among 'morally degenerate' groups, black people included. The implications of the low rates of mental illness among black people created such a furore that the source of madness itself was entirely redefined. It was to the new biological sciences that the establishment now turned. Insanity ceased to be associated with moral degeneracy and instead increasingly attributed to organic sources in the brain. Madness now became linked to 'evolutionary complexity' rather than degeneracy, and mental illness was re-theorised as an unavoidable result of the stresses of being civilised, as a by-product of the greater sensitivity and creativity of the white race. In a re-hash of noble savage ideas, black people's brains were now said to be too simple and retarded to be affected, and their apparent lack of insanity was taken as being further evidence of mental inferiority.

The new statistical methods were unashamedly deployed to bolster the anti-abolitionist cause. The 1840 census went so far as to manufacture regional variations among black people, so that it presented Southern blacks (mostly still enslaved at this time) as having lower rates of insanity than freed Northern blacks. Anti-abolitionists then used such 'facts' to argue that black people were constitutionally unfit for freedom, and that it was in the best interests of all that slavery should be continued. Many of those in support of abolition were stumped by this apparently factual evidence, and those who refused to be defeated by it were to be ignored for some time to come. For example, in 1842 Jarvis found the 1840 census figures to be inaccurate, if not completely bogus. He found that in the Northern state of Maine, where the highest rate of black mental illness had been found (1 in 14 blacks had been reported as mentally ill), there were no black people at all. The fact that Jarvis's findings were ignored by an ensuing Congressional inquiry is a clear example of the way in which some knowledges gain credence over others, as and when conditions demand.

Arguments about how damaging liberation was going to be for the Negro continued to abound. Thirty years after emancipation there were still those who construed slavery as a golden age for black people, scientists such as Dr A. Witmer who is on record as saying:

> Previous to their emancipation, the health and morals of the slaves were carefully preserved and inebriety, excessive venery and venereal diseases were closely guarded against; since their liberation, through overindulgence, exposure and ignorance of the laws of health, many have suffered from the effects of these fruitful causes of insanity.
>
> (cited in Prudhomme and Musto 1973: 37)

By the late nineteenth century, mental illness was almost universally attributed to organic causes. Where the 'stress of civilisation' argument could have led to the conclusion that increasing rates of mental illness meant that black people were indeed becoming civilised, others cited new arguments which were to do with measurements of skulls and ideas about 'earlier cranial closure', 'fewer cortical layers' and other constitutional fabrications. All argued that black people were biologically inferior to white people and therefore unlikely ever to adjust to freedom.

Fears of contamination and the unhealthy preoccupation with racial purity evident in early medical science also fuelled early psychological discourse on black people. Carl Gustav Jung would have probably found himself extremely unpopular if he had been in America when, in 1910, he postulated the existence of an 'American complex', which he thought to have been caused in Americans by their living in close proximity to the inferior races, most notably the Negroes, a sort of 'drag-down' effect. One might have thought that daily involvement in upholding the brutalities of racism would be more likely to cause psychological damage than mere proximity to black and Amerindian peoples. After all, Jung wrote at a time when, although slavery had been condemned, the public lynching of blacks was still a common white pastime. Needless to say, this was not one of the symptomatic behaviours he identified as cause for concern and he makes no mention of any guilt complex. None the less he was among the earliest theoreticians to consider the effects of relations between the races on the psychology of *white* people. This aspect was to be ignored for a great many years to come, for throughout the first half of the twentieth century, attention was to centre on examining the damaging effects of white racism on black mental life (see Chapter 3).

Evarts (in 1913) and Lind (in 1913–14) shared Jung's excitement about the opportunity for study afforded by the intimate coexistence of whites and Negroes. In keeping with the ontological approach of psychoanalysis, and the Darwinian theory of human evolution from low to higher stages, they set out to investigate the psychology of races assumed to be at a lower evolutionary level. Studies of 'the Negro' were therefore conducted in the hope of producing phylogenetic evidence for the stages model of development that had already been developed by Freud.

Lind (1913) identified a peculiarly Negro complex which he referred to as a 'colour complex' and viewed as resulting from white domination. He derived his ideas from his observation that the Negroes he came into contact with assumed God to be white, and fantasised that after death their black skins were cast off at the entrance to heaven. Lind further postulated that all those Negroes who exhibited the opposite pattern, by insisting (as the Garveyites and the Universal Negro Improvement Association were soon to do) that God and the angels were black, suggested 'a note of defiance' and were no more than the exceptions that proved the rule. While he did note that not all black people were psychotic, he found the 'Negro complex' central to virtually all the mental abnormalities that manifested themselves.[7]

We can conclude from this discussion that by and large, early psychology constructed the Negro as a unitary subject, in simplistic and obviously expedient ways, producing imaginary notions which reaffirmed a status quo in which only white people had the power to define, and to articulate knowledges that were taken as scientific truths. The effective suppression of any contrary evidence that emerged (e.g. that of Jarvis) illustrates the interplays that occurred between the knowledge produced (the psychology of the Negro), the dominant social order (of white supremacy) and the practice (of slavery, of medicine). Although times were changing, the dynamic interplay between knowledge, power and practice, which upheld a particular regime, was to continue as that regime was gradually subverted. Jarvis may have been ignored in 1842 but the Emancipation Proclamation was still issued on 1 January 1865, the result of a coalescence of forces too numerous to list here. The process of change was to continue into the twentieth century but with psychology and psychiatry continuing to play a contradictory role in generating knowledges about black mental life, as we shall see in the following chapter. But before moving into the modern post-slavery and post-colonial period, let us examine what was happening in the field of psychology in the African colonies, and how this resonated with the ideas being propounded in Europe and the Americas.

IT TOOK MORE THAN THE MAXIM GUN: PSYCHOLOGY IN THE AFRICAN COLONIES

The links between the Negro psychology that emerged in the slavery-based societies of the West and the psychology of the colonised Africans which developed in the colonies are worth considering. Studies of black Americans make frequent reference to African origins, whether this be to highlight the innocence or the depredation of black people. What all such references have in common is simplistic assumptions about Africa. Africa is invariably construed as a jungle inhabited by primeval tribes, for whom time is arrested and development inconceivable. Evidence that contradicts this depiction of Africa and her peoples is attributed to outside influences or viewed as exceptional. Even black psychology, albeit for different reasons, refers to a simplified Africa (see Chapter 3). For black people worldwide, eternal Mother Africa has been viewed as the source of an essential African culture and philosophy, from which roots can be replenished and identities reinvigorated.

The facts are very different. While American Negroes were experiencing slavery, great changes were also occurring on the continent from which they had been taken. However, the profound changes in the culture and psychology of African peoples have not been the subject of colonial psychology. Instead, here too a racial paradigm has masked the complex realities of the colonisation process and led 'the African' to be construed in ways that are, in the end, not very different from American constructions of 'the Negro'. Indeed one can argue that the one has been used to feed and sustain the other. None the less, the practical exigencies of colonisation and colonial rule were different from those directing the truth-claims of scientists working in antebellum Southern states of America, and this has directed the production of knowledge concerning the African mind along different routes.

Scientific interest in the psychology of Africans dates back to the beginning of the colonial incursions into the continent. In the introduction I noted how Africa, construed as the dark continent, functioned largely as a repository for white fantasies and self-discovery, as is apparent in both early and late colonial literature. By the nineteenth century, the 'blank darkness' of early reports was being filled in, not so much with factual or anthropological knowledge about Africans or dream-like fantasies but with conjectures that emanated from the emotional, political and administrative needs of colonisers whose role it was to govern the colonies.

During the earlier phases of colonialism, which took the form of slave trading and military conquest, it had mattered little to the Europeans what went through the minds of Africans. Practically speaking, there was little reason for the colonisers to consider whether they even had minds as such. The superiority of military hardware, combined with an unquestioning conviction that the mighty western civilisation had a divine mission to conquer and rule, simply overruled any need to consider whether indigenous cultures existed, or whether these constituted a source of resistance. This situation persisted into the twentieth century, upheld by the findings of various theologians and anthropologists. Raoul Allier, eminent Protestant theologian, typifies the overt nineteenth-century racial values that still prevailed in the 1920s:

The negro is content with vague[r] ideas, he [does not] allow himself to be troubled by the flagrant contradictions which they contain. He is not precise, does not reason, knows nothing of logic, does not go so closely into things ... these negroes have no theories: they have not even convictions, only habits and traditions.

(Allier 1929: 27)

Belief in the universality of humanity was an anathema to Allier and his cohorts. He attacked the noble savage school of thought:

To picture the life of uncivilised man as a joyous idyll, cadenced by the jerky beating of the tom-tom and the frenzied gesticulations of the bamboula, is to confess that we have not taken the trouble to examine into his terror-stricken soul.

(Allier 1929: 20)

For Allier, Africans were 'backward individuals who know nothing of our culture and whose customs may at times border upon bestiality' (Allier 1929: 21). For him it was not a question of education or development but one of radical difference between 'civilised' and 'uncivilised' mentalities. He took it upon himself to challenge the theory of the noble savage and the postulates of those whom he accused of making the doctrine of the universality of man proverbial instead of supporting white supremacy.

During the period of colonial rule, missionaries and evangelists were among those colonialists who first realised the importance of penetrating the minds of Africans. Motivated by more than a mere lust for military power or crude economic ambitions, these servants of the Church had loftier goals. Many of the missionaries who were so deeply concerned to convert and uplift the 'heathen' found their good intentions thwarted by the existence of complex and diverse religious and cultural systems. They correctly identified these as being at the heart of the resistance many Africans showed towards conversion. The unwillingness of the natives to 'see the light' piqued their curiosity and provoked not only prayers but also research and reflection. Reverend Father Placide Tempels, a Belgian missionary who spent many years in the Congo in the first half of this century, was well aware of the importance and political implications of his work *Bantu Philosophy*. He clearly stated that it:

concerns all colonials, especially those whose duty is to hold administrative or judicial office among African people; all those who are concerning themselves with a felicitous development of tribal law, in short, it concerns all who wish to civilise, educate and raise the Bantu.

(Tempels 1959: 23)

In other words, Tempels saw that administration and regulation required an understanding of the mental life of the target group.[8] His insight was as much the result of changing historical conditions as of an evangelical agenda. In the Belgian Congo, as elsewhere in Africa, colonial administrations were being established, and these increasingly sought to involve Africans in more than mere brute labour. A class of collaborators was needed, intermediaries and junior administrators who would further the governing of African societies by European order. A more benevolent, paternalistic style of domination was a more effective way to achieve this.

Missionaries, until then more of an irritation to the colonial administrators, because of their dedication to saving the souls of the natives, now proved to be ideal vehicles for this new approach. For in their quest to convert the 'heathen', missionaries necessarily focused on the psychology and cultural life of their target group. Our well-intentioned Reverend Father expressed his frustration at the failure of the Belgians really to penetrate the minds and hearts of the Africans:

> How many fully civilised persons or evolues can we count amongst the natives of the Congo? Of *deracinés* and degenerates the number is legion. . . . The majority however remain *muntu* under a light coating of white imitation.
>
> (Tempels 1959: 27)

Father Tempels was, despite his obvious historical and racial location, a man far ahead of his times in his conviction that 'Bantus' *had* a philosophy, at a time when scientists were insisting that Africans had inferior brains. In many ways his work pioneered the study of African philosophy, at least in Francophone Africa. The position he took in asserting that there was such a thing as an African philosophy has continued to feature in contemporary debates.[9]

My argument that the African mind became a subject for scientific research at exactly the time when the continuing development of colonial rule and an increasingly industrialised labour market generated new administrative and regulative needs, casts new light on the development of ethnological interest in psychology. The development of anthropology as 'the handmaiden of imperialism' has already been well documented, and has highlighted the influence of colonial interests and concerns on both the subject matter and the methodological assumptions of colonial social science (see, for example, Ake 1979, Huizer and Mannheim 1979). The high level of interest that developed in the psychology of the so-called primitive races can be understood as an integral part of the changing form of imperialism.[10] Anthropologists, ethnologists, ethnopsychologists and ethnopsychiatrists followed the explorers, merchants, soldiers and missionaries. Most of them used what can best be described as a 'tribal paradigm' which treated dynamic and changing African societies as if they were static, ahistorical, atomised units, ignoring the profound impact of colonisation and the complexity and multiplicity of societies which had evolved over thousands of years, in constant contact with other civilisations. Isolated and necessarily increasingly remote communities were used to typify Africa – an Africa constructed within this limiting framework and which was more a product of western imagination and projection than anything else. Ethnopsychiatry came into being as the psychiatry of this imaginary Other, and owes much to both colonial medicine and anthropology.

Vaughan (1991), in her insightful study of colonial medicine, notes that although psychiatry in Africa was introduced by the colonial powers, it evolved under conditions very different from those which prevailed in Europe. The most obvious difference was the lack of resources for mental health provision, so that there was never a period comparable to the 'great confinement' which took place in eighteenth- and nineteenth-century Europe, during which all categories of those deemed socially undesirable were confined in asylums and poorhouses (Foucault 1967). In Europe the whole emphasis of psychiatry was on distinguishing the 'abnormal' from the 'normal' but in Africa a very different situation existed. Here the European psychiatrist, confronted as he was with a plethora of diverse cultures of which he had no real knowledge or understanding, found himself unprepared to make this kind of differentiation.

This may explain why by the 1960s major studies found it necessary to devote some of their resources to establishing at least some basic facts about the societies in which they were conducting psychiatric practice and research. Teams at the Fann Hospital in Dakar and the Aro Community Hospital in Nigeria, for example, both included social scientists as well as medical researchers and local informants (Collignon 1982, Leighton *et al.* 1963). Despite these efforts, colonial ideas about the African mind were heavily influenced by early physical anthropology and phrenology. They retained and developed the tribal paradigm, polarising it into two schools of thought: one insisting that there were essential differences between Africans and Europeans rooted in predetermining ethno-biological factors, and the other, more liberal school, advocating universalism of humankind. Proponents of the liberal school found it necessary to deny differences altogether in order to challenge a colonial order which insisted on fundamental differences between the races. Any work which did not fall into either side in this dualism was largely ignored. It was not until the post-colonial period, with the interventions of African psychiatrists, that more discerning approaches began to emerge.

As a result of its focus on racial differences between Europeans and Africans, colonial psychology did not concern itself so much with differentiating between normal and deviant Africans as with pontificating on the specific characteristics of Africans in general. As such it became a major site for theorising 'the African'. Whereas European psychiatry has largely been concerned with diagnosis and treatment of psychopathology, in Africa psychiatry has propagated as many ideas about healthy Africans as about the mentally deranged. This is clearly evident in the work discussed below.

J. C. Carothers, the eminent South African-born and British-trained psychiatrist, devoted much of his professional life to colonial service in Kenya, first for nine years as a government medical officer and then for a further twelve years in charge of the Mathari Mental Hospital and HM Prison in Nairobi. It was after his retirement from colonial service that he conducted the research for his famous monograph *The African Mind in Health and Disease*, published by the World Health Organisation in 1953. In his prefatory remarks, Carothers reveals himself to be firmly committed to the tribal paradigm. He carefully pays lip service to the cultural diversity of Africa and notes the profound and pervasive impact that 'alien influences' have had across the region, even going so far as to observe that very few Africans have been untouched by the tides of trade, invasion and change that have swept the region for centuries. However, he goes on to point out that his monograph does not consider any but this imaginary few:

> This monograph is not concerned with the Christian, the Mohammedan, the urban or the 'educated' African as such, not even with those groups (such as the Yoruba) who have developed that diverge from the usual rural pattern.
>
> (Carothers 1953: 8)

Not satisfied with excluding all who could contradict his fundamental idea of the African, Carothers also uses the racial typologies of his time to exclude all the 'non-Negro races' of Africa, who are listed as Pygmies, Hottentots, Hamites, half-Hamites and Semites. Carothers defines his work as addressing itself to whoever is left but none the less refers to his subject as 'the African mind'. According to Carothers, Muslims, urban dwellers, Pygmies and all the rest are simply not really African.

Carothers reviewed western psychological work on the African mind, providing us with a fair summary of the findings of his colleagues:

> The African accordingly has been described as conventional; highly dependent on emotional stimulation; lacking in foresight, tenacity, judgement and humility; inapt for sound abstraction and for logic; given to phantasy and fabrication, and in general, as unstable, impulsive, unreliable, irresponsible, and living in the present without reflection or ambition. To counteract these ruderies, he has also been described as cheerful, stoical, self-confident, sociable, loyal, emotionally intuitive, and eloquent, and as bearing no grudges, and having an excellent memory, a large vocabulary, and an aptitude for music and dance.
>
> (Carothers 1953: 87)

One can be forgiven for identifying the conclusions of scientific psychology with the rantings of Gobineau and his cohorts over a century ago. Carothers himself is convinced that Africans are fundamentally different from Europeans, elsewhere characterising them as suffering from 'cortical laziness' and as having the intellectual capacities of 'lobotomised Europeans'. Most recently he has reaffirmed his racist ideas on the basis of parallels he draws between Africans and African-Americans, implying that this evidence suggests a biological basis for differences between the African mind and the European mind rather than a social one (Carothers 1953, 1972).

Like many other Europeans, Carothers viewed Africa as a disease-infested place with a hostile climate, held in check by the persisting legacies of 'tribal' culture. The fact is that he was well aware of social changes occurring during his stay in Kenya but viewed them through the blinkers of a colonial psychiatric paradigm, even in his work on the Kenyan resistance movement, a monograph entitled *The Psychology of Mau Mau*.

Psychoanalysts, like psychiatrists, played as much part in colonial psychology as we saw them play in early American race psychology. It was the French psychoanalyst Octave Mannoni who, during a sojourn in French-occupied Madagascar, produced the first major work on the psychology of colonisation, *Prospero and Caliban*, published in English not long after the Carothers monograph, in 1956. Mannoni, in contrast to Carothers, was not concerned with a remote imaginary tribe of Africans untouched by history but with psychological study of the relationship between the colonisers and the colonised. Unfortunately, he too takes up the position of an objective scientist, assuming that 'psychology' has nothing to do with wider social processes:

> The colonial problem is one of the most urgent of those confronting the world today – and France in particular. But though it is my intention to throw some light on its psychological aspect, that is not because I hope or even wish to contribute either directly or indirectly to the search for a practical solution.
>
> (Mannoni 1956: 17)[11]

Like his predecessors in North America, Jung and Lind, Mannoni too discovers complexes. According to him, the Malagasy suffer from a 'dependency complex', exhibited in dependent behaviour towards the colonial masters. He does not consider this a likely product of colonial system but instead traces it to the local culture, namely the Malagasy religious and family system, which he atavistically refers to as 'the cult of the dead' because of the emphasis on ancestors. He then theorises that for the Malagasy, the white man arrived and immediately came to symbolise the dead ancestors, so that infantile emotional dependence is then displayed towards whites. In plain language, the Malagasy were psychologically predisposed towards being colonised long before the French ever landed! As Fanon (1967a) points out, in Mannoni's analysis of the dreams of Malagasies, no notice is taken of the fact that some eighty thousand (one in five of the total population) were killed during the colonial period, and torture was a widely used means of repression. Furthermore, the possibility that this may have affected the local psychology, or permeated the dreams of those he interviewed, is not even considered. In short, Mannoni ignores the actual process of colonisation, preferring to conjure up anthropological anecdotes about cults and super-stitions in order to analyse the Malagasy psyche. It is a thesis of the status quo, a narrative which must have been quite soothing to the French conscience and which overlooks the atrocities they committed.

Less palatable to the French but equally deterministic is Mannoni's theory that the colonisers suffered from a complementary 'Prospero complex'. Rejection of his own world leads the colonial to flee, complete with a deep urge to dominate and control, an urge which (lo and behold!) finds a whole society ready and waiting in Madagascar. It is in their 'natural' role as dependants of the Europeans that the Malagasies become the repositories of all that is feared and projected outwards by the Europeans, making the Malagasy a child to the colonisers' paternalism, a sexually licentious native to the colonisers' repressed sexuality and so on. The texturing of his own perceptions by the same projective processes that he described for his countrymen becomes apparent in his depiction of Malagasy women as erotically licentious, archetypal and yet rumoured to have mysterious powers which sap the will of the French men who are so drawn to them. In short his comments on women come straight out of boy's own colonial fiction of the Rider Haggard genre (see Stott 1989).

Mannoni's conclusion about the colonial relationship is that it cannot be psychologically healthy for Europeans to have their projections indulged so constantly, a point which implies that he did not really favour the colonial system, even though he does not address any deleterious effects it may have had on the colonised. Mannoni saw the Malagasy through the lenses of his own position, as a French man (with a special word of condemnation for the allegedly even worse racism of French *women*) and from within a psychologically determinist frame of reference that failed to consider the possibility that the colonial subject may have been a product of the colonial system itself.

AFRICAN NATIONALISM AND THE RETREAT INTO EMPIRICISM

The end of the colonial period occurred when empiricist psychology was at its zenith. This has been reflected in African psychology throughout the post-colonial era. The discipline of psychology did not address the intellectual challenges that nationalist transformations engendered in the way that, for example, history and philosophy did. Psychologists did not address themselves to the ways in which African nationalist discourses challenged European constructions of Africans. Instead they appear to have retreated into scientism: uncritically applying the techniques and tools of the western scientific paradigm. In the West this form of psychology emerged in the context of the rapid growth of science and industry that accompanied the war years (Rose 1990) but these were now applied in Africa, under very different social and cultural conditions, in keeping with the notion of science as something that was objective and value-free, and therefore universal in its application.

One result of this carry-over was that the theoretical base of Africanist and early African[12] psychology did not change significantly. What did happen was that psychology in Africa as elsewhere became increasingly atheoretical and reductionist, in accord with the tenets of empiricist scientific method. Empiricist science is anti-theoretical in the sense that it is premissed on the belief that the observation of 'facts' is the only way to advance knowledge scientifically, an approach which assumes that such facts exist in isolation from the precepts and perceptions of the objective observer, man the scientist and his tools. By the 1950s and 1960s, the discipline of psychology had become much more institutionalised in the western world and, as an accompaniment to this, had adopted a set of methods and practices based solely on the observation and measurement of what was observable.

In the case of psychology, what was observable was external behaviour. This meant that internal psychological processes were left untheorised in a 'black box' model of man which rendered the mind unamenable to scientific investigation. Since psychological processes cannot in fact be directly observed, the subject matter of the discipline itself shifted from the psyche to behaviour. Psychology became for many the science of human (and very often animal) behaviour, and was now more often referred to as behavioural science. Psychologists adopted natural scientific methods of experiment and devised arsenals of quantitative techniques with which to measure human behaviour, on the assumption that they would ultimately be able to predict and manipulate it. At the heart of the paradigm the individual is assumed to be unitary and fixed, and to live in a society which is a single cohesive structure (Henriques *et al.* 1984).

The new scientific psychology was applied wholeheartedly to the study of African people. Indeed it is fair to say that it faced fewer challenges here than in the West, where humanist philosophy and the radical social movements of the 1960s generated competing discourses. These alternative psychologies have not been taken up in the colonies and former colonies with the same enthusiasm as psychometric and experimental psychology.

At the end of the colonial period, conditions on the African continent were undergoing profound changes. Nationalist movements erupted to challenge the white supremacist order on every front, to protest at economic systems solely designed to extract African material resources; education systems which excluded the vast majority of the population; racially segregated social systems which deprived Africans of decent standards of living; and indeed the entire political order which continued to treat Africans as inherently inferior to the white man. African scholars began to protest at the negative effects of colonialism, not least on the psychology of 'the native':

> Colonialism is not satisfied merely with holding a people in its grip and emptying the natives' brain of all form and content. By a kind of perverted logic, it turns to the past of the oppressed people and distorts, disfigures and destroys it.
>
> (Fanon 1967b: 169; see also Memmi 1965)

The history of African nationalism is well documented and will not be reiterated here, beyond pointing out that this upsurge in nationalist consciousness also heralded profound psychological changes and a radically different articulation of what it meant to be African, by African and diasporean black intellectuals (see Cabral 1980, Fanon 1970, Garvey 1983, Nkrumah 1964, Padmore 1956 and Senghor 1971). It was during the nationalist period that African redefinitions of what Nkrumah refers to as 'the African personality' and what it means to be black were thrust into the international arena to fuel the existential and philosophical crisis that the demise of colonialism provoked in the western world and which ultimately led to the emergence of poststructuralism. In the English-speaking black world, black nationalism was most visibly formulated as the philosophy of pan-Africanism often identified with Kwame Nkrumah, George Padmore and other leading participants at the early pan-African congresses. In the French-speaking world, the most prominent form of black nationalism was referred to as 'negritude'; its proponents included Aime Cesaire from the Caribbean, Leopold Sedhar Senghor and Sekou Toure from Africa, and a great proliferation of poets and artists from all over the French-speaking black world (see Cesaire 1950, Senghor 1971).

Without going into the details of the many variants of black nationalism and the many ideas that were contained and contested within it, it can be said that the unifying feature of it all lay in the compulsion to redress the humiliations endured by Africans during the centuries of racism and colonialism, both by articulating a new African-centred understanding and vision of the continent and its peoples and by engaging in the political struggle for the liberation of all the nations of the region from western domination and exploitation. Within this, the concept of African personality became a way of expressing the concern with celebrating the collective African past as well as articulating a collective will and vision for the future. Within it, personality was both a philosophical and political concept, very different from personality as it has been defined in psychology (see below). Let us now return to the question of how psychologists responded to the major cultural and psychological changes that accompanied African nationalism. To answer this, the results of several decades of such work are briefly discussed below.

Starting with research on early development of Africans, we can see the persistent reference to Freudian ideas. However, these are not treated theoretically or historically but as abstract mini-hypotheses which could be studied using testing and measurement techniques. For example, a large number of studies have sought to account for the assumed characteristics of adult Africans by studying newborn infants and weaning practices. An example that illustrates this focus is the theory of infant precocity, which Wober (1975) attributes to Geber. Geber is said to have noticed that newborn African infants displayed more advanced psychomotor reflexes than European babies. Her observations gave rise to numerous studies which tested the reflexes of newborn Africans, many of which replicated her findings. Researchers set out to uncover the basis of this particular observation, concentrating on the study of weaning and early child-care practices. It is worth noting that the observed precocity of African infants mystified psychologists only because they assumed Africans to be more backward. As a result, research was carried out in South Africa, Cameroon, Ethiopia, Zambia, Nigeria and Botswana. The majority of these studies affirmed the finding of advanced psychomotor reflexes in African infants but were inconclusive as to the causes and contradictory in what they considered to be the implications for adult Africans. Some advanced genetic explanations, others social ones. Few posed the question the other way round, to ask themselves why it was that European infants have slower psychomotor reflexes than the babies from all the other races that were tested.

A second area of research has been devoted to assessing the cognitive growth of African primary-school-age children through the administration of psychological tests, a research area that owes much to Piagetian theory. The aim has been to test for racial differences in cognitive development. The initial search for biological and anatomical distinctions soon gave way to a search for cultural determinants. For example, the harsh weaning hypothesis, which recurs again and again in the literature, suggests that the differences in African intelligence can be attributed to 'African' weaning practices, defined as being universally late, sudden and severe. Another favourite was the 'puberty hypothesis' which attributed differences between adult Africans and Europeans to the initiation rites performed in some societies to signal entry into adulthood, rites that Europeans viewed as traumatic enough to retard Africans.[13] Despite the number of studies, Wober concludes that the research has failed to prove the existence of any constitutional disadvantage, instead pointing to the role of early schooling and parenting in advancing cognitive development. African culture is given short shrift in most studies, since it has invariably been invoked to account for the inferiority or backwardness of Africans as compared to Europeans.

With regard to African adults, extensive resources have been devoted to the measurement of intelligence. The first tests are reported to have been administered in South Africa in 1915, with subsequent studies being carried out throughout the 1920s, and then in Kenya during the 1930s, and in the Spanish and Belgian colonies in the 1950s (Wober 1975). Most of this work has assumed that tests do measure intelligence and that they can justly be applied to persons from social and cultural contexts quite different from those for which the tests were designed and standardised. This assumption was first challenged in the 1940s by the South African Biesheuvel, who thus opened a long-standing debate on the possibility of developing 'culture free' or 'culture fair' tests. In the field of intelligence research, as in early infancy and child development research, differences between Africans have been largely subsumed to the preoccupation with finding and measuring racial differences in test scores and to debates about the possible source of such test score differences.

The debate on race and intelligence has similarly preoccupied western researchers at home as well as abroad. Numerous studies have also been done on black populations in Europe and North America, research which has provoked enormous controversy because of the insistence of some that there must be a link between test scores and genetic make-up, and that lower test scores are therefore a measure of the inherent inferiority of people of African descent (see, for example, Block and Dworkin 1977, Jensen 1969, Rose 1976). Intelligence testing was used to facilitate a resurgence of the old arguments asserting the intellectual retardation of black people as compared to white people. In most African countries (apartheid South Africa being an exception) such arguments have had little impact on educational policy, perhaps because the emphasis has been on achieving mass education and distributing resources as equitably as possible under dire economic conditions. Although African researchers have acknowledged that Africans generally score lower on so-called intelligence tests than Europeans (Otaala 1971, Yoloye 1971), they have generally interpreted this finding differently. Others (present author included) prefer to challenge the validity and basis of the tests themselves and the rationales for using IQ tests in educational practice. Generally speaking, the application of psychological tests has been more limited here than in Europe, presumably because of the under-resourcing of psychology and the marginal place afforded to the discipline in African educational policy development and practice.

A substantial amount of research has also investigated the possibility of using psychological tests to meet the needs of the military and corporate industry; that is, for selection purposes. Wober (1975) reports the first large-scale study to have been conducted during the Second World War, by MacDonald, who was working with the British forces in East Africa.[14] MacDonald is reported to have compared the scores of nearly 2,000 men in 14 tests with ratings of their military performance and found correlations.

From the 1950s onwards, tests have been deployed in relation to the needs of industry, with several studies directing their efforts at the selection of mineworkers for skilled as compared to purely manual labouring jobs. The South African National Institute for Personnel Research has played a leading role in developing such tests – tests suited to the concerns of the apartheid society and its industrialisation needs, rather than to the human and vocational needs of the predominantly African workforce.[15] During the 1960s several studies were carried out in West Africa, the largest reported by Wober (1975) having been carried out between 1961 and 1963 in Nigeria under the auspices of an American Aid for International Development Project. Erroneously claiming to be the first such study in Africa, Schwarz's project collected a million words used in schools, out of which 20 tests were developed using the most familiar vocabulary. These were tried out on 15,000 examinees. Fortunately or unfortunately, the study remained incomplete as it was never followed up, although others subsequently applied these or similar tests in studies of primary school leavers in Nigeria and nearly 2,000 students in Rhodesia and Uganda. It was found that tests could act as predictors of school performance, although this depended on the quality of the school, and that examination performance could predict later career success. Wober (1975) also reviews the large body of research on using tests for selection carried out in Uganda during his stay at Makerere, in which several Ugandan psychologists participated.

The final area – which should be the most relevant to a consideration of subjectivity – is that of personality research. I have noted that the term 'personality' has been deployed by African scholars and writers as a philosophical and political means of expressing a collective will and vision of the future. In scientific psychology, personality could not have been defined more differently. Here it refers to a highly individualised self, which has a core of possibly inheritable essential characteristics that distinguish him or her from other individuals and which are fixed by adulthood. Perhaps the most interesting psychometric study of personality was that reported in the *Authoritarian Personality* by the philosopher Theodore Adorno and his colleagues (Adorno *et al.* 1950). Working in the post-Hitlerian era and heavily influenced by Freud, these researchers sought to identify the personality correlates of fascism and to elucidate the ways in which these were produced in the bourgeois family.

Mostly, however, the emphasis has been less theoretical and more statistical, concerned with devising measures and finding correlations between scores, and between scores and other variables. Personality is in general considered to be measurable and quantifiable, and it is to this end that personality tests have been developed, following the pioneering work of Raymond Cattell in the United States (Cattell 1946). In many ways, personality has come to be defined by the bipolar scales that measure it: in terms of introversion and extroversion, aggressivity and passivity.

Personality research in Africa has borne a heavily Freudian legacy, apparent in the popularity of designing and administering tests for dependency, anal behaviour, lack of self-control, over-aggressiveness, impulsiveness, strong egos, weak egos and the like. Thousands of Africans all over the region have been subjected to Rorschach tests, thematic apperception tests, Rosenzweig's picture frustration test, Goodenough's draw-a-man test, Eysenck's personality tests, Cattell's scales, McClelland's achievement motivation tests and probably many others (see Wober 1975 for a review). The results of personality testing in Africa are as contradictory as they are inconclusive, with different researchers contradicting each other and struggling but failing to come up with the definitive African personality type, as distinct from the European. It appears not to be taken very seriously in the region where it is probably granted less credence than astrology.

We can conclude that psychologists have tended to ignore the changes heralded by African nationalism and the demise of direct colonialism. Instead they seem to have buried their heads in the sands of empiricist methods, travelling about the continent administering questionnaires and tests to obscurely defined groups of subjects, and then using these to make all manner of generalisations about an African subject who has remained entirely mythical. The initial emphasis on finding scientific support for the racial differences that were assumed to distinguish Africans from Europeans meant that little attention was paid to studying African psychology in its own right. At its heart, the Eurocentric paradigm deployed by psychologists continued to assume the African (like the European) to exist as a unitary subject, a static and eternal entity about whom the grossest generalisations could be made, a simplified Other against whom the European subject could be contrasted and so reaffirmed in his supreme position at the centre of the universe.

In Africa (as in the West) applied psychology appears to have been motivated by a 'Brave New World' vision of a highly ordered society in which people could be selected to fit into the jobs for which they were best suited, in the interests of maximising production and efficiency. The main emphasis was on using scientific psychology to fit men (not women) to jobs rather than perhaps developing workplaces or training to meet the needs of the workers of both sexes. In Africa more person-centred styles of management have been slow in coming, and where they exist it is not, in my view, due to the insight and efforts of industrial psychologists but rather due to the sustained activism of workers' organisations.

We can see from this discussion of modern empiricist psychology in Africa that there has been a great emphasis on what we can loosely refer to as psychologies of control, concerned with behaviour manipulation, mental measurement and screening techniques, all of which characterise the 'scientific psychology' that has predominated in the West as well as in Africa. South African psychology has focused particularly in these areas (see Bulhan 1981).

This pattern of psychology developing in the service of corporate industrial and managerial interests was not specific to psychology in Africa, as Bulhan implies. The history of industrial psychology in the West and the proliferation of psycho-technologies in the administration and regulation of industrial capitalist societies has indicated a similar relationship, with psychology developing in directions devoted to servicing and playing regulatory and administrative functions for war machines and corporate bureaucratic, institutional and managerial interests (Rose 1979).

Thus we see that in Africa too, psychological expertise was increasingly deployed, not merely to inferiorise and subordinate Africans but also to meet the needs of the late colonial and early post-colonial African economies for carefully calibrated and controllable workforces.

CONCLUSIONS

The long history of slavery and colonialism, and the perfection of racist regimes at home in North America and abroad in the various colonies, must thus be seen as a major influence on the twentieth-century psychological discourses on black people. By the 1930s, the imperial powers controlled as much as 80 per cent of the world. We should not underestimate the institutional power of the discourse which construed black people as unquestionably mentally inferior and as exhibiting racially specific forms of pathology. Nor should we underestimate the repressive practices that accompanied this global expansion. The pervasiveness of these practices meant that they became normalised, equated with an order that was seen as 'natural' and 'God-given': the black people of the world were an underclass, the 'white man's burden' of writers such as Rudyard Kipling. This ubiquitous system meant that even if any of the early psychologists thought differently, they were likely to be dismissed as quacks or madmen. Black mental inferiority had the status of a God-given and scientifically proven truth. The unquestioning (and some would say *un*scientific) reproduction of dominant racial assumptions in psychological theory results from the uncritical retention of Eurocentric philosophical premisses. Psychology has echoed these assumptions and so contributed to the reaffirmation, production and legitimation of racist discourses on Africa and Africans.

Psychologists working in Africa in the early years of independence applied a European post-war empiricist paradigm. Here it has re-inscribed archaic racist ideas in the language of science and enabled psychologists not to realise that their idea of the African was imaginary and that in reality African peoples and societies were diverse and constantly changing. In any case, the evidence reviewed here suggests that the paradigm they came with was ill-equipped to theorise the multiplicity and dynamism of Africans either during colonisation or nationalist transformations. Some years were to pass before the old frames of reference were to give way to new approaches containing epistemological and methodological possibilities more suited to theorising black and African subjectivities. But we jump ahead of ourselves, to matters that are explored in later chapters.

The following chapter examines the psychological constructions of black people that have emerged in the West, and how black psychologists have set out to develop non-racist theories of black identity.

NOTES

1 Key texts addressing this history in more detail include Boahen 1985, Chinweizu 1975, Rodney 1974 and Williams 1964.
2 Appiah (1992) addresses some of the commonalities between the Africanist discourses of the colonisers and the early pan-Africanism articulated by Crummell and DuBois, drawing attention to the persistence of the race paradigm across the boundaries of European and African thinking. Similar ideas have been evident amongst the earlier critics of negritude and racial essentialism in black thought (e.g. Fanon 1967).
3 Baudelaire is well known for the poems in which he writes exotically about his black mistress, Jeanne Duval.
4 This idea does, however, appear in black narratives of slavery, e.g. Caryl Phillips's *Cambridge*, Toni Morrison's *Beloved*, to name only two.
5 The emphasis was on the black *man*, since psychologists did not at first take much notice of black women.
6 Years later, in 1905, G. S. Hall, one of contemporary psychology's founding fathers, was to proclaim that medical treatment of different races was as different 'as the application of veterinary medicine for horses is from that applied to oxen' (cited in Thomas and Sillen 1974: 3).
7 What is striking about this particular theorisation is not just that it has persisted in one guise or another to the extent that any black person in the West today will recall having been accused of suffering from colour complex, but that it has also permeated a great deal of contemporary black psychology (see Chapter 3).
8 Although Tempels writes of people he refers to as 'the Bantu', it is worth noting that he has no hesitation in declaring that his findings are relevant to all who work among the broader category of 'African people'.
9 See the work of African philosophers such as Mbiti, Hountoundji, Wiredu and

Kagame. Mbiti, a Kenyan theologian, has shown the greatest adherence to Tempels' view that there is indeed a single essential 'African philosophy'. This is worth noting because, perhaps as a result of his presence in the United States, his work has had the greatest influence on the thinking of black Americans unversed in the complexities of contemporary African philosophical thought, black intellectuals who are hungry for an African source.

10 See Allier 1929, Boas 1911, Levi-Strauss 1966 and a great many other titles available in any anthropology library.

11 Alas for Mannoni, it was not to be so. Ten years later, he was to write of his unpleasant surprise at finding himself attacked for his psychology and being 'compelled to realise that his book was bound to be interpreted in a political sense' (1966: 328–9).

12 Here used to mean psychological work conducted by psychologists of African origin, most of whom were trained in the West until the advent of psychology departments in African universities. There is strong evidence that psychology in independent Africa has been slow to challenge the premises of the discipline and develop its own terms of reference, instead continuing to rely heavily on the uncritical application of western concepts, methods and measuring devices to African subjects.

13 Both hypotheses indicate the influence of anthropological studies in empiricist psychology in Africa, something which perhaps differentiates it from psychology in the West.

14 Interestingly, in the West too, aptitude tests were also first developed within the military (Rose 1990).

15 For example, Biesheuvel was considered to be highly successful in developing and using aptitude tests to classify African recruits for work in the gold mines into 'boss-boys', mechanical and non-mechanical categories of occupation, and he subsequently was appointed to direct the National Institute for Personnel Research in Johannesburg.

Female Quadroon Slave of Surinam.

Chapter 3

Inventing black identity

Negroes today are experiencing an inner transformation that is liberating them from ideological dependency on the white majority. What has penetrated substantially all strata of Negro life is the revolutionary idea that the philosophy and morals of the dominant white society are not holy or sacred but in all too many respects are degenerate and profane.

(Martin Luther King, 1968)

In this chapter we shall examine the emergence and development of academic psychological research and theory about black people in North America. Before doing so, it is perhaps worth noting that the use of 'black people' as a conceptual category is something that has developed in societies in which 'race' – however that is constructed – has been a major social division. We saw in the previous chapter that racist discourses have had a long evolution and how these permeated colonial psychological theory, so that the discipline has often legitimised dominant racial assumptions and construed the African as a single generalised Other, in stereotyped ways. In this chapter, North American studies of the psychology of black people will be examined as a means of further investigating the relationship between psychology and race politics. I shall demonstrate that both mainstream and black psychology assume a unitary subject – the black man – about whom a great many generalisations have been made.

The main questions I address are these: how have psychological theories been influenced by the legacies of slavery, emancipation and contemporary white domination? What have psychology, and later 'black psychology', had to say about African-American identity, in the context of all the enormous changes of the twentieth century? How have black psychologists intervened in these constructions, and have their theorisations of black people been fundamentally different from those of white psychologists or not? What changes have been brought about by the civil rights movement and the new racial assertiveness heralded by the Black Power movement?

Until the 1920s, psychological research had been the exclusive preserve of white academics, with black people as their objects of study. In that year Francis Sumner became the first black person to obtain a Ph.D. in psychology. Subsequently, he supported Kenneth and Mamie Clark's research on 'Negro identity' during the 1930s and 1940s. By the 1950s there were still only fifty black Americans with doctorates in psychology, and although there has been a steady increase since the 1960s, black people are still grossly underrepresented in the discipline. Furthermore their participation during the 1950s and 1960s was largely concentrated in ethnic specialisations and community psychology, with very little involvement in the burgeoning mainstream of theory and research. Although a similar situation has prevailed in other areas of scholarship, suggesting that the academies reflect the racial divisions characterising the rest of American society, it has been suggested that there are characteristics of established psychology which have made it an unlikely choice for black students:

> Mainstream (that is, behaviourist) psychology was not amenable to investigating such issues as racism and oppression, the psychosocial reality of Black people, or the consequences of being an Afro-American. Thus it is readily apparent why so few Black Americans saw psychology as an attractive occupation. It was seen as a narrow, stifling field and in particular as insensitive to the themes most directly pertinent to Black Americans.
>
> (Boykin et al. 1979: 5)

It is also possible that the limitations of the psychological research conducted on black people until the end of the 1960s were also offputting. In the last chapter we saw how racist psychological theories were used to argue against abolition. The next step is to consider the development of Negro psychology (as it was known) after abolition and during the first half of this century. What were the ensuing changes in American society, and how did these affect psychological theories about black people?

By way of background, it is worth noting that after emancipation massive northward migrations of black people occurred, as people left the rural farms of the South and the legacies of slavery and headed for the expanding urban centres elsewhere in the United States. Hundreds of thousands headed for the West, where there had been relatively few black people during the earlier epochs. By 1910, 1.7 million had moved from the state of their birth, and during the First World War, half a million headed north (Frazier 1949). The conditions that precipitated such massive movements cannot be detailed here but it is clear that emancipation did not bequeath great things to freed slaves. Indeed, in many parts of the South, things continued much as before emancipation, with black people either remaining on the plantations as heavily exploited labour or constituting a landless underclass of drifting casual labour. The few that managed to obtain a little land were obliged to scratch out a living under conditions of great hardship; women and men alike suffered and endured. Those who left in search of better lives in the North, in the cities in particular, found work as artisans, domestics, seamstresses and as casual labourers on farms and building sites, and formed a new black proletariat in the developing industrial centres of Chicago, Detroit and the like.[1]

The enormous diversity of black social and family life is revealed in the work of E. Franklin Frazier, whose sociological study of the Negro family highlights the emergence of an array of family forms during and after slavery, out of the various social contexts in which black people lived. He details the dynamics that produced both female-headed ('matriarchate') and male-headed patriarchal ('patriarchate') family forms. The 'matriarchate' was produced under conditions of slavery during which the white slave-holders showed no respect for black kinship. The 'patriarchate' was equally produced by multiple factors including loyalty to the dominant Christian form of marriage, the needs of male former slaves to assert themselves as 'kings' of their own hearth (a prerogative long denied them by the slave-masters) and by the assertion of extreme male-dominance within the waged urban proletariat.

Two main schools of thought can be discerned within the emergent 'Negro' sociology. Frazier was a social constructionist rather than an essentialist, who took the view that the American 'Negro personality' was constructed out of prevailing social conditions, during and after slavery, particularly reflecting the role of the Negro in the plantation economy (Frazier 1939: 360). He had little time for the alternative school of thought, which emphasised the connection of the Negro to his native habitat, to 'savage life' or to the 'primitive' Africa then being documented by colonial anthropologists. Without denying the African past, he rejected the idea that African culture had anything to contribute towards understanding American Negro life in the modern, post-slavery period:

> Probably never before in history has a people been so completely stripped of its social heritage as the Negroes who were brought to America ... of the habits and customs as well as the hopes and fears that characterised the life of their forbears in Africa, nothing remains.
> (Frazier 1949: 15)

By taking this position Frazier was able to reject both biological and culturally deterministic arguments that posited a unitary, essential Negro rooted in racial and cultural survivals. Instead he theorised that varied life-styles and family forms were constituted out of the changing and diverse social conditions of black people's lives. In other words, he rejected the idea that there were fundamental differences between the races, preferring the view that American Negroes would eventually assimilate and acculturate as full citizens of the United States. The history of slavery and extreme suffering was to be left behind, and moving forward meant breaking with the past to establish new positions in American society.

The dramatic changes in American society that Frazier and his colleagues in the field of sociology were writing about soon generated new interest in 'Negro psychology'.[2] While the first studies were conducted by Jewish psychologists, it was not long before black psychologists entered the field. We shall now examine how the psychology of black people became a field that, narrow and stifling though it may have been, was certainly a place of influence regarding 'the race problem'.

WHAT PSYCHOLOGY HAS SAID ABOUT THE NEGRO

> There is not one personality trait of the Negro the source of which cannot be traced to his difficult living conditions. There are no exceptions to this rule. The final result is a wretched internal life.
>
> (Kardiner and Ovesey 1951: 81)

This remarkable statement indicates the prevailing view of the psychological establishment prior to the 1960s. I shall argue that this view of the Negro as damaged concurred with dominant post-slavery discourses, and can be understood in terms of the changing race politics of the time. In order to understand why certain theorisations of the black person gained enough currency to become unquestionable, it is necessary to consider what the wider social conditions and institutional concerns were at the time. How did these conditions enable certain ideas to prevail to such a degree that they would be accepted as truths?

As a consequence of the migrations mentioned above, the black urban population grew enormously in the first decades of the twentieth century. The labour needs of industrialisation subsequently fell off, so that as America entered the Great Depression of the 1920–30s, urban black people found themselves constituting a new underclass deprived of work and, subsequently, of other necessities. This was a period in which social welfare came into its own, in the USA as in Europe, and with it, new ways of regulating and governing the urban masses.[3]

In 1935 the American Youth Commission was established, and by 1938 it was so widely accepted that black children suffered from psychological problems that a special advisory committee was set up. Powell (1973) describes the mandate of this committee as having been to help organise an enquiry into the specific problems facing black youth in their individual development. In other words, by this time it was already officially understood that black children were damaged. Just what these 'distinctive problems' were was to be the subject of much investigation in the years to come.

The special advisory committee commissioned a number of researchers to undertake studies in various parts of the United States. The question was not whether black children were damaged or not. For psychologists the issue was not so much to question what everyone assumed but to conduct empirical research and to find a conceptual language for the 'distinctive developmental problems' black children were already widely assumed to suffer from. Psychologists aware of the high level of official interest would also have been anxious to get in on this emerging field of social research. The results of their efforts can be grouped under two headings.

The damaged Negro

These construed the Negro as a psychologically tormented individual whose entire identity was dictated by white racism. Kardiner and Ovesey preface their study with a quote from the 1950 UNESCO Statement on Race that asserts 'the universal brotherhood of mankind' (sic). They acknowledge a great debt to Frazier's work, thanking him for his advice concerning the book as a whole, and to a number of others, who include Kenneth and Mamie Clark (see below), for help in finding subjects for them to interview. It is therefore a study that has been conducted with the support and assistance of leading black social scientists and that is antiracist in its intentions.

So how is it that even as they caution against over-generalisation and stereotyping, their own conclusions end up being simplistic statements about a generalised and pathologised 'Negro personality', statements that reaffirm black inferiority? Part of the answer lies in their use of a clinical methodology and the fact that their subjects were hardly shining examples of black success. The American Negro they describe is a character that they have constructed on the basis of interviews with 25 black men and women, 11 of whom were undergoing clinical therapy at the time. Others – generally the poorest subjects – were paid by the hour for their time. The individual portraits that Kardiner and Ovesey draw are detailed and cast some light on the role that racism plays in the psychodynamics of individuals. The problem lies in the way that they use individual particularities as a basis for making general statements about 'the Negro personality', statements that simply cannot justifiably be drawn out of such material, even if theorising about the process of individual development can be advanced. The generalisations that they make presuppose that 'the Negro' is a unitary personality type and that all black people conform to this construction. Most of the challenges to Kardiner and Ovesey's portrayal of blackness-as-stigma have objected to the negative content, not to the philosophical premiss of a unitary 'Negro' personality. Rather than challenging the singularity of the black subject, Kardiner and Ovesey's detractors merely reject their portrayal.

None the less, Kardiner and Ovesey's approach discards the old bio-logically racist arguments of essential differences between white and black people. Like Frazier, they view the human subject – in this case the Negro personality – as socially and historically constructed rather than geneti-cally programmed and unchangeable. The gross generalisations that they make are not biologically based assertions of black pathology but socially and culturally deterministic ones, whose theoretical invalidity emanates from the premiss that there is a unitary 'Negro personality' that can be defined solely in terms of its difference from 'the white man'. Despite their professed wish to avoid stereotyping, the result is a simplified and reduced construction of an essential, stereotyped, 'Negro' subject.

Kardiner and Ovesey's 'Negro' was not just an artefact of their para-digm. The notion of black people as scarred and damaged by their unhappy experience is one that had already been articulated in literature and one which here as elsewhere, was intended to demonstrate the social injustices of racism. Black protest writers such as Ralph Ellison, James Baldwin and Richard Wright also captured the suffering that has been one of the most salient aspects of what it has meant to be black in America. As such, Kardiner and Ovesey (and all the others who similarly constructed 'the Negro' as damaged) merely reiterated an existing portrayal, transposing it into psychoanalytic and sociological jargon. The problem lies not so much in the truth or falsity of their construction but in their assumption that this is all there is to the 'Negro personality', an assumption that flies in the face of the complexities of Negro cultural and social life and that casts black people as passive victims of white racist social structure.

Kardiner and Ovesey's work overlooks the fact that as early as the 1920s and 1930s there were competing portrayals of Negro life. By the time they were conducting their research, the Harlem Renaissance had occurred. Langston Hughes, Zora Neale Hurston and the others had produced great literary works that celebrated and lauded the culture and achievements of black Americans and realised the existence of an autonomous African-American cultural space. Psychologists have limited their theorisations to the deleterious effects of racism on the psyches of black people, writing a reductionist psychopathology, without first knowing what black social life and psychology might broadly be about. Nowhere in their work is there any acknowledgement of the various collec-tive (cultural) responses to the long black experience of oppression, or the fact that they might have had any experience apart from that of racism. Racial oppression itself is inadequately conceptualised as monolithic, total and homogeneous in its effects. The nuances and intricate sets of social etiquette and behaviour, of betrayal and collusion, of inversion and resist-ance that constitute racism as a social process are barely touched upon.

Today, clinical and psychoanalytic techniques such as those adopted by

Kardiner and Ovesey have for the most part been superseded by more reductionist methods. In adherence to empiricist philosophical tenets, research psychologists have concentrated on the measurement of observable behaviour. They have therefore been obliged to rely greatly on 'scientific' methods, using experimental and psychometric techniques. This has meant that grand theoretical questions about the relationship between personality and society have by and large been replaced by examinations of micro-hypotheses and the testing of more experimentally manageable concepts. The psychological study of the self-concept is one result of the reductionist imperatives, which have led to a focus on measurable and testable experimental constructs. Self-concept theory has particularly preoccupied black psychologists and psychologists studying blacks, and it is to the development of more empirical psychological constructions of black people that we now turn.

The negative self-concept

Ruth and Eugene Horowitz, like Kardiner and Ovesey, worked in the context of the profound racism of the 1930s. Racial segregation was upheld and enforced by the law, while a biased criminal justice system tolerated and condoned the public lynching of blacks who 'stepped out of line'. In other words racial inequality was perpetuated through acts of tolerated terrorism and intimidation, and through constant denigration of black people.

It was in this context that psychological research conducted by both black and white researchers between the 1930s and the 1960s repeatedly constructed a unitary black American subject: a self-hating person who rejected his (*sic*) own ethnic group. The first of the self-concept studies was conducted by the Horowitzes (see R. Horowitz 1939). They developed and used racial preference tests, which consisted of presenting photographs to infants and young children and asking questions such as 'Who do you like best?' and 'Who would you sit next to?' The first racial preference study (E. Horowitz 1939) focused on establishing a social rather than an instinctual basis of racial attitudes and, indeed, found that children reared in a commune did not show the same racial preference that both black and white children raised in ordinary households did. Ruth Horowitz was so intrigued by her husband's finding that Negro boys showed a slight preference for white photographs that she proceeded to conduct further studies on infants. She was less interested in the fact that white boys, raised in the same American society as the black boys, showed the same preference for white photographs. Part of her interest lay in her conviction that racial preference was suggestive of deeper dimensions of personality. She went on to conduct a number of experiments to investigate the ability of children to self-identify correctly (in racial terms) and their preferences for photographs of light or dark people. On the basis of some of her findings, she concluded that black boys suffered from what she called 'wishful thinking'; that is to say, although they knew from an early age that they were black, they wished they were white instead. Cross (1991) has provided a detailed re-analysis of Horowitz's studies, in which he exposes the methodological errors and unsystematic nature of studies that actually ignored the results of any tests on black girls and white boys that did not affirm the hypothesis of black self-hatred. Small sample sizes and selective interpretations of the results of the tests she administered, not to mention the very young age of the subjects, are among the weaknesses that should have undermined the theorisation of the 'Negro' as a damaged, self-hating creature, instead of giving it scientific legitimacy.

In addition to the above-mentioned official climate regarding urban blacks as a problem, the Horowitzes were probably heavily influenced by the growing European literature on the psychology of their own Jewish people, literature that construed Jews as self-hating and owed much to the context of rising fascism and anti-Semitism. Cross (1991) implies that this couple may well have been preoccupied with the self-hatred thesis on their own account, when he draws attention to the fact that they changed their name from the identifiably Jewish Horowitz to 'Hartley' during the Second World War. It seems fair to suggest that because they hid their own Jewish origins, the Horowitzes expected other oppressed minorities to feel the same way about themselves: wishing to be Other and masking their identities to avoid detection and slip ahead of their compatriots. Of course this is not an option for those who are as visibly different as black people, and for whom fantasies of whiteness – 'wishful thinking' – would be the only way out.

Whatever the case, the Horowitzes' work might still have faded into insignificance if the ideas and testing techniques they developed had not been pursued by another couple, this time not Jewish but black, who in the end were to become far more renowned for their work on the psychology of black Americans than the Horowitzes/Hartleys ever were.

Psychology and civil rights: the Clarks

Kenneth and Mamie Clark began their research on the black self-concept during their student days in the 1930s. Since they are best known for empirically demonstrating that black people wanted to be white, it is worth noting that in concluding their first study – which was not a study of racial preference in any case but a study of children's ability to identify correctly their colour from a choice of variously shaded dolls – actually challenged the whole idea of black people wishing to be white. They did not do further work on the subject until 1947–50, and it was then that they found black children did exhibit white preference. By 1955, without conducting any further tests but having reanalysed the 1930s study, the Clarks were arguing that they had found stable, persistent and important dimensions to the 'Negro personality'.

Cross's (1991) critique of the studies conducted by the Clarks identifies various anomalies and methodological weaknesses. They also appear to have ignored the fact that even the white preference they did find disappeared after the age of 7 years. On the basis of a careful scrutiny of their data, Cross demonstrates that their conclusions were not borne out by their own experimental data. In order to affirm the self-hatred hypothesis they instead drew on clinical observations made on some other children, who happened to be undergoing psychiatric treatment. It would seem that the negative remarks made by some of these children had such an impact on the Clarks that they interpreted them to represent pervasive themes, not only in the racial identities of other young children but in Negro identity in general. None the less, despite the flawed nature of these studies, the thesis of black self-hatred became widely accepted. For answers to the question as to why this was so, we must turn to the wider social conditions and institutional needs.

A historical reading of the published findings of the Clarks indicates the way in which the hypothetical construction of black Americans as self-hating resonated with the emergent discourses of the black civil rights movement and the political agenda of desegregation. The idea of blacks as damaged by racism was the one that became a central theme in the battle over desegregation. Kenneth Clark was asked by the NAACP to help them develop a case against segregation, and the fact that his monograph was included in the brief to the Supreme Court of the United States of America, provides us with a fine illustration of how the institutional uptake of a particular finding may have influenced the course of psychological theory for years to come. In this example we see that the psychology of the 'Negro personality' as being damaged by racism was being used not only by the white establishment but also by the black civil rights lobby, committed to assailing the institutional bedrock of racism: segregation.

The struggle for black people to be given the same rights as white American citizens that became known as the civil rights movement was the first major movement for black liberation to take place since the end of slavery. Black people in the United States were still being excluded from housing, jobs, health-care and education by institutional discrimination: an apartheid system of segregation that had developed in the post-slavery years. By 1963, support for the movement protesting against the continuing oppression of black people had grown so much that 500,000 people were mobilised in what became known as the March on Washington. This peaceful demonstration was both a culmination and a beginning. It was the culmination of the growing desire of black people to express dissatisfaction with the lack of progress on the race question. It was the beginning of a new era of protest, a march on the centre of government that was to be followed by sit-ins, strikes, school boycotts and other forms of mass action across the nation. The leadership of the NAACP, personified in Martin Luther King, was perhaps accurate in articulating the desire of most black people for integration – a desire to enjoy the same rights and freedoms as white Americans.

It was a position supported by all the social and economic evidence that indicated without a doubt that black people were disproportionately deprived. In 1964, 60 per cent of black families survived on less than $4,000 per annum, a great many living far below the poverty line, and all the evidence suggested that the gap between white and black people was growing all the time. The year following the March on Washington saw the government beginning to respond: President Johnson's State of the Union message declared 'unconditional war on poverty' partly in response to the growing fear of black revolt. This fear was well founded – not only by the continuing material evidence that black people were oppressed and dehumanised in American society but also because the peaceful protests of the civil rights movement had been responded to by white communities in the South with a series of violent attacks and bloody murders. The 1964 Civil Rights Act was rushed through Congress and made law, superseding all other business. In 1965 this was followed by the Voting Rights Act and the Anti-poverty bill, which was intended to ameliorate the crisis of urban poverty. These legislative accomplishments were major victories for the civil rights movement. None the less, high levels of black frustration and suffering were not wiped away overnight, and the white backlash continued. While the leadership of the civil rights movement continued to campaign for peaceful protest and to appeal for calm, a new and more militant black politics was being born in the cauldron of urban poverty and black deprivation.

We can sum up this discussion of black self-concept psychology by noting that psychological studies of black identity initially took up and selectively reaffirmed certain historical legacies, while ignoring others. Blacks were now viewed as being damaged by racist society, rather than as innately inferior – something of an improvement. None the less it meant taking white racism to be the sole factor in black identity formation and ignoring the existence of the diverse cultural referents available to many black people. The result was a narrow and mono-dimensional view; in short, a stereotype that was to permeate psychological discourses on black people well into the 1970s and 1980s.

The affirmation of the self-hatred hypothesis by America's largest and most influential black organisation indicates that it was neither just a question of racist discourses finding happy consonance with these new, scientific psychological findings, nor a matter of white scientists reaffirming their prejudices. Institutions of opposition, too, have had an interest in particular constructions of the black person, and it is in these that black psychologists have played a central role.

Over time, further studies of the black self-concept produced mixed results, with a great many failing to confirm the thesis of black people as having negative self-concepts (for example, Deutsch 1960, Pettigrew 1964, Rainwater 1967) and some studies actually finding white Anglo-Saxons to have lower self-esteem than blacks (Powell 1973, Rosenburg 1972). Explanations of these contradictory findings have also varied. Some (for example, Kardiner and Ovesey 1962, Powell 1973, Pugh 1972) attributed the fall-off in results confirming the negative self-concept idea to wider social changes having enabled black people to become less self-hating, rather than suggesting that there was any problem with the thesis of black self-hatred. Others (Banks and Grambs 1972, Cross 1991) concentrated on the methodological weaknesses of the earlier studies, presuming that improvement and refinement of these would lead to the discovery of the truth of the matter.

In light of the methodological critique, which suggests that scientific method was not adhered to in any case, it is clear that conditions and climates outside the laboratory were playing a major role. These included the institutional needs of both welfarist and civil rights organisations, and the political expediencies of those difficult times. There was little space for richness and diversity, or for the subtle nuances of multiplicity in the struggle for resources and programmes for the black urban poor and against racism and segregation.

Ultimately, the validity of deducing pervasive conclusions about black identity from identification and preference tests also came under increasingly critical scrutiny. Wider social and cultural transformations and changes in American race relations are likely to have contributed to the decline of the self-hatred theories. Although even today self-hatred theories continue to have currency in some circles, a great many other ideas about black identity and black psychology in general have since developed (see Boykin *et al.* 1979).

What all the above work has in common is the assumption that there is a unitary black subject, or, in the case of colonial psychology (Chapter 2), a unitary African subject. It is this that accounts for the gross generalisations that have been made about 'the Negro', often on the basis of very inadequate evidence. Even where 'the Negro' was viewed as being socially constructed, this was only in terms of a monolithic concept of racism. Other aspects of social reality and the diverse experiences that can be grouped together under the heading of the 'black experience' do not feature in any of the work that has been discussed so far. This cannot be explained away as being due to the absence of evidence. Even a cursory reading of African-American history reveals it to have been complex and varied, textured by an array of cultural and other responses to the highly oppressive situations that prevailed both during slavery and after abolition. Yet psychological studies have invariably reduced this complexity, in order to generate simplistic 'truths' about 'the Negro' that conformed to the dominant ideas and practices of the times.

One dimension of diversity within the category 'Negro' that has not been addressed in the above-mentioned constructions is gender. 'The Negro' is assumed to be male, and considerations of gender are not addressed. In fact, where Ruth Horowitz's early experiments found less evidence of 'self-hatred' among girls, she decided to drop girls from her sample, in order to achieve the results she desired. All of this work has been gender-blind, but the damaged black at the heart of it all was a male subject. This paved the way for subsequent social science work that was to focus on the black male's poor self-concept and in some cases to place the blame for this squarely on the shoulders of black women.

1960S–1970S: THE EMERGENCE OF BLACK PSYCHOLOGY

What were the social conditions which led psychologists to posit the need for a 'black psychology', distinguishable from white psychology? What led black psychologists to form their own organisations outside the existing professional and academic forums that existed for psychologists in general? The racism of the psychological establishment provided more than enough reason for black psychologists to organise themselves as professionals but this alone did not make for black psychology. Black psychology has come to mean psychological study of black people by black people, and has by and large been based in the United States.[4] Within it, serious questions have been raised about whether modern psychology is adequately equipped for the study of black people and the issues of interest to black psychologists. Many felt that psychology, despite its claims to scientific neutrality, was racist because of the kinds of knowledge which it has generated about black people. For some, 'black psychology' meant using the existing theories, methods and practices of psychology but adapting these to use on black people. Others felt that it would have to invent new approaches. Black psychology has not generally referred to the studies of black people that have been carried out by white psychologists, ethnopsychologists or anthropologists. The differing positions on how it should be defined and developed continue to be debated among black psychologists, particularly in the *Journal of Black Psychology*. For present purposes, we are concerned only with the psychological studies of black identity. My purpose in this chapter is to explore the evolution of black psychological discourses on identity and their possible relations to changes in black popular cultures and wider social and institutional developments. To this end the relationship between psychological discourses and the institutional needs and practices of both the mainstream establishment and the black movement are traced.

The 1960s were years of intensifying struggle and suppression, years in which the pacifism of the civil rights movement was superseded by the militancy of the Black Power movement. Questions of identity no longer centred on integrating into white institutions, culture and society but on the assertion of black identities as distinctively different and separate. Whereas the 1950s cultural change manifesting itself as the Harlem Renaissance concentrated on celebrating blackness and claiming the humanity of 'the Negro', the Black Power movement added to this a rejection of whiteness as corrupt and undesirable, and asserted a philosophy which concentrated on the acquisition of power by black people. It was an idea which terrified the white establishment and white society in general. A diverse array of new organisations sprang up in black communities, expressing this militant attitude in various ways. The Black Muslims, for example, used Elijah Mohammed's highly racialised interpretation of Islamic philosophy, which Malcolm X first propagated and subsequently developed into the broader political ideology he called Black Nationalism. During the same period black community organisations coming under constant physical attack from the authorities proclaimed their willingness to take up arms and fight back, and formed the Black Panther Party for Self Defense, with Eldridge Cleaver and Stokely Carmichael as main spokesmen.[5]

With regard to social science during this period, the best-known work was being undertaken by the white establishment in the form of Moynihan and Arthur Jensen. The Moynihan Report was published in 1965, only a year after the Civil Rights Act, and provoked a heated controversy over the way in which it construed 'the Negro family' as a pathogenic, matriarchal institution, to which most of the problems of black people could be traced. In 1969, Jensen's article in the prestigious *Harvard Educational Review* reactivated old genetic arguments when he argued that the lower IQ scores of black children were the result of genetic rather than social factors and that social intervention was therefore futile.

The National Association of Black Psychologists was founded as black radicalism, and the establishment responses to it, reached their zenith, in 1968. Jensen's notorious article on IQ and black underachievement in the education system sparked off a renewed debate on race and intelligence that was to preoccupy behavioural scientists and wider society well into the 1970s.[6] Because of this onslaught of anti-black research, one finds that black people who became professional psychologists during the early 1970s did so with a somewhat defensive, problem-solving orientation, rather than out of a proactive engagement with the positive aspects of what it meant to be black in America. Therefore it is not surprising to find the black psychologists of the 1970s described as being:

(a) dedicated to critiquing the academic myths concerning the psychological reality of black people, and

(b) 'watchdogging' their communities, and trying to protect them from further invasions by white social scientists and the detrimental social policies and actions that emanated from their studies.

(Boykin *et al.* 1978)

In short, it was a period of damage limitation exercises and ground-clearing, peppered with a few attitude surveys on black militancy. Needless to say, the bulk of this work did not develop radical new paradigms for research, nor did it challenge existing psychological methods. This may have been because most black psychologists lacked the institutional support and strength to develop ground-breaking research. Instead they concentrated on diligently applying the methods they had been schooled in, methods that carried the most legitimacy within the empiricist paradigm. Although they addressed themselves to issues of concern to black communities such as mental health, personality assessment, education, intelligence and achievement, racism and racial integration, they did not challenge the premises of empiricist psychology. Psychology, even more than other social sciences, concentrated on a narrow, dualistic paradigm which fell back on biologistic explanations of human behaviour and which took 'the individual', 'the family' and 'society' as given, rather than attempting to study or theorise how they came to be. At that time there was no reason not to assume that once there were enough black psychologists, psychology would cease to reproduce the dominant racist ethos of the times. This would be done by adding a black perspective to the existing theories and methods of mainstream psychology.

Although black psychologists may have been more concerned with social, and particularly racist, conditions, their methodological thrust therefore continued to be reductionist. The complaint reflected in the title of Guthrie's study *Even the Rat Was White* is more a charge of neglect than a challenge to the dominance of rat behaviourism. Others have called for the development of 'black behaviourism' (e.g. Hayes 1980). The predominantly empiricist thrust of the emerging black psychology is evident in leading collections produced during the 1970s (e.g. Banks and Grambs 1972, Boykin *et al.* 1979, Wilcox 1971). The subject at the heart of black psychology, like that of mainstream psychology, was still assumed to be a unitary, static and rational subject, and the emphasis here too was on what was measurable, quantifiable and observable.

None the less, black psychologists did begin to address the concerns of black people and, even if their conceptual frameworks limited their efforts in some ways, they did succeed in opening up a new intellectual field of enquiry within black studies. They also took concrete steps to limit the negative effects of psychotechnology on black people, such as when the Association of Black Psychologists imposed a moratorium on the use of mental tests which showed black children to score lower than whites. Black psychologists set about constructing new measures that tried to take black social and cultural realities into account.

There were also some who wanted to push black psychology beyond the existing paradigm. Wade Nobles (1980a), for example, rejected mainstream psychology as 'white' and therefore inapplicable to black people, arguing that black psychology should embark on its own course, drawing on a philosophical base that can be derived from the African origins of black culture. He and other advocates of Afrocentric psychology owed much to the Afrocentric school of thought propounded within North American Black Studies. However, the African philosophy that is identified as the proper framework for black psychology is defined in essentialist and simplistic ways. This has tended to rely on the work of one or two African philosophers (see Mbiti 1970) and to overlook the wide-ranging philo- sophical debates that have occurred among African intellectuals: debates which demonstrate that there is no single set of principles that can be defined as the essential African philosophy.[7] The size and cultural diversity of the region cannot be reduced to the list of concepts that Nobles uses to describe 'the African self'. None the less, black psychology makes continual reference to an unproblematised African philosophical base upon which it is assumed black psychology should draw (for example, Parham 1991).

The struggles and victories of the civil rights movement, and the back- lash which led to the more militant rebellions of the late 1960s, thrust the African-American intelligentsia (including psychologists) into a new era of self-questioning and exploration. Black radical discourses led black psychologists to pose new questions, their early theses having been over- turned by the black liberation movement. After all, self-hating Negroes do not rise up in their thousands and riot to protest against their oppres- sion. This particular construction had been superseded by dramatic and revolutionary behaviour, as well as by the proclamations of self-love that characterised the Black Power era. Even within psychology, the scene was at last set for new areas to be explored.

THE PSYCHOLOGY OF NIGRESCENCE

In the 1970s a series of theorists developed racial identity theories, that addressed themselves to conceptualising the process of black identity formation (Cross 1971, Milliones 1980, Thomas 1970 and others already reviewed in Phinney 1990 and Helms 1990). Helms (1990) points out that many of these authors do not refer to each other's work, so that there is a certain amount of repetition. General to all is the proposition that black people move from a less 'healthy' state of white-defined identity to a more healthy, racialised identity. They also all depict black identity as developing in a series of stages which the individual passes through in a linear fashion. Only the details of these stages vary between authors.

Thomas (1970), for example, hypothesises that white racism has generated an existential pathology in black people, which he calls *negromachy*. Drawing on the much earlier work of W.E.B. DuBois on black alienation (DuBois 1920), and taking up the idea of black people as damaged people, he describes negromachy as being symptomatised by a confusion over self-worth, over-dependency on white society for self-definition, compliance, subservience and over-sensitivity to racial issues. This unhappy first stage obviously bears a close similarity to the self-hating figure who dominated the 1930s–50s work on black identity and led to the pre-occupation with the black self-concept. What distinguishes the racial identity development theorists from the others is that they did not stop here but instead developed models for black identity as a dynamic and developmental aspect of selfhood which emerged within the black community rather than being defined by the external forces of racism. In other words, while they do not question but in fact reaffirm the pre-existing idea of black self-hatred, this is now taken to be the starting point of black identity formation rather than a permanent psychological accompaniment to blackness.

Nigrescence is defined by Cross as the process of becoming black (1974, 1980). His model has received the most attention from researchers, something which he suggests may be due to its having proved to be the most amenable to empirical investigation (1991). This does seem a likely explanation, given the continuing dominance of rather narrowly defined empiricist methods in North American psychology.

The Cross model of nigrescence delineates five stages in the process, which can be summarised as follows:

1 *Pre-encounter*, a stage which bears a marked similarity to the self-hating Negro idea and to Thomas's depiction of *negromachy* in that it involves being deracinated, dominated by the Euro-American world-view which inferiorised blackness.
2 *Encounter* stage involves 'a shocking personal or social event that temporarily dislodges the person from his old world-view, making the person receptive (vulnerable) to a new interpretation of his identity and his condition' (Cross 1980: 85).
3 *Immersion–Emersion*, described as 'the vortex of psychological metamorphosis' (ibid.), is typified by a struggle to remove the old perspectives and clarify the new world-view, which includes 'glorification of African heritage, either/or thinking, blacker-than-thou attitudes' and a 'tendency to denigrate white people and white culture while simultaneously deifying black people and black culture' (ibid.). This

sometimes reactionary and rather dramatic stage is said to level off after some time, leading to:

4 *Internalisation*, a stage which signals the resolution of conflicts between the old and the new world-views and is characterised by self-confidence, psychological openness, pluralistic and non-racist perspectives.

5 An *Internalisation-commitment* stage which is restricted to those for whom the ideological change has lasting significance, some of whom become social activists.

The Cross model has been tested and developed by a number of researchers (including Cross himself) since it was first published in 1971. The most detailed reviews of all this work have also been produced by Cross (1980, 1991). Only key points will be mentioned here, largely for illustrative purposes.

The earliest studies of the Cross model sought consensual validity. For example, Hall *et al.* (1980) did this by deriving a series of single-sentence descriptors from each of the five stages in the Cross model and presenting these to 90 black and 90 white college students as a sorting test, to see if they would group them according to Cross's stages. Both black and white students were found to cluster the items into three or four groups of items that correlated with Cross's stages, results which were taken as evidence for the stages in the Cross model of nigrescence. In a similar vein, Cross (1974) conducted a retrospective recall study of a group of 44 male and 21 female black students from Ivy League colleges, all of whom were activists in the Black Student Movement. This used a fifty-five-item Stages Questionnaire composed of forty-five items generated to represent the stages of pre-encounter, immersion–emersion and internalization. By this time, Cross had modified his model so that 'encounter' was no longer regarded as a stage but rather as catalytic events or experiences. Once again both the results of the stages questionnaire and the post-test interviews offered support for the model.

These studies seem to be unbelievably tautological, and even when they have been conducted in collaboration with others, it seems rather unsurprising that they offer support for the Cross model in view of the fact that Cross lived, worked and derived his model from the same social milieu as the participants being used to test it. Cross was himself a postgraduate student at the time. Furthermore, having come up with a model, generating items for each stage that others would group similarly seems a likely possibility. In interview situations it became apparent that most black activist college students saw themselves as having gone through stages of transition, militancy and finally a mellowing in their consolidation of black identity.

Regarding gender difference, Cross did find that the men reported a more intense immersion–emersion stage and suggested that this may have been the result of male bias in the items. It may of course have simply reflected a bias in the very movement whose members he was researching. Generally samples have used students of both sexes, and found very little gender difference; both men and women seem to produce generally similar results in their grouping of items and their perception of themselves as having passed through stages of development.

After conducting a very similar experiment to the one described above, Krate *et al.* (1974) pointed out the problem of inferring any relationship between racial identity and the changing social climate purely on the basis of data generated by studies of students. Taking urban, low-income, black youth to be a more representative group, they conducted a study on students at their own, northern state college but their results also offered support for those of the Cross studies of the Cross model.

Most of the research that has involved testing for the plausibility of the model offers support for it. But the conclusions that can be drawn are limited in their experimental character by the fact that most have continued to rely on easily accessible black college students as subjects. It is also hard to avoid the conclusion that this kind of work, in keeping with much empirical psychology, has a pronounced self-fulfilling element to it. Research serves to replicate experimentally what researchers already know of their social milieu.

The Cross model has also been used as the basis for the development of at least two psychological tools, devices for measuring and determining which stage an individual is in at a given point in time. Milliones (1973) developed a 66-item device that she called the Developmental Inventory of Black Consciousness (DIBC), while Davidson (1974) developed a 20-item attitude scale, the Black Group Identification Index (BGII).

Thomas Parham (1991) is the only researcher in this tradition to have moved beyond empirical tests of the model's validity. It cannot be coincidental that he is also the first to have proposed major reconceptualisations. In so doing, he addresses a number of the limitations that became evident during the 1980s (see Mama 1987). For example, he too draws attention to the inadequacy of a linear stage model that posits a unitary subject passing through finite identity changes. Correspondingly, he takes a different methodological approach. Using biographical material from the lives of William DuBois and Malcolm X, he notes that these two men, operating in two different eras, have passed through discernibly similar stages in their identity development, DuBois having lived and grown up during the turn of the century and Malcolm X during the post-war period and into the 1960s. Using these examples, and bringing adult development theory to bear on the matter, he argues that identity development continues throughout adult life. Whereas Cross conceptualises 'nigrescence' as a discrete process, occurring as a result of a particular social change (the advent of Black Power in the 1960s), Parham finds that there is a need to theorise identity development in relation to the life cycle. Whereas Cross regards the process of nigrescence as a finite thing that has ended once a person has become black-identified, Parham addresses the need to consider adult identity (and racial identity as an aspect of this) as a continuous process.

Correspondingly, he then develops the Cross model to encompass the stages of early, middle and late adulthood (Parham 1991). He suggests that nigrescence be considered not as a finite process but as a cycle that may be repeated, with somewhat different content, at any of the stages of adult development. This recycling through the nigrescence stages is conceptualised to take in the different circumstances of early, middle and late adulthood. The pre-encounter mid-life adult is depicted as a highly individualistic achiever who has adopted Eurocentric standards of individualism and materialism, denies the effects of race on his or her life, socialises more with white people and is more conscious of his or her 'identity choices' than an adolescent at the pre-encounter stage. His or her children are likely to have grown up as integrationists but would be expected to know of the struggle that their parents went through during the civil rights era and to be proud of who they are. Pre-encounter adults may then be startled by the realisation that this history is not shared and that their children are not black identified, a realisation that provokes a new phase of self-questioning, renewed guilt and anger. They may then change their social habits, for example by moving away from white friends or introducing racial issues at their own workplace. Eventually the intense emotional aspects of their encounter will fade, as the changes are internalised. In late adulthood, recycling may be provoked by reflecting back over a lifetime and perhaps realising that their white peers are far ahead of them, and experiencing a heightened awareness of the role that race may have continued to play, and so to feelings of disillusionment or anger, which may once again lead to recycling through the stages of nigrescence.

Parham further suggests that there are various 'resolution alternatives'. A given person may do either of three things: stagnate at any of the given stages, proceed through life in a stage-wise linear progression, or recycle through the stages at various stages in the life cycle. He does address the possibility of individual diversity, not only through the various listed options but also in his proviso that individuals may start at different levels, depending in part on the racial identity of the parents and surrounding communities within which the individual grows up.

This is clearly a more sophisticated model of identity development than Cross's original version and one that does succeed in providing a framework for conceptualising racial identity changes throughout adulthood. It is also a model that recognises that it is only addressing an aspect of subjectivity and that there are a great many other areas besides racial identity. Parham's extended model recognises the important role of racism but he also claims that 'Black/African identity is an entity independent of socially oppressive phenomena' (Parham 1989: 195), a claim not very well upheld by the processes he details, since these do in fact centre around racial experiences. While he may well be correct to suggest that there is more to black identity than reactions to racism, the content of this non-racial aspect – what he refers to as 'the values and fabric of Black/African culture itself' – is assumed rather than described or theorised. In this he is uncritically taking up the essentialist proposition that there is an 'essential African core', and remarks that his model is intended to be theoretically consistent with this position.

We can conclude that although Parham's model is a significant advance on earlier models, and has been recognised as such by Cross (1991), he none the less does not transcend the essentialist assumptions of its pre-decessors: namely that there is a 'natural' black self. Parham's essential self is not a self-effacing 'Negro' but a prouder 'African' self. While as a whole Parham's model can encompass much greater diversity of iden-tities within the black American community, in the end it still posits a unitary black subject, even if this is one who moves through defined stages of nigrescence again and again, or who may stop (or stagnate) at any given stage. The most important advance Parham makes is that he puts forward a theory of the black person as a dynamic subject, constructed in the course of interaction between the internal and external worlds and located in the African-American experience. It is therefore a theory of subjectivity that moves some way beyond the simpler, linear stage models of black identity development. The individual can change over time, and different individuals will start, progress and end in different places. What he does not encompass is the possibility that multiple stages (or positions) may coexist within (or be available to) a given individual at any given moment. In other words, while diversity is considered a distinct possi-bility, multiplicity is not yet on the theoretical agenda. The theorisation of the subject as not only socially constructed and changing over time but also multi-layered and non-unitary is advanced in the second part of this book.

While theorists of nigrescence as a whole have made a major break-through in theorising racialised identities as being produced out of the interaction between the individual and the society, they are dualistic because they still presume the essential separateness of the internal and external worlds. What has yet to be advanced is a theory of subjectivity as a process that is both individual and socio-historical at the same time. The way in which individuals act on and use social history and experience to invent their own identities along the interrelated dimensions of race and gender, to constitute themselves as racialised and gendered individual subjects, is also left to later chapters.

The psychology of nigrescence links psychological change to social change. The psychodynamics of the process of racial identification are not theorised in these models and this aspect of identity has become separated from internal psychological processes. Perhaps as a result of the empiricist paradigm being utilised, the focus is on measurable attitudes, not the analysis or theorisation of subjective processes.

NOTES

1 Toni Morrison's novels *Beloved* and *Jazz* are informative on this period, the first being about a household headed by an escaped slave woman, and the second concerning characters who have migrated to a Northern city.

2 Frazier's book, first published in 1939, was followed by other major works; see Collard 1937 and Myrdal 1944.

3 The role played by psychological theory in the development of social welfare in Europe has been studied in detail in France (Donzelot 1980) and Britain (Rose 1990). Although these analyses are race-blind they do detail class dynamics in welfarism, and one presumes that a similar proliferation of welfarism and social intervention occurred in the USA. Here a great many programmes were designed to address the 'problem' of the urban poor, a disproportionate number of whom were, and continued to be, black, as Muse (1968) notes.

4 In Britain there have been very few black psychologists and they occupy marginal positions in the establishment. They have not separated their professional work out as 'black psychology' although they have formed support groups among themselves to discuss and consider the race implications of British psychology, and some, but by no means all, have concentrated on working on and with black communities.

5 More detailed information on this period can be found in Cleaver 1965, Davis 1974, Jackson 1970 and Malcolm X 1965.

6 This debate is extensively covered elsewhere: see, for example, Block and Dworkin 1977.

7 Useful sources on African philosophy include Appiah 1992, Hountoundji 1983, Kagame 1956, Towa 1971 and Wiredu 1980.

Chapter 4

Researching subjectivity

In the foregoing chapters we have seen the way in which psychological discourses have construed black people, and the relationship between these discourses and the dominant regimes of truth which prevailed during the history of slavery and colonialism. I focused on the role played by the emergent science of psychology, a role which has predominantly operated in the direction of upholding and legitimising the practices of slavery and colonisation. I observed that since independence, psychology in Africa has become increasingly reductionist in its concepts and methods, and has failed to address the social and psychological transformations that accompanied the emergence of independent nation-states. I ended that section by looking at the responses of western-based black psychologists to the racist functioning of psychology, seen in their efforts to appropriate psychological concepts and methods, and to apply psychology in the service of the black American community. Such initiatives have aimed to use psychology to counteract racist stereotypes instead of reaffirming them, and to generate more complete knowledge on and about the psychology of black people. Instead of psychology being used solely by advocates of racism and anti-racism, black psychology has sought other reference points in black cultural and political life, as was exemplified through my discussion of the close and recursive relationship between 1950s' and 1960s' self-concept research and the civil rights movement, and the psychological study of nigrescence in the context of the post-1960s black movement.

In examining what has gone before from the perspective of the epistemological and political concerns I outlined in Chapter 1, I have engaged in a deconstruction of psychological constructions of colonised and black people. In so doing, some of the key elements of a different approach to the psychological study of black people have also been indicated and will now be developed.

At the epistemological level, I have taken the position that knowledge is situated, and specified the contexts and concerns which guided my research into black women's subjectivity. In this chapter I propose to detail the methodological consequences of this position and to outline the measures I have taken to ensure that I did not generate theories that would simply reaffirm the status quo: a status quo in which gender, race and class are major dimensions of oppression.

CHOOSING TO RESEARCH BLACK WOMEN

The foregoing discussion of colonial and black psychology has revealed the almost complete absence of women from consideration in both of these fields, by both white and black researchers, most of whom have been male. I noted that the colonised, the Negro and the black subjects have been assumed to be male and that women have barely been mentioned.[1] This alone makes the study of black women a worthwhile enterprise. Studies of and with black women are also likely to generate material that has implications for the ways in which both race and gender have so far been theorised and for social theory in general, just as studies of other hitherto unconsidered groups have done. We have already seen (Chapter 1) that the emergence of a black women's movement in the West affected the fundamental categories of feminist thought by forcing a reconsideration of the unitary woman subject, as well as a re-theorisation of particular issues (work, reproduction, sexuality, etc.).

However, choosing an oppressed and omitted group for study does not necessarily alter the kinds of knowledge that are produced. Many studies of the psychology of women, for example, have reaffirmed rather than challenged the patriarchal status quo. More generally, it must be said that traditional research has often taken less powerful groups as objects of study, whether these have been students studied by university professors, working-class youths investigated by white male sociologists, the 'natives' harassed by western anthropologists or middle-class women on the couches of psychoanalysts. The vast majority of social scientific research, particularly in psychology, has utilised students, a captive, cheap and easily available population, even if they are perhaps not highly representative of humanity in general. Studies of 'Other' groups have lent themselves to an unequal relationship in which the Other is kept at a distance and objectified, in the interests of science. Whoever has been studied, the fact is that the power relations of orthodox research processes have vested complete authority in the scientists, who have usually been male and white or western. This has had the effect of silencing the researched – whether these have been colonised people, black people, women or members of other less powerful groups – or at least of orchestrating whatever it is that they are heard to say. In other words the power relations of the research process have acted in the same direction as those in the wider society, a fact which must have had major effects on what has been perceived and what has not been perceived in the course of the research, and so on the type of knowledge that has been generated within this paradigm.

The alternative scenarios are those which have been advocated by radical scholars of anti-imperialist, feminist and leftist persuasion. In the first of these, members of less powerful groups research 'upwards', bringing their differently situated vision to bear in their conceptualisation and theorisation of those more powerful than themselves (see Chapter 1). Kum-Kum Bhavnani (1990) provides us with a rare example of this reverse direction method. She, as an Asian woman, chose to research white youths, arguing that she was able to generate different but valid material and derive theoretical insights that might not have been available to a white male researcher, because of her social difference from the subject group. The second alternative is to conduct within-group research, in which researchers research members of their own social group, or people of similar status, as a way of rectifying the constant reproduction of the status quo within knowledge production. My choice of black women of similar class background and age to myself places it within this option. It reflects my commitment to generating knowledge out of more egalitarian power relations between researcher and researched.

In addition to contributing to an under-researched field (black women's studies) and conducting research within my own ill-defined social group, there was also a rationale that emanated from the socio-historical context. I began the project during my own involvement with a black women's movement in which black women were collectively and individually embarked on a voyage of self-discovery. For this reason a study exploring black women's views of themselves, their identities and their social-historical situation would be a contribution to this ongoing social process and something that black women would willingly participate in and, I hoped, benefit from. I saw my responsibilities as a researcher as being about learning how to observe and analyse in such a way as to assist the participating group to know more about themselves and the social conditions of their existence and formation. This meant facilitating a growth in collective and individual self-awareness, a growth in consciousness of the past and present sources of our various identities and cultures, of our African, Caribbean and European-nesses, of what has enriched and inspired those identities, as well as what has stifled and oppressed them. This places my research within what Mies (1979) has defined as partici-patory research. My use of the term 'research participants' indicates that the women who took part in it also shaped it in important ways, both at the level of generating the information on which the theorising was based and in influencing my conceptualisation of it.

Choosing a multiply oppressed group to research does not in itself ensure that one's research does not affirm the status quo, however, even if one is a member of that same social group. Given my training and experience in psychological and psychiatric research, I could, in theory at least, quite easily have conducted a traditional piece of research taking whomever I chose to define as black women as objects of study and producing knowledge that reaffirmed dominant ideas about black people and women. If I have not done this, it is more the result of the epistemological and political positions I have already outlined and identified with than of my personal characteristics. However, these commitments do not come with a list of procedures attached. The rest of this chapter documents the various steps I took to concretise these commitments in the research process – to translate them from being expressions of intent into a method of enquiry, analysis and theory-building.

DERIVING A RESEARCH PROCEDURE

Traditionally, research procedure is portrayed as a sequence of clearly definable steps. First, hypotheses are formulated. Second, the methods of data-gathering are chosen and designed. Third, data is gathered. Data is then studied and analysed, and finally hypotheses are confirmed or rejected and theory so developed and scientific knowledge advanced. The truth of the matter is that research seldom progresses in such an orderly, sequential manner. Hypotheses are often amended and rewritten during the research process and ideas about how data will be interpreted are often present long before the information has been collected. What is actually presented in research reports is usually a highly sanitised and ordered account of what the rules of procedure suggest *should* have occurred, while the actual processes and events that have occurred in generating this knowledge are considered to be irrelevant, or, worse still, flagrant violations of proper procedure.

I started out this research with some research experience, having worked on a large project in social psychiatry, as well as having conducted two smaller pieces of research of my own, and therefore had to decide whether to uphold what I now knew to be a fiction of sorts, or to jeopardise my career prospects and address myself to the earnest business of exposing some of these fallacies and taking a different approach. In view of the major questioning of social scientific orthodoxy that was occurring as a result of and in step with the various anti-colonial, black liberation and women's movements, and the presence of a like-minded supervisor on the early doctoral dissertation, it was not too difficult to break with tradition on this score. The fact that my first research projects were studies of black people living in South London also had a major influence on my choice of method. The community living in and around Lambeth at that time was not sympathetic to academic research, or to formal interview procedures. In fact, in my first encounters with members of the community there I came in for cross-examination and was intimidated by accusations of my allegiance being to 'Babylon'. The terms on which I eventually won the co-operation I sought were not those of a research student seeking assistance with research projects conducted for academic and institutional reasons. Instead it was the interpersonal commonalities and differences that existed between myself and those I wanted to write about. In the first instance, during the late 1970s, it was the fact that I came from Africa that endeared me to the Rastafarians of Brixton. When I was taken around and 'shown the runnings' it was because I was defined as an 'African daughter' (albeit from Nigeria and not the favoured Ethiopia). And indeed, I later reflected, was my interest not a result of that African background – a background that made me curious to know more about a group of people generations removed from the continent and living in inner-city London, yet embracing a back-to-Africa philosophy and inventing an African life-style? Similarly, when I sought to do a dissertation on 'Social representations in black women' in 1980, people co-operated with me because I was another black woman and had met them at the local black women's centre in my capacity as an active member of that community centre, rather than because I came from the London School of Economics and Political Science.

In short, choosing marginalised groups who are often less than sympathetic to academic pursuits in itself provoked me to adopt less formal methods and to use research techniques that were more about using than about masking my social attributes and interests. Below I go into a more detailed discussion of the social relations of the research process I developed and used as a means of studying black women's subjectivity but first a few comments on the overall process.

I did not start out with neat hypotheses that I then went out to test. The absence of pre-existing material on my chosen subject group and area of interest would, in any case, have made this difficult. This meant that I was conducting a preliminary or pioneering study rather than contributing to an existing body of knowledge, and that my aim was to develop theory rather than to test existing theory. Even if there had been a theory of subjectivity to test, the fact that I take the view that theory must be grounded in social realities would in any case have inclined me towards starting from the hitherto ignored social reality of black women. This meant that I wanted to study first and formulate theory on the basis of what I saw, something that demanded an open mind rather than a pre-formulated set of hypotheses. I started conducting my research with the hope that theoretical ideas would be generated and refined during the research process, rather than imposed on it from the beginning.

With hindsight it is now clear to me that although I may not have had a theory in the formal sense of the term, my common-sense understanding of identity was influencing my methodological choices. I already viewed identity as dynamic and multiple, and had long observed that people were not rational and were often contradictory. It was in the course of my reading that I adopted the term 'subjectivity' to indicate this and stopped

using the term identity.[2] What I started out with, therefore, were preliminary ideas about subjectivity, derived from experience and observation
of myself, other people and the changes we were going through.

I began the research having chosen a social group and a topic – black
women's subjectivity – but little else. I began reading widely in a quest
for approaches, concepts and ideas that I might be able to use in this
uncharted territory. Some of what I read has been considered in Chapters
2 and 3 but these bodies of literature in colonial and black psychology
told me more about what I wished to avoid doing than what I should do,
and, as we have seen, mostly referred to men without acknowledging that
they were doing so. Feminist psychology was only just emerging at that
stage and its precursors – the psychological studies of women and of sex
differences material – were not substantially more illuminating. I derived
more inspiration and insight from the psychoanalytic, Marxist and later
post-structuralist theory than from theoretical psychology. I also reviewed
existing sociological and anthropological studies of African and Caribbean
people. My ideas developed gradually throughout the research period. In
short, theory-building occurred throughout the entire process and gained
momentum during the time I spent writing and rewriting to produce the
work in its present form (an earlier version can be found in Mama 1987).

COLLECTING BLACK WOMEN'S CONVERSATIONS

It will be apparent from my discussion of the research process as a continuous development of ideas that I did not use the standard research tools
at the disposal of trained psychologists. Since I was developing rather than
testing ideas about black women's subjectivity, I needed a method that
would generate material rather than one that would impose a formalised
set of questions on the research participants. I shared many of Anne
Oakley's objections to the accepted methods of interviewing. She
succinctly pinpoints the contradictory nature of the textbook prescriptions
for interviewing:

> The motif of successful interviewing is 'be friendly but not too friendly'
> [sic] . . . the contradiction at the heart of the textbook paradigm is that
> interviewing necessitates the manipulation of interviewees as objects of
> study/sources of data, but this can only be achieved via a certain amount
> of humane treatment. If the interviewee doesn't believe he/she is being
> kindly and sympathetically treated by the interviewer, then he/she
> will not consent to be studied and will not come up with the desired
> information. A balance must then be struck between the warmth
> required to generate 'rapport' and the detachment necessary to see the
> interviewee as an object under surveillance.
>
> (Oakley 1981: 33)

Within this paradigm, proper interviewing is about creating a highly artificial social relationship in which the interviewer asks the questions and the interviewee answers and does not ask questions back. The interviewer is not to give away his or her own opinions, values or ideas, lest these influence the interviewee in some way and lead to what is regarded as 'bias' in the results. If asked, he/she is to evade giving any straight answers, at least until the interview is over. In drawing attention to the gender relations of interviewing, Oakley observes that methodology textbooks invariably assume the interviewer to be male and depict this mode of interviewing as 'masculine', as reaffirming the existing relations of dominance and subordination which disempower and objectify the interviewees.

Whether formal interviewing procedures are to be characterised as masculine or not, it is clear that they have disempowered the researched and allowed researchers to direct the production of data. Neither of these is acceptable within the epistemological and political commitment I have expressed, or in any project that aims to empower the research participants and generate knowledge which is centred on their reality and experience rather than on the presuppositions of the researcher.

Nor are such methods suited to the study of subjectivity. Indeed, the whole rationale for traditional interviewing protocol has been about excluding subjective factors, which are viewed as sources of distortion and bias. This has been especially true of survey research, in which respondents are taken to be exemplaries, individuals chosen more to represent a wider population than because the idiosyncrasies or details of their particular experience are of interest to the researcher. It also needs to be said that although psychology has addressed the individual, it has had concerns very different from my concern with theorising subjectivity. For example, in the study of individual differences, psychology has defined these in accord with a statistical paradigm. Individual variation is addressed but only insofar as it can be reduced to statistically definable differences: standard deviations from statistical norms and statistically significant correlations. Variations in test scores are generally correlated with other variables – which may include gender, race and class – but these are taken as already constituted social factors, that is, as independent variables. Differences between individuals are reduced to differences in test scores.

According to Cronbach (1957), the other main paradigm utilised in psychological research is experimental psychology. Here there is a different approach to individual variation:

> Individual differences have been an annoyance rather than a challenge to the experimenter. His goal is to control behaviour, and variation within treatments is proof that he has not succeeded. Individual

variation is cast into that outer darkness known as 'error variance'. For reasons both statistical and philosophical, error variance is to be reduced by any possible device. You turn to animals of a cheap and short-lived species, so that you can use subjects with controlled heredity and controlled experience. You select human subjects from a narrow subculture. You decorticate your subject by cutting neurons or by giving him an environment so meaningless that his unique responses disappear. You increase the number of cases to obtain stable averages, or you reduce N to one, as Skinner does. But whatever your device, your goal in the experimental tradition is to get those embarrassing differential variables out of sight.

(Cronbach 1957: 674)

The assumptions underpinning the traditional correlational and experimental paradigms that Cronbach challenged in the 1950s still pervade scientific psychological research four decades later. When, as here, one is actually concerned to study the conscious and unconscious thoughts of the individual, her sense of herself and her ways of understanding her relationship to the world, then clearly a different means of collecting, analysing and thinking about one's subject matter is required.

It should by now be clear why I adopted a non-directive and open-ended approach. While I was considering how best to go about gathering material that was not generated under contrived social and relational circumstances, I realised that I was surrounded by exactly the kind of material I needed and participated in producing it each time I went to a women's meeting or spent time with other black women. What we called 'consciousness-raising' was a practice in which subjectivities were explored, shared, changed and constructed. The kind of discussions I chose to use for my research and theorising were happening in kitchens, lounges, bedrooms and community centres – wherever one found two or more black women spending time reflecting together. I chose to record and document an ongoing slice of a social practice that all the research participants and I were involved in, and to use this as a basis for theorising. I have already described how identity was a central concern of the black women's movement at the time of the research (Chapter 1). Consciousness-raising was one of the activities that black women were constantly engaged in during that period of our history, one which reflected the influence of both the black liberation and feminist movements that had preceded the 1980s.

In order to record the kind of material I was interested in, and knew to be available from my own involvement in a great many discussions in and around the London black women's social scene, I arranged sessions with one or more women, contacted through the same network. I generally indicated my particular interest in researching and theorising on the subject of black women's identities and my wish to record discussions between black women.[3] We met at one of our homes, setting aside an afternoon or an evening to reflect on our identities and on those aspects of our personal histories which we felt to have been influential in making us the people we were. We settled down over cups of tea, or over a meal one of us had prepared. Often I initiated the conversations by explaining my interest in doing a study of black women's identity formation, as simply and directly as possible, and responded in an open and honest way to any questions or challenges. Since I either knew or had been introduced to all by mutual friends, and had by the time of meeting already established their interest in participating in the research, getting discussions going was unproblematic.

I used a small tape recorder which I left running throughout the session. Discussants soon became less conscious of, if not oblivious to, this equipment, since I took responsibility for ensuring that the tape was running. The advantage of recording these sessions far outweighed the disadvantages, particularly because it left me free to participate fully, something which would not have been possible if I had had to take notes.

Sessions took the form of open-ended exploratory discussions in which participants compared and contrasted experiences that they felt to have had some bearing on their identity and on their awareness of themselves. My role was a dual one, as both researcher and participant. However, since we shared the goal of exploring black women's identities, and I took care not to claim any expertise in this area, I did not pose questions for other participants to answer, or restrain my own participation when questions were directed at me. In keeping with the commitment to power-sharing in the research process, discussions were conducted in the spirit of mutual exploration, much in the style of consciousness-raising or co-counselling. Since most of the participants had some experience of group work, most were accustomed to giving one another the space in which to speak and develop thoughts aloud, so that there was no need for any mediation to ensure no one was silenced, although levels of verbal participation varied between individuals. There was never a shortage of things to talk about, and the majority of the conversations flowed freely and enjoyably, occasionally getting heated and intense but never acrimonious.

All in all, 14 women and I participated in the fully recorded discussions, in small groups of between 2 and 4, in sessions that lasted between 2 and 3 hours. One participant, Theresa, shared my interest in the study and also had a background in psychology. She set up and hosted several sessions at her home and at the homes of others, and therefore participated in more than one. Otherwise, participation was on a one-off basis for the purposes of the research, although some of us continued to meet socially and to continue discussing issues raised in the recorded sessions, in the ensuing years. A follow-up study would be extremely interesting to carry out, ten years on. In addition to these 14 women, there were a number of others whom I referred to in the thesis as secondary part-icipants. These were women with whom I had ongoing friendships in the course of which we had many discussions like those I recorded for the research and with whom I often discussed ideas on subjectivity, the black women's movement, feminism, racism and any number of other relevant areas. I have not quoted from these but mention them as having been influential in shaping my ideas.

I stopped holding recorded sessions when I had material from dis-cussions with 14 women, amounting to 29 ninety-minute cassettes, aware that I had a vast amount of material to work from, a great deal of which I did not use or quote directly, although all of it was part of the research experience and thus played a more or less explicit role in the process of reflection and theory-building. I played back and listened to these tapes repeatedly and began the process of transcribing and reflecting on the material while I was still gathering both written and recorded material. In the end I did not transcribe all the tapes in full – to do so would have taken an inordinate amount of time and produced far more pages of tran-script than I could ever use. After completing the first hundred pages of typescript I became more selective as to which sections of each tape I transcribed. The transcript of forty-five minutes from one session is given in the Appendix.

CHOOSING PARTICIPANTS

Individual participants were not chosen through the approved methods of statistical or random sampling. These would not have been appropriate for research which was partly about defining who black women are. To select a representative sample of a group that is in a continuous process of self-definition and which is clearly not homogenous on any major social dimension would have been impossible. Claims regarding the representa-tiveness of the research participants were also likely to facilitate stereo-typing. Given the ease with which limited and partial knowledges about black people have been taken up as absolute truths and generalised, this was something I wished to avoid.

I chose participants using a method that would be referred to as cumu-lative or theoretical sampling. Random sampling was quite inappropriate to an own-group study of this nature, since there were no listings of black women to use as a frame. Ensuring the representativeness of the research participants was also not my concern because of the exploratory nature of the research. This is the same as saying that in the study of the group 'black women', there has been so little research that we are not in a posi-tion to define the parameters on which representation should be based. Random or representative sampling is designed so that general statements can be made about a designated group. This project was not about making general comments on the group defined as 'black women' but, on the contrary, about studying subjectivity – how individual black women have developed their particular identities. In view of this, orthodox sampling methods would have been inappropriate and increased the likelihood of the information about the research participants being misused and taken up in new or old stereotypes about the group 'black women'. Furthermore, representative sampling assumes a certain homogeneity across the group and, in the case of a newly emerging social group, this would not escape presuming certain answers to the question of what constitutes the identity of black women and presuming an already defined 'black community'. Establishing what a representative sample would have comprised also posed particular problems because of the fact that most of the black women contacted self-identified with more than one group and as such were multiply representative; that is to say they could have been taken as representative of women (although in Britain 'women' are assumed to be white) or of blacks (although in Britain the typical black is a young male) or of Afro-Caribbean women (although they were all in fact British and few could have said they were of African descent alone), African women and so on. It is unlikely that any of them would have been deemed to be 'representative' of British women, although all were British. The situation was not made any simpler by the fact that not only were all the research participants only partly defined by the prevailing ethnic categories but also by the fact that ethnic categories have been changed repeatedly over the years, both as a result of the imperatives of the attempts to monitor Britain's communities ethnically and as a result of the assertions of new (and sometimes reassertions of old) collective identities. While I describe the participants as all being black women who self-identify as such, their accounts were in no way taken as definitive or typical and, as the conversations soon showed, this was not an identity which precluded any of the others I have mentioned, or which prevented individual innovations. Each was a unique individual, whatever collectivities she identified with. In other words, my approach was more of a case-study approach than a survey of any kind.

The selection of research participants departed from orthodoxy in another important way, namely in not having a control group of white women, or of black men. My rejection of the comparative method is based on the fact that studies of oppressed groups have generally done them a disservice by taking the dominant group as the norm. Black women cannot only be defined in relation to the difference between them and white women, as is implied in existing literature. Just as feminist scholars study women in their own right, and black scholars reject a paradigm that marginalises black experience and centres on white experience, this study investigates black women in their own right. The comparisons that are drawn are of similarities and differences between black women. Given the enormous diversity of experiences and backgrounds within the group, this provided more than enough material for a study of this scope. The focus on black women and the rejection of a comparative method also aimed to ensure that there was time and space to do a depth study. For the same reasons the sample size of 14 was deliberately small.

The minimal criteria for inclusion were as follows:

1 that participants identified themselves as black women and were willing to talk about what that meant to them and how they had come to define themselves as such;
2 that they fell in the early twenties to mid-thirties age group at the time of the research;
3 that participants were of African-Caribbean or African descent (including individuals of mixed parentage in which one parent was of African-Caribbean or African descent and the other European).

For circumstantial reasons all lived in London at the time of the research, and had lived there throughout their adult lives, that is to say, for at least 10 years prior to the research period.

Once the first few sessions had been held, participants were asked to suggest other women whom they felt it would be interesting to include, either because of what they shared with them as self-identified black women or because they differed in aspects of their identity and background.

THE WOMEN IN THE STUDY

Here I present a brief description of the research participants, as they were at the time of the research. They are introduced under the pseudonyms that are used to identify them wherever they are subsequently being quoted. More is learnt about some of them in the course of the following chapters, while others make less of an appearance. None the less, all are listed here to indicate some of the basic facts about the fifteen primary participants.

Theresa is single and in her early thirties. She trained and worked as a nurse and then took a degree in psychology and a master's degree in medical psychology. She is highly committed to her work which involves training, counselling and consultancies for her local authority and community organisations. She grew up in the Eastern Caribbean. Her parents emigrated to England during her childhood, leaving Theresa and her brother and sister to be raised by her grandmother until the age of 16, at which point she and her younger sister were sent for and came to join their parents and younger siblings in Britain. She was active in the black women's movement during its peak years.

Angela is in her mid-thirties and is raising a 4-year-old son. She was born and raised in Britain by her English mother. Her father was a Ghanaian who did not marry her mother but returned to Ghana and established an African family there. Angela visited her father and step-family in Accra for school holidays several times in the course of her teenage years. She teaches in adult education, writes and does art. Like Theresa she has been extremely active in black women's organisations and the two of them are friends who exchange social visits and generally keep in touch with one another.

Asha is of Ghanaian parentage and has lived in Britain since her early childhood, about thirty years ago. She trained as a teacher but then moved into working with a black women's project set up by the group she was a member of. She is married to an African who lives on that continent, while she remains in England with their two primary-school-age children. She is very concerned to provide them with sufficient African cultural enrichment in their home environment, to mitigate the effects of the racism they experience at school. Ultimately she would rather they lived in Africa but at present she is dedicated to her work with the black women's project and keen to preserve the autonomy her full-time employment in this affords her.

Mona is 27 and was born and raised in London by her Jamaican migrant parents. She has never visited Jamaica and has limited knowledge of the Caribbean, her upbringing having been focused on enabling her to succeed and integrate into British society. Her mother appears to have been a very dominant figure in their family life, and Mona left home in her teens. She has worked with a number of black community projects in various parts of London. She has a white English boyfriend and they plan to buy a flat together.

Rosaline is a teacher who lives alone in a small West London flat. She has been in Britain since her migrant parents brought her to join them when she was in her early teens. She has been back to visit Jamaica once, in 1976, but has no plans to live anywhere but Britain. Her social life centres on the Caribbean community.

Mary is 26 and was born and brought up in a small Northern English town by her Jamaican migrant parents. Like Mona, she was brought up to see herself as English, to speak properly and fit in with British society. After secondary school she moved to London and has since held several jobs. She currently works at a South London community centre, where she has worked at establishing a black women's group and become increasingly racially aware.

Martha was born in Britain, her mother English and father Nigerian. Her parents separated and she and her siblings grew up with their father and his family in Nigeria until her early teens. Her mother then sent for her and she spent the ensuing years in London, until she left home. She has two young children by a Jamaican partner and works full-time in a community organisation to support her home and family. She visits her family in Nigeria from time to time.

Dot is a youthful 24-year-old who was born and raised in East London by her Eastern Caribbean mother in a large family of siblings and half-siblings. She lives with her white English boyfriend and has taken time off from college to pursue her interest in music, as a singer.

Gloria is a 36-year-old community worker who was born in Britain of Jamaican migrant parents. She has lived in this country for all but two years of her childhood, at which point the family returned to Jamaica. She strongly identifies with Africa and black culture, and is a community worker, mostly with young black women. She is single and has one son by a West African partner.

Halima is 23 and was born in Nigeria of a Nigerian father and a Welsh mother. She is the second of five girls. She came to boarding school and then to college in England, visiting Nigeria regularly until her parents' divorce. She has a well-paid job with a private company and one of her younger sisters lives with her in London. They visit their older sister in Nigeria regularly and are fluently bilingual.

Priscilla is a 26-year-old who was born and raised in England of Eastern Caribbean migrant parents. She has made one visit to the Caribbean. She works with a community theatre company that produces plays concerned with black women's history and experience.

Beatrice has a white English mother and a Nigerian father who still live in this country. She was born and raised here and has never visited Nigeria. She is also single, and works with Priscilla in the theatre company.

Iscara was born in Jamaica of Jamaican parents who brought her with them when they migrated to England in her early childhood. She has lived here ever since but visits Jamaica regularly. She has two children by different Jamaican fathers who both live there. Although she lives in England, as a Rastafarian she strongly identifies with Africa and would ultimately choose to live there, as her religion prescribes. In the meantime she lives in as African a manner as possible under her circumstances, and spends her time writing and performing poetry.

Penny, in her early twenties, was born in Britain of a Ghanaian mother and a white British father who worked in the British army serving in West Africa during the colonial years. She is the second of two girls. The family lived in Ghana during her childhood. After her parents' divorce the two sisters were sent to an English boarding school by their father and their mother subsequently died. Their father then married another Ghanaian woman and has continued to live in West Africa, while Penny and her sister live and go to college in England.

Amina, the researcher on this project, is also of mixed parentage, with a Nigerian father and an English mother. They are still married and both have lived in Nigeria since I was 2 years old. I am the first of three children and now in my mid-twenties. After early childhood years in Kaduna, all three of us came to schools and subsequently to colleges in Britain. One brother has returned to Nigeria to live and set up a business, the youngest is still studying and lives with me in London. I work, study, am involved with the black women's movement and work with other black organisations involved in anti-racist activities and African solidarity work. One thing that distinguishes me from the rest of the participants is the fact that I have some knowledge of all three cultural sources: I am African and British, and have lived in Britain's black communities, and have also travelled and stayed with families in Jamaica and the Eastern Caribbean.

SOCIAL RELATIONS AND THE RESEARCHER'S ROLE

Having introduced myself as a participant, I will elaborate on what has been meant by participatory research in the context of this project. Participatory research has been embraced by both feminists and radical anthropologists as methods which enable a more egalitarian relationship to prevail between researcher and researched (see, for example, Carasco 1983, Huizer and Mannheim 1979, Lather 1988, Mies 1979).[4] The term 'participatory' has come to mean a great many different things to different researchers. Without my going into lengthy discussion of the matter, it is clear that subject participation has very often been sought at the level of data gathering but seldom at the levels of data analysis, interpretation or publication. Since it is readily apparent that higher levels of subject participation yield richer and in many ways better types of data, there are perfectly good grounds for sharing power during this stage of the research process, even if one is not concerned with transforming social research into a more democratic exercise. Allowing or securing participation beyond this level is rare and has been less easily effected, for good reasons. The first of these is that unless the research agenda is collectively established, the researcher is in the position of demanding people's time and energy, not to mention their intellectual and other resources. Other reasons stem from the fact that researchers have professional and intellectual rationales for undertaking research, and these involve delivering research products such as publications in forums and styles not necessarily accessible to those who have been sought as research participants. One way round this is to produce research publications that are accessible, as well as the more academic papers, either in the form of books or manuals that are of use to the participants or that they may participate in producing.[5] Others have designed projects that have the participation of community members in producing publications or implementing social changes. Research that involves participants in effecting some kind of personal or social change is often referred to as 'action research'. Kielstra (1979) usefully defines action research as research which seeks to link the research to the aims and aspirations of the researched community and use it as a tool for effecting social change. In short, there are a great many possibilities along the spectrum from purely academic research that centres around production of theory and knowledge, to social development and policy research that has an action-oriented focus, to activist research that seeks to empower its target group and effect social change.

In the present project, by choosing an agenda that I saw as already existing in the context of the black women's movement, I sought to use and work with an ongoing social practice. The fact that a great many black women were undertaking self-exploration, and that my project was about furthering our understanding of what it was to be a black woman, meant that there was a common interest. As a result I found women willing to participate in discussions during which they reflected on matters of identity and personal and collective history, and to have me use these for a research project that I was undertaking, with a view to writing a book and obtaining a doctorate. It can be seen from my description that participation was sought and granted at the level of data collection. Since I did not set out to test pre-existing theories of my own but to have my theorising emanate from the debates in which we engaged, the process of thinking about identity was also to some extent a shared one. It was not a fully participatory research process (if such a thing can be said to exist) because the further development of the ideas started in the discussion process, the background research and all the writing up were undertaken by me, with no participation from the rest of the participants. This has been true of most of what is referred to as participatory research, but exponents have seldom made the limitations of their subjects' participation so explicit, so implying that the issues of power are democratically resolved by using a two-way data-gathering method. Since most power lies in the interpretation and allocation of meaning, and in the analysis, theory-building and in the production of publications, participation in data-gathering is a long way removed from power-sharing, but still a major change from the complete exercise of power that has characterised traditional social and psychological research.

One common response to the exercise of power in the process of analysis and theory-building has been to withdraw from doing either: to view research as a means of giving voice to previously silenced views on the world but to refrain from theorising. The method most commonly adopted is one in which women are directly asked for accounts of their experience, which is what Hollway refers to as descriptive interviewing. As she notes:

> The method of descriptive interviewing represents a consistent application of the political principle that women's experience can provide a direct route to women's consciousness or identity. That principle provides the answer for feminist method: ask women directly for an account of their experience ... the assumption is the idealist one that the knowledge is there, based on experience, and can be represented in an account.

> (Hollway 1989: 40–1)

The same author points out, as Wilkinson (1986) did before her, that this principle was nothing new, having been applied in ethogenics and personal construct theory. It is a method that has gained enormous popularity in women's studies, particularly in studies of non-western women in which feminist researchers have been doubly reticent about theorising as a result of the anti-imperialist critique. Such an approach assumes that accounts accurately reflect experience, that they unleash 'truth' in a pure form unadulterated by the assumptions and values of the researcher. Feminist post-structuralist thinkers have challenged this assumption, instead pointing out that any number of accounts can be given by an individual and the reading of such accounts is never empty of theory but always discursively positioned, as are the accounts themselves (Hollway 1989, Weedon 1987). What this means is that while these open-ended methods may indeed reveal previously suppressed voices and rich experiences, a theory of how such material is produced, and what it means, is still required if we are to move beyond assuming that what is said is the truth and that whatever truth is revealed is somehow absolute, rather than a historical production that is one of many possibilities. In other words, open-ended research techniques tend to evade the epistemological and theoretical dilemmas raised by the feminist critique of science instead of addressing them.

THEORY-BUILDING

Usually very little is said about where hypotheses come from, although reference to the work of well-known scholars and theorists in the field of enquiry is common. The research most acceptable to the establishment is that concerned with testing and falsifying or verifying the theories of great men of social science. Original hypotheses will have a much harder time gaining acceptance by tutors, colleagues or funders, particularly if the researcher is youthful, or otherwise uninfluential. Postgraduate researchers are told that they must conduct work that is original, but the truth of the matter is that when original hypotheses or theories are presented as subjects for enquiry, these are unlikely to be given the institutional support afforded to less adventurous proposals. When those who are entitled and empowered to conduct original research present their work to the rest of the world, theories and hypotheses often seem to have emerged out of thin air, or in a flash of inspiration of the Archimedes-in-the-bath variety. Theorising is an unexplained area of the research process. In short, there is a great deal of mystification going on. While research students may be thoroughly trained in all manner of data-gathering techniques and statistical analyses, little is said about the processes of reflection and theory-building, or about the mental activities that go into the inter-pretation and use that is made of the information that has been gathered.

I have already noted in this study that theorising occurred throughout the research process. This had the advantage of ensuring that whatever ideas I came up with were generated by the material I was accumulating. They were not presuppositions that I sought to verify or falsify and thus did not direct my research so much as emanate from it. This approach is in keeping with the idea of 'grounded theory' put forward by Glaser and Strauss (1967), one that seeks to reunite theory and method and to reject the separation of the two that has traditionally characterised social research. In addition to using the recorded discussions as a source of theory-building, I also used published material from the fields of African, Caribbean and ethnic studies, particularly the social historiography of black people in Britain. These sources were used alongside the data while I sought ways of analysing and making sense of what people said, in social historical terms. I also read literature (fiction and poetry) from all these places. Once I had decided to use a method of discourse analysis (see next chapter), these sources proved valuable in identifying discourses. My travels in the Caribbean and my personal knowledge and experience of Africa were also important in giving me insights into the background cultures of participants, particularly when it came to the different sig-nifications of race in these places and the transposition of these into contemporary British racial identities.

To develop my theorising I spent a great deal of time going through both written sources and the recorded material, as well as reflecting on and discussing questions of subjectivity with my peers. It was some time before I was able to decide on how best to theorise subjectivity in a way that would incorporate collective history. I would do this by taking subjectivities as positions in discourses that are historically generated out of collective experience. Before that I looked at my material in terms of similarities and differences between the various participants. The dimen-sions of sameness and difference that I worked with included:

- time spent in Britain;
- time spent in the Caribbean or West Africa;
- social orientation towards black or white communities;
- parentage;
- own racial or ethnic identification;
- sexual and racial orientation.

With hindsight I realise that my capacity to occupy several different social positions was important in helping me to reflect on the material generated in the research process. This capacity may well be available to all people, but it is something that has been particularly developed in members of oppressed and minority groups as a result of the duality imposed on them by the need to understand the dominant society from the position of an outsider, however long they may have lived in the country. This is something imposed by unequal power relations such as those prevailing between black and white people in racially divided contexts, relations that mean that whereas black people are obliged to understand white people in order to succeed and survive the reverse is not true.

In the research process, although the relationships were all between black women living in Britain, differences among the participants were an important force in the discussion process. Participants constantly compared experiences and feelings, either identifying with or distinguishing themselves from what another participant might have said, or at least from their interpretation of it. This is illustrated in the following extract, in which four participants are considering what it means to be black and British:

AMINA: Caribbean people have a really scornful attitude towards black Britons who visit the Caribbean (*turning to Theresa*) – like your attitude towards the black British.

THERESA: Yes. That's because my foundation is from the Caribbean. I don't understand black British people actually, from what I see of a lot of them.

BEATRICE: What do you mean by black British – people who were born and brought up here like me?

THERESA (*laughs, a little embarrassed*): No, I think it's more than just being born here actually. I don't want to be. It's something to do with the way they see themselves. They detach themselves from their parents' roots a lot.

AMINA: But you heard what Mona was saying – her parents didn't want her to know anything about the Caribbean –

PRISCILLA: That's right – and the thing about not talking Creole, dialect – it isn't allowed.

AMINA: So you can hardly condemn the black British for that.

THERESA: No! Condemn is such a strong word.

AMINA: But you do look down at them.

THERESA: I've been rethinking that since that discussion – you know where I got this thing about black British from? I'm thinking about OWAAD. The women that came there were so, so *western*. Not just because they were educated here but their whole view on everything – they all looked down on Third World cultures, that's what I felt from them, and that's what I resented – them not wanting to find out more about their parents.

PRISCILLA: But it's also what those women were exposed to. Some women just aren't exposed to the alternatives. They don't look for it either, because it's a lot easier to just get by.

THERESA: But it isn't.

PRISCILLA: No, it's not, but that's what they've been fed and they've learned how to cope with that so it is easy ...

THERESA: It's easier, and they go around with that. That's what I refer to as black British women.

PRISCILLA: The ones who conform without challenging?

THERESA (*to Beatrice*): I wouldn't say you were – because you challenge.

PRISCILLA: Well maybe if you spoke to them all?

This rather terse exchange indicates that within this group of black women living in London, there are different identifications. Theresa identifies herself as Caribbean, taking distance from those she defines as 'black British'. The way she defines 'those' women is challenged by Beatrice (who does at this moment identify as black British) and Priscilla (who defends and explains the black British without explicitly identifying as such). Theresa explains her initial feelings of resentment. Since all the participants are British citizens who have lived in Britain for a great many years, in theory any of them could self-identify as British, but they in fact take different positions and have different understandings of what the term connotes. These different positions underpin the whole discussion, which went on for some time, clarifying and comparing meanings and considering the cultural identity of black people residing in Britain.

I deployed my own differences from and similarities to the participants when I came to analyse material. The fact that I was not of Caribbean origin can be said to have enabled me to perceive some things as Caribbean and others as not being Caribbean, something that was essential for me to do in order to identify and separate discourses from one another. My ability to take distance and abstract myself from a conversation in which I had participated depended on this capacity. I was able to do the same thing – by positioning myself as African – when it came to identifying what 'black British' was. My dual racial background enabled me to see 'black positions' from within and from without. At the same time, my commonalities with other participants gave me enough empathy and identification to share and exchange with participants at one moment and to theorise about the processes that were occurring at another. In a previous piece of work I described this as follows:

> I have exploited the fact of my own multiplicity by taking up different available positions throughout the course of this research (as black, as a woman, as a Nigerian, as someone who has visited various parts of the Caribbean, as someone with a white English mother, as a British resident, etc). I have played with all these similarities and differences in the course of discussions with participants.

(Mama 1987: 368–9)

Doing this did not involve pretence or affectation: all the positions I took up were legitimate aspects of myself, that I utilised both in generating discussion and in theorising.

DATA SAMPLING

The first problem I confronted was the quantity of material generated by my chosen method of tape-recording free-flowing conversations and then laboriously transcribing these sessions. Initially I had no framework for selecting, and so transcribed the first few sessions in full. It soon became clear that I would never be able to use all of the material I had gathered, since once I started contextualising excerpts of conversation, my commentaries, initially devoted to identifying the historical and contemporary cultural sources (identifying discourses) of the identity positions and experiences being described, also ran to great lengths. I therefore selected what seemed interesting, by setting the transcripts against my then growing background knowledge to identify discourses. Discourses were identified from a very wide base of information about black and Caribbean culture and then used to chart paths through my data. I went through the tapes and transcripts selecting excerpts which enabled me further to elaborate the discourses I had sketched out and, more importantly, to understand better the processes and the contextuality of those subjectivities manifesting themselves in the conversations, or, to put it simply, where they were coming from, socially and historically, and what power relations had permeated these personal and collective histories.

The second stage of my analysis of subjectivity concentrated more on the role of individual history. The later chapters are therefore devoted to in-depth study concerned with the psychodynamics of the subjective process. The rationales for this mode of analysis are presented at that point.

I refer to this process of selecting information from both written sources and recordings as data sampling. As was the case in my selection of participants, I did not sample extracts at random, or in accordance with a predefined sampling technique. Instead I chose to transcribe and subsequently to select extracts for quotation on the basis of the ideas that I was developing. I make no claims about the use I made of the material at my disposal being the best or only use that could be made. On the contrary, I regard the material as having a potentially infinite number of possible interpretations and uses to which it could be put. What I have done is select a small amount of it to put forward and develop my ideas concerning the subjective processes of the research participants, processes that I suggest may be of use in conceptualising the subjectivity of other groups of people, once their specificities have been taken into account. The same process of information sampling takes place whenever a writer chooses a quotation to illustrate or affirm an idea she or he wishes to convey.

Quotation and analysis were not the only uses to which material was put. In an important sense, all the reading and listening to the participants (and to other black women not directly participating in the research) formed the 'data base' that has influenced my thinking in this field. None the less, I suggest that the idea of data sampling be borne in mind as another form of theoretical sampling that has occurred in conjunction with theory-building.

The following chapters continue depicting the research process; they also begin the substantial work of charting black women's subjective processes, developing a way of reading and understanding them, and forming a theory of subjectivity as socially and historically constituted, as a process that is at once collective and individual, multiple and dynamic.

NOTES

1 E. Franklin Frazier's sociological study, mentioned in Chapter 3, is one of the few which has addressed gender. Since then there have been other sociological and historical studies, but black psychologists have continued to work without theorising gender beyond passing mention of sex differences. The more recently emergent feminist psychology has yet to address itself to considerations of race and culture.
2 I continued to use the term 'consciousness' for much longer, since this connoted the collective and social dimensions, and had the advantage of having been used within radical social theory and Marxism, and in African social philosophy, in ways that were not too far removed from the kind of theorisation I started out with. Colleagues in psychology, however, eventually succeeded in persuading me that it signified the opposite of unconscious in the Freudian sense, and that this would be misleading.
3 In two cases, recording was not consented to, and although lengthy and interesting discussions were held (which may well have influenced my thinking), I have not quoted from these out of respect for the fact that these individuals were clearly not as willing as others to share their feelings, thoughts and

experience, anonymously or otherwise. Nor was it necessary, since I had an abundance of material.

4 Action research, in addition to this, has sought to link research to the aims and aspirations of the researched community and use it as a tool for effecting social change (Kielstra 1979).

5 A community research project such as that which produced *The Hidden Struggle* (Mama 1989b) was undertaken with the participation of the Women's Refuge Movement and over 100 abused women. Although the subject group could not be called upon to write up the research, the report was written in such a way as to make it a resource for Women's Aid and other organisations working in the field of woman abuse. To this end, I secured a publication agreement in which one third of the printed copies were made freely available to women's refuges and community organisations. The production of more academically written articles was a secondary activity that I undertook in my own time (see, for example, Mama 1989a).

Chapter 5

Locating the individual in history

The central concern of this chapter is to theorise subjectivity as being constituted, socially and historically, out of collective experience. I theorise subjectivity not as a static or fixed entity but as a dynamic process during which individuals take up and change positions in discourses. I further propose that these discursive positions can be located in the collective history of the social group in question. Theorising subjectivity as a discursive process concurs with the epistemological commitments set out in Chapters 1 and 4. In particular, it enables us to transcend the dualism which has so far separated the individual and the social in psychological and social theory. I suggested that we need to start with viewing individuality as socially produced, while at the same time viewing sociality as produced within individual subjects. I also noted that earlier theorists developed the concept of subjectivity to bridge the theoretical divide between the individual and the social (Henriques *et al.* 1984). In what follows, I develop this theory of subjectivity by exploring the social and historical production of the subjectivities of the black women who participated in the research process. In order to do this, I begin by outlining the social history and origins of black women in Britain, before going on to define what I mean by discourse and to derive the particular discourses positioning black women from this material. On a methodological note, it is worth mentioning that I began theorising subjectivity as discursive in the early stages of the research, while I was reading in the fields of ethnic, Caribbean and African studies and trying to see and conceptualise the ways in which history (in this case black history) features in people's identities. In other words, I began to develop a way of using the concept of discourse as a heuristic device I could use to read people, to comprehend their subjectivities. Put at its simplest, I identified discourses that enabled me to see links between the history of colonial Africa and the Caribbean, present-day social relations and what my research participants were saying.

SOCIAL HISTORY OF BLACK WOMEN IN BRITAIN

The history of black women is in many ways a history of contemporary British race and gender relations, and derives not just from Britain but also from the collective experience of the colonial Caribbean and Africa. Black women living in Britain have diverse origins, and those which are identified depend partly on whom one chooses to include in the term 'black'. This has been the subject of many debates about race, politics and culture, which we will not re-open here. I could, for example, have included black-identified women of Asian descent, a choice that would have required me to conduct research into the large areas of the world that Britain's Asian communities have come from (East Africa, Bangladesh, Pakistan, India, Iran, Afghanistan and Sri Lanka, not to mention China, Hong Kong and the Philippines). For brevity, and because of my own African origins, I chose to limit this study to women of African and Afro-Caribbean descent. The discussions indicated clearly that African, Caribbean and British sources featured in the subjectivities of the participants, often as references to their childhood experiences, to their parents and to the felt need for a strong cultural identity. Participants invoked ideas about their roots as a way of identifying and locating themselves, and in distinguishing themselves from white people and white British culture and behaviour.

Since the community of black women is itself a nascent and self-constituting collectivity, my use of the term 'community' does not denote a taken-as-given set of people with particular physical, social or cultural characteristics. Instead it refers to those who have described and asserted themselves as members of the group 'black women', and to the particular collective vision of themselves and their location in the world that has been most explicitly articulated by the black women's movement described in Chapter 1. The precursors to that contemporary movement, however, lie in the longer history of the black presence in Britain as well as in post-colonial social relations. Although the black presence has been the subject of a welcome series of publications, few of these have addressed the gendered aspects of black history, or the particular experience of black women in British society (see, for example, Fryer 1984, Gilroy 1987, James and Harris 1993, Rogers 1967, Shyllon 1974). It is worth briefly considering the background to the contemporary conditions of black women's lives.

Diverse trajectories

Black people have been present in Britain from Roman times or earlier. The sparse documentation of the early existence of black women leads the researcher into mythology and religion – the worship of a black goddess by the Celtic people during the sixth century AD, the reported presence of Moors in medieval Scotland – and to occasional references in court history, such as to Ellen and Margaret Moore, two black women who worked for Queen Elizabeth in the 1500s (see Fryer 1984, Rogers 1967).

London, like Cardiff, Bristol and Liverpool, has one of the oldest black communities in Britain, partly owing to its port and the arrival of black men – initially mainly Somalis and Asians – as sailors and Lascars employed on imperial ships during centuries of sea trade. Perhaps some of the earliest black British women were the locally born daughters of liaisons between black sailors and local women.

Others were imported as slaves and servants brought over from the colonial territories and American slave plantations. Phyllis Wheatley, for example, was born in Senegal, captured at the age of 7 and survived the middle passage and enslavement in the Americas. Her owners discovered her to be a particularly talented child and she rapidly learnt to read and write both English and Latin, before coming to Britain as a young free-woman in 1773, where she astonished high society with her talents as a poet (Busby 1993: 18–22). Mary Prince was another slave-woman, exceptional in having managed to acquire literacy and so to write an auto-biography chronicling her heart-rending experiences as a slave in Bermuda, the Caribbean and England, culminating in her dramatic escape in 1828 (Prince 1831). Both of these chronicles give us valuable insights into what it meant to be a black woman in those days.

African women were also imported as objects of curiosity. Saartje Baartman, a South African woman, was brought to England in the 1800s and displayed in fairgrounds across Europe, billed as 'the Hottentot Venus' until her premature death in 1816. Much of the attention she attracted, caged and shown in a semi-nude state, was centred on her physique – a fascination which led to her being made into a sexual fetish, featuring on many bawdy postcards. She also attracted the scrutiny of scientists such as Baron Cuvier, who probed and examined her while she was alive and later dissected her corpse and preserved her genitals. A plaster cast was made of her body and, until recently, displayed in the Musée de l'Homme in Paris, where it continued to attract unsavoury attention.[1] Her ugly fate illustrates the role that Africans played in the nineteenth-century European imagination but tells us little of how they might have seen themselves.

Mary Seacole had a very different fate. She was already widely travelled and accomplished as a businesswoman and healer of some repute when she arrived in Britain from Jamaica, in the dank October of 1854. Seacole was determined to continue to carry out her healing vocation (already practised during cholera and yellow fever epidemics in Central America and the Caribbean) by travelling to Crimea. Although her enthusiasm met a frosty reception at the Nurses' Enlistment Centre in Belgravia,

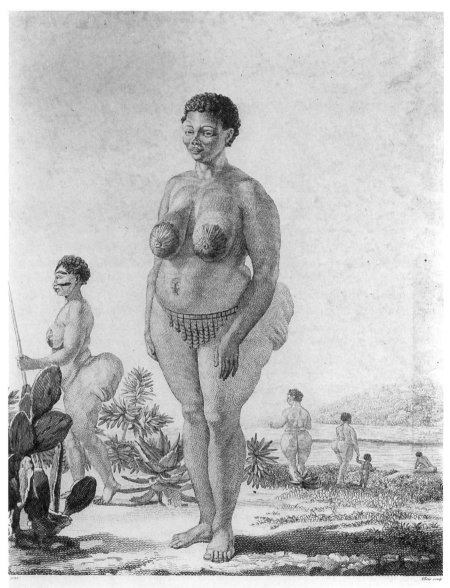

LA VÉNUS HOTTENTOTE.

Sara, femme de race Hottentote agée de 25 ans, observée dessinée et peinte au Muséum d'histoire naturelle en Mars 1815.

she used her own resources to travel to Crimea. There, unhampered by the restrictions and prohibitions circumscribing the activities of Nightingale and other white nurses, Seacole, 'an elderly mulatto woman', became well known among the troops, even if she was not to be granted quite the same public acclaim as the white lady with the lamp (Alexander and Dewjee 1984: 26).

As early as 1731 there were enough working Negroes in London for the Lord Mayor to think it necessary to protect white labour by passing a decree that 'no Negroes should be taught trades' (Rogers 1967: 201). In 1746 it was estimated that there were 20,000 slaves in London alone, and a great many more so-called free mulattoes and black servicemen in the army and navy. Black women, whether they were of pure or mixed origin, appear to have lived among the rest of the working classes in the towns and cities, under conditions not too different from those of white working-class women – many in various forms of servitude and prostitution but others as working women, mistresses and wives further up the scale. At the beginning of this century black women still came as domestic workers, some from plantation societies barely emerging from slavery, others from trading centres and ports. Many of these took care of the children of the bourgeoisie, working as ayahs from India, or as nannies from Africa and the Caribbean.

During the present century, black women (and men) have continued to travel to Britain from all over the former British empire, some believing the imperial myths of the motherland as a land of milk and honey, others coming in search of jobs and in the quest to build better lives for themselves and their families. As a result of this constant immigration, the indigenous black communities were constantly replenished by new migrants, bringing with them attitudes and values deriving from cultural and political conditions in Africa and the Caribbean, which themselves have been constantly changing.

The First World War saw tens of thousands of black men coming to Britain as sailors, soldiers and munitions workers. The survivors established themselves in large cities and continued the process of intermarriage and black settlement. Hardly had the war ended before the 1919 race riots occurred, during which the white people of London, Liverpool, Cardiff, Manchester and Hull attacked the homes and workplaces of their black neighbours.

Since the 1940s, many women have been among those recruited as migrant workers from the English-speaking former colonies, while still others have accompanied or followed migrant parents or husbands. Williams (1993) draws our attention to the fact that when the *Empire Windrush* docked in June 1948, bringing the first shipload of workers from the Caribbean, on board was a 25-year-old woman stowaway: Averilly Wauchope, Kingstonian dressmaker. Subsequent ships brought other black women: fifteen on *The Orbita* only three months later, and then forty-nine more in 1949. Soon women, too, were being directly recruited by London Transport and British hotels.

From the 1950s onwards, more privileged sons and daughters of independent nations also came to study in Britain, some of whom stayed on and embarked on successful careers as an emergent black élite, or joined other black settlers in the services and industries that rapidly expanded after the Second World War. Others stayed because of deteriorating economic conditions in their countries of origin, or because they had married Europeans reluctant to move to the tropics. African refugees have also spent varying periods of time in Britain and, although most of these return home at the earliest opportunity, for some independence or victory has come too late, as has been the case with elderly South Africans, or the children of refugees who have grown up in Britain. Furthermore, many of the black men in Britain, for any of the above reasons, have had children with white English women: children who have grown up with or without the input of their black parent, to constitute a community of British-raised children of mixed ancestry.

A denied presence

It is not an exaggeration to say that throughout the history of the black presence in Britain, there have been recurring movements dedicated to its removal. The earliest recorded expulsions of black people were carried out during the reign of Queen Elizabeth in the sixteenth century. Her efforts to cleanse and purify the nation included a series of edicts calling for the forced removal of 'blackamoors' from the realm and the employment of a merchant fleet to carry out the said removal on her behalf. There followed nearly three hundred years of slavery during which significant numbers of black people continued to find themselves in Britain, either directly from Africa or from the brutal Caribbean plantations, to be kept by the aristocracy as servants or as objects of curiosity, imparting status to their owners and, later, employers. During this period – a period in which Britain had an ever-increasing involvement with Africa and Africans – racist ideologies grew in strength and complexity, systematising relations in which Africans were dehumanised and objectified; whites therefore felt entitled to perpetrate brutal oppression and exploitation in order to enhance their wealth and advance the economic and political interests of their civilisation.

If, in earlier epochs, the racial superiority of white people was seen as a God-ordained truth, the nineteenth and twentieth centuries saw the doctrine of white supremacy being substantiated and legitimised by the emerging sciences: by biology, phrenology, evolutionism and, later, by anthropology, all of which reified racist sentiments which accorded with imperialist interests, giving them the incontestable status of scientific truth (see Chapters 2 and 3, this volume). There is abundant evidence for the thesis that racism developed as ideological justification for the inhuman aspects of imperialist expansion (Fryer 1984, 1988, Williams 1964).

In the twentieth century, many of the pseudo-scientific bases of racism have been exposed and discredited. None the less the contradictory process through which black people have been brought into Britain, and yet the history of their presence continuously denied, has continued. During the First World War, black people were recruited from the colonies to fight for King and country, only to be left destitute on the streets of London, where they became known as 'the St Giles Blackbirds'. Similarly, when the Second World War broke out, black soldiers were once again called to serve the imperial flag, and did so. At the end of the war, many felt entitled to live in the country they had fought for and many others had died for.

Even with active recruitment going on during the post-war boom, racial contradictions persisted. While workers were needed, they were excluded from housing and other social amenities by a colour bar. It is telling to note that the first shipload of workers arrived to be welcomed off the *Empire Windrush* by the Mayor of Lambeth, only to find there was nowhere for them to sleep, so that they had to be accommodated in the hastily prepared Clapham air-raid shelter. In other words, the entry into Britain during the last phase of immigration was always selective: labouring hands were needed but no consideration was given to the human accompaniments to that labour. The history of the Welfare State is one in which there has been a constant preoccupation with limiting access to benefits to those deemed to be most deserving of them. Black people have not been viewed as 'deserving' but rather as parasitic, despite the fact that the same Welfare State has depended so heavily on black labour.

It is for these reasons that for a long time black social and cultural life developed largely outside the mainstream of British life. The intermittent occurrence of race riots throughout the inter-war years and in the 1950s and 1960s has served as a reminder that most of British society has continued to equate Britishness with whiteness, and that certain sections of it have continued to argue for the expulsion of black people from the nation.

Since the 1960s, successive British governments too have fomented racial divisions by exploiting race as a party political issue and competing with one another to introduce increasingly restrictive legislation designed to exclude people of colour from settling in Britain. The first such legislation was the 1961 Commonwealth Immigrants Act. Once primary immigration had been successfully controlled by the subsequent series of legislative changes, government began to shift its attention towards internal administration: to preventing overt discrimination in the highly ineffective Race Relations Act of 1969, and to the regulation and control of minority communities through social policy and administrative practices.[2] Internal immigration controls have also been developed, circumscribing the access of black people to public services and subjecting them to surveillance, intimidation and, where possible, deportation.[3]

We can see that the British state has increasingly curtailed black migration to Britain. Partly as a result of the changed administrative and political circumstances, the small numbers of black people being allowed entry to settle in Britain in the 1980s and 1990s are those who have been categorised as refugees, or who already had British nationality before the latest round of legislation. As a result of the closure of Europe's borders to new immigration from the developing world, the growth of the black communities through new arrivals has been curtailed. This, combined with the fact that ever increasing numbers of second and third generation British-raised blacks have reached child-bearing age, has meant that the black community has grown increasingly British in its cultural make-up. Although contacts with Africa and the Caribbean have continued, the primary location of the majority of black people in Britain today is uniquely British, however much it may differ from the dominant white cultural order. Black British culture, with all its sources in history and in contemporary British racism, is therefore the main backdrop to the identities of black people in post-colonial Britain.

Given these diverse and contradictory trajectories into British life, what can we say to have been the collective experience of black women in Britain? Most of those who would identify themselves as black women today are of African, Caribbean or Asian descent. Many are of mixed origins, and a large proportion were born and have been raised in Britain. British-born black women may have migrant parents, or they may be daughters of British-born black parents. Exact numbers elude statistical monitoring, not least because of the high degree of intermarriage and the dubiousness of ethnic and racial categories in a heterogeneous and changing society.

One thing that we do know is that black women appear to have occupied positions in the labour market that clearly reflect the race and gender divisions that have persistently characterised British society. Three black women's movement activists trace black women's experience of work in Britain over the last five centuries. They describe it thus:

> [O]ne long tradition of back-breaking labour in the service of European capitalism. . . . [I]t was as slaves that Black women's full labour potential was first established, and as slaves that our response to exploitation was first tested out.
>
> (Bryan *et al.* 1985: 17)

Perhaps this legacy explains why, despite being a highly educated segment of the population, most black women continue to hold poorly paid jobs, and why they worked under extremely exploitative conditions (see Lewis 1993, Mama 1984). Most have remained within the 'feminine' professions, as teachers, midwives, nurses, and performing various low-grade tasks in the public services. Little wonder then that the social lives of black women have been addressed mainly in terms of the oppressive impact of exploitative work conditions and Welfare State structures. Occasional policy studies have taken a superficial look at the situation of black women within the British legal and criminal justice system (Mama *et al.* 1986) or as recipients of social services (Mama 1989b), both revealing extremely disturbing conditions and great injustices. No social scientific studies appear to have addressed themselves to the leisure and cultural pursuits of black women, although a number of recent compilations indicate the cultural creativity that has for so long been suppressed in British social life (see, for example, Busby 1993, Grewal *et al.* 1988). None the less, much remains to be told about the past and present-day lives of black women in Britain.

A similar paucity of information prevails when we consider the sources on women in Caribbean and African history, important because the participants in this research made constant reference to these places as cultural and historical sources of their identities. If British experience is articulated mainly in terms of racial oppression, it is to their knowledge of the Caribbean and Africa that many black women turn for inspiration and ideas. These are the alternative sources that feature in their constructions and visions of what black womanhood is about, once the silencing burden of racism is rejected. This becomes increasingly apparent as we listen to what black women say, and identify the cultural and historical sources that they refer to. Where this knowledge is not readily available, there is an inevitable reliance on fictional accounts and the deployment of creative skills that synthesise whatever piecemeal bits of information have been disseminated through the mass media, or percolated down the generations, or simply been picked up from one another.

DEFINING DISCOURSE AS A TOOL FOR ANALYSING SUBJECTIVITY

In the first part of this book we conducted a discursive analysis of the science of psychology to reveal how the interplays of knowledge, power and practice have affected the construction of colonised, African and black subjects. The remainder of this book also involves using the concept of discourse, but to analyse subjectivity itself, instead of as a means of criticising what psychology has had to say about black people.

In theorising subjectivity as discursive, the discourses I am concerned with here are those that embody the collective knowledges, attitudes and beliefs of social groups. I will be identifying discourses as a way of charting the cultural and historical locations of the research participants. This is a prerequisite for the real concern of the remainder of this book, which is to develop an understanding of subjectivity as dynamic and multiple, and as collectively and relationally produced. In this chapter, different subjects are theorised as being positions in discourses, and changing subjectivities as the movement of the individual through different discourses. Within this framework, discourses carry the content of subjectivity, which means that subjectivity can only be approached through the particular histories and cultures of those being studied. There is no universal subject but only particular subjectivities and subject positions that are located in discourses – and so in the social sphere – in history and in culture. Subjectivity is a process of constitution and movement through already constituted positions.

I define discourses as historically constructed regimes of knowledge. These include the common-sense assumptions and taken-for-granted ideas, belief systems and myths that groups of people share and through which they understand each other. Discourses articulate and convey formal and informal knowledge and ideologies. They are constantly being reproduced and constituted, and can change and evolve in the process of communication. A discourse is a shared grid of knowledge that one or more people can 'enter' and through which explicit and implicit meanings are shared.

This use of the concept is derived from Foucault, but whereas he was concerned with the study of the relationship between knowledge practice and power – with the evolution of social institutions and the production of regimes of truth (Foucault 1967, 1972, 1976, Gordon 1980) – I use it for the purpose of analysing subjectivity.

Discourses, as they are defined here, position individuals in relation to one another socially, politically and culturally, as similar to or different from; as 'one of us' or as 'Other'. They exist within and transmit networks of power, with dominant discourses exercising their hegemony by resonating with and echoing the institutionalised and formal knowledges, assumptions and ideologies of a given social and political order. On the other hand, subaltern discourses also exist in contradiction to hegemonic ones, which subvert the dominant symbolic order and empower oppressed groups through their resonance with alternative ideologies and cultural practices. In other words, discourses do not only transmit cultural content but also power relations, both relations of oppression and subordination and relations of resistance.

Discourse analysis in this context is an interpretative technique, in which subject positions are located and the collective assumptions and shared meanings and values that have been cumulatively built up through the collective experience of the group are described. Individual subject positions are thus simultaneously social moments, in which the individual takes up particular social positions.

Having implemented the concept of discourse to serve as a heuristic device – an analytic tool for reading particular subjectivities – I then immersed myself in the historical and cultural material I had gathered in order to isolate those discourses likely to feature in black women's subjectivities. These I then applied to conversation transcripts in order to locate the subjectivities of the participants within them.

This study focuses on the subjectivities of a number of women who have self-identified as 'black women' and, in accordance with that identification, makes recourse to specific histories and cultures and experiences of contradiction. It is through the process of identifying discourses that we begin to chart the social life of the research participants and elaborate upon this with reference to other sources. Because of the nature of the society they live in, it soon becomes apparent that the social experience (and therefore the subjectivities) of the participants is unique in its combinations of cultural content, content which is articulated and conveyed as being highly racialised and gendered – and structured by the divisions of British society.

In what follows, it will become apparent that individuals have many discourses and discursive positions available to them, and the positions they take up are momentary, changing with the different social contexts and relations they find themselves in. Analysing subjectivity as positions in discourse allows for the person to be conceptualised historically, as changing over time and in different contexts. It also advances the idea of people having multiple subjectivities; since various subject positions are available to a given individual at any given moment, she or he may adopt different positions simultaneously, and display contradictions as a result of this. Subjectivity is therefore taken to be a process of movement through various discursive positions, as something which is constantly being produced out of social and historical knowledge and experience.

IDENTIFYING DISCOURSES AND LOCATING SUBJECTIVITIES

I have already noted that the published sources I used to identify and describe discourses were necessarily diverse, and included the existing literature on colonial Caribbean and African history and culture and the emerging literature on black people living in Britain. I read both literary and social scientific material. The recorded conversations between women themselves provided useful oral histories on the contemporary period. Using the recorded conversations as oral historical sources became particularly important when the paucity of published documentation of the contemporary history and experience of black women became apparent.

Two main and oppositional themes appeared to qualify as discourses in the way that I have defined the concept. These I have named *colonial-integrationist discourse* and *black radical discourse*. Both have long histories that transcend national boundaries but include the experience of colonisation, during which African ways of life were subjected to the cultural and social interventions that accompanied military conquest and the penetration of capitalist economic interests. The impact of the imperialist and patriarchal systems that profoundly affected most of Africa and created the Caribbean as we know it survives in the discourses that embody black cultural and intellectual life, and in the collective consciousness of black people today, be they in Africa, the Caribbean or in Europe. Colonial-integrationist discourse conveys a message of conformity and an acceptance of white hegemony, while black radical discourse conveys a politics of resistance and subversion, and the assertion of a cultural politic that draws on African, Caribbean and British minority group experience. Before elaborating the genealogy of these two discourses in Chapter 6, I propose to illustrate the way in which they manifest themselves in black women's accounts.

Colonial-integrationist discourse

MONA: I think in a lot of ways I quite resented my father when I was a kid, because um, I think that we – we were brought up with a perception of what a family was supposed to be. For me a family was like something I saw out of a Bisto advert – with the old man standing at a table and carving the roast beef on a Sunday morning – and my Dad was down at the booky! (*laughs*) So in that sense he didn't actually play that kind of role, even though he was terribly important.

As a child, Mona, a British-born black child, wished to conform to the dominant order as symbolised by the 'Bisto-ad. Father' carving the Sunday joint. In wishing for her family to conform to the hegemonic idea of a nuclear family with particular gender roles and customs, we can now say that Mona is recalling her position in colonial-integrationist discourse. She was being positioned by her British experience, which her family does not really conform to; she resented the fact that her Caribbean father went off to the betting-shop instead of doing what she felt (and the dominant white society said) fathers should do on Sundays. She is not alone in feeling the tension between what one is supposed to be and what one is. Another participant describes feeling embarrassed and ashamed when white friends came to her home, afraid that they would see yams and bananas and liken her family to monkeys (cited in Chapter 7).

Elsewhere, Mona describes her mother as being committed to 'fitting in', and in fact being quite oppressive towards her children because she is so fearful of what the neighbours will think:

MONA: It would be nice to go to Jamaica and fit the family tree together. My mother never talked about it – she never talked about being in the West Indies and what it's like there at all.

AMINA: Mary said her parents refused to talk about it – as if they tried to wipe the slate clean and start again.

MONA: That's right. Oh yes. I think my mother's got this whole idea into her head that, in order to be accepted by white people, there are certain things you must do and certain things you must not do, to become – you know – English. She would deny her own roots by not telling us anything even when we asked. She was outrageously strict to the point of silliness. You couldn't play – she would actually ban you from playing ball in the back yard in case the neighbours heard you hitting the ball against the fence.

Here she makes it explicit that her mother's strictness stemmed from her desire for integration. She wanted her children to become as English as possible, to adopt white English behaviour. To this end she was more than willing to discard her own Caribbean past. Colonial-integrationist positions may be in tune with the wider society, but they are somewhat uncomfortable insofar as they jeopardise the harmony of this black family: Mona resents her father for not conforming, her mother sanctions her children in fear of the neighbours' scorn. Mona is within the discourse in the first of these two extracts and then steps outside it when she considers her mother and the relationship they had. This illustrates movement in and out of a given discourse and the fact that multiple positions are available. She is able to distance herself from her mother's colonial-integrationist position by taking up other positions (described below).

Other participants recount similar tensions between themselves and their parents, one of the most extreme examples being provided by Angela, the mixed-race daughter of a white English mother. She recalls her mother feeling so oppressed by the real or imagined racism of her white neighbours that she denied her, telling them she was not her daughter but her ward and describing her as 'Sudanese' because this seemed less negroid than Ghanaian. Angela recounts how she and black male visitors were obliged to enter the house through the back door, because her mother wanted to avoid being stigmatised as a prostitute. This mother was incapable of standing up against racism. Instead she remained completely positioned by racist discourses, hankering for acceptance from white people who rejected her because she had had sex with an African. Angela is irrefutable physical evidence of that union.[4] This example brings us to consider the importance of race in the colonial-integrationist discourse. In the following extract we see that not only white parents can suffer from remaining positioned by the dominant racist discourses.

MONA: We used to get into massive arguments when I'd say to her 'That's someone being racist towards you', and she'd say 'No it's not'. She's very hard on black people. Her own people. She's one of those people who will – her favourite saying used to be 'You don't want to work with black people, 'cause them never do any work.' ... You can't come out and say things like that!

AMINA: But that's fairly typical though.

THERESA: Believing all the stereotyping about black people. I think it's a way of wanting to be accepted.

Being positioned within colonial-integrationist discourse means accepting what white society says, including what it says about black people. Mrs Smith takes up this position, despite her own non-white Caribbean origins and despite the fact that she is talking to a daughter who is very dark-skinned. Mona's awareness of her own appearance (and her mother's origins) has made it very difficult for her to relate positively to her mother. Her experience of such contradictions may well have facilitated her radicalization: she rejects her mother's colonial-integrationist position and takes up a position in black radical discourse. Mrs Smith, because of her own history, and presumably her personal experience as a light-skinned Caribbean woman, does not identify with black people at all.

The colonial-integrationist position enables Mrs Smith not to identify with black people because in the Caribbean of her youth the world was not divided into the crude categories of black and white in the way that British society is. Instead there was an elaborate system of colour gradation – a pigmentocracy – in which elaborate distinctions were made between people on the basis of their racial ancestry and physical attributes. This placed the pure white at the apex of a complex listing of the races and the pure African at the bottom. The British institutionalised these categorisations all over the colonies. They included the following bizarre list:

Negro: child of Negro and Negro
Sambo: child of mulatto and Negro
Mulatto: child of negress and white man
Quadroon: child of mulatto woman and white man
Mustee: child of quadroon (or pure Amerindian) and white man
Mustiphini: child of mustee and white man
Quintroon: child of mustiphini and white man
Octoroon: child of quintroon and white man[5]

(cited in James 1993: 235)

Little wonder that Rodney characterised the Caribbean as 'the society in which modern racialism was engendered' (Rodney 1969: 9). He went on to note the manifestation of this legacy in 1960s Caribbean culture:

The language which is used by black people in describing ourselves shows how we despise our African appearance. 'Good hair' means European hair, 'good nose' means straight nose, 'good complexion' means light complexion. Everybody recognises how incongruous and ridiculous such terms are, but we continue to use them and to express our support of the assumptions that white Europeans have a monopoly on beauty, and that black is the incarnation of ugliness.

(ibid.: 33)

James (1993: 239–40) vividly depicts the shock that people coming from such an elaborate system of racial gradation experience on arriving in Britain to find that they are all categorised together as 'coloureds', 'West Indians' or 'wogs'. He is not alone in identifying this homogenisation as a major stimulus towards the realisation of a common Caribbean or black identity (see also Patterson 1965).

Black identification was less an option for the white mothers of black children, however. It also appears not to have been Mrs Smith's response to her new situation in Britain. Instead she continues to display derogatory attitudes towards black people and repeats all the easily recognisable racist stereotypes: for her, blacks are lazy, morally corrupt and unclean. For Mrs Smith these are truths and she appears to have been haunted by the fear that her children may 'revert to type', not least because she only has to look at them to see that they are black. The 'strictness' that Mona describes is her attempt to avoid this eventuality. This discussion leads to a consideration of why Mrs Smith has remained so embedded in the colonial value system:

MONA: My mother actually said something about being white. She's very fair – very light-skinned and she has light brown eyes and straight hair.

THERESA: Aha! I know exactly what you're talking about!

MONA: She was joking, 'cause she was grinning all over her face and I said 'Stop!' When I was a kid we used to row – she used to say to me, 'Mona, how come you'se so black?' (*laughs*) and she used to joke about it, because I take after my father. I've got his colouring. I really think she really disliked the fact that I was born as dark as I was. It's one of the reasons I developed my helluva mouth, because I used to turn round and say 'Yes, black but comely'. She once said my Dad was lucky to marry her. I can imagine her – she was small, slim, very pretty. I suspect that what was happening was that she carried status by dint of the way she looked.

THERESA: Yes, they do.

MONA: Therefore, like me Dad – dark bush boy – was doing well to marry this amazing sort of straight-haired and whatever woman. I think she still holds it against me Dad actually. That's why the woman is so bitter (*laughs*). I think that in parts of her head she doesn't actually see herself as black. If you want she sees herself as 'coloured' – as if she can actually see herself as a separate entity. So she can quite justifiably sit there in the house and slag off black people: 'All the girl dem ever do is getting pregnant' and 'All the boys dem ever do is get into trouble' and so she ended up with kids who are very careful about what they let her see them do. We all got into trouble but she never knew about it, that's all (*laughs*).

Theresa's exclamation at the beginning of this passage is one of 'recognition'. This is not surprising when one considers that she may actually understand Mona's mother even better than Mona, because she was herself brought up in the Caribbean with a near-white maternal grandmother, who disapproved of Theresa's mother's marriage to a darker-skinned man. Theresa's grandmother shared the same race politic as Mona's mother, and both are light-skinned Caribbean women raised during the colonial era. This interpretation is borne out in another discussion session which gives us more information on Theresa's experience and so how it is that she can 'read' Mrs Smith so clearly:

THERESA: My grandmother would never actually see us as black. Her father was white and her mother was both, of mixed parentage.

ANGELA: Yes.

THERESA: So she sort of looked white, among black people. I'm sure we thought of her as 'brown-skin'. And when we started to actually say – my brother started saying he was black quite early – she used to say 'No, you're not black, you're brown-skinned.' It's really difficult. [1] I remember when I was younger, my grandmother used to comb our hair – because she didn't want anyone else to do it and she couldn't do it properly – she couldn't plait properly. Every time she was combing she'd go 'Your nigger-hair'. (*laughs*) 'You've got real nigger-hair!' And I used to pray for the day to come when I could actually press my hair and have it straightened, because I thought if I could have straight hair I would be so much more beautiful. I thought I was ugly because of this. But yet she didn't want it straightened. I asked her and she said there was no way. It's really very painful, though. Someone is saying to you that you're not actually right. There's something awfully wrong with you. You're *ugly*. [2]

ANGELA: That's it. I mean blackness and ugliness always went together. At school I was never one of the girls who was fancied. I first started having a lot of boyfriends when I went to Ghana – when I come to think of it – of course!

[1] I have already noted that finely graded racial categorisations permeated colonial Caribbean life. Theresa is describing the discomforts of

adjusting from being 'not black' in colonial Caribbean discourse to being 'black' in black radical discourse.

[2] This point is concluded with an explicit statement of the aesthetics of colonial-racist discourse which the discussants have worked out in the course of sharing experiences: [black/nigger] = ugly.

This extract not only addresses race but introduces some of the gendered consequences of being a black woman in a racially stratified society.[6] At the age when everybody else had boyfriends, and having one was a sign of status and success, Angela was 'left on the shelf'. 'Never being fancied' is the experience of many black girls, since in white-dominated situations black and white boys alike tend to conform to the prevailing aesthetic, and fancy white (if not blonde) girls more. I return to consider some of the gendered aspects of black women's subjectivity in Chapter 7.

For women of African parentage the story can be different but in Angela's case was remarkably similar, because she was raised in Britain, by an English mother with white supremacist values like Mrs Smith's. Even if she had not been, the fact is that the idealisation of 'fair' skin and 'soft' hair is prevalent in some African societies, still marked by their own colonial heritage and a contemporary order in which Africa and her peoples have failed to live up to the dreams of nationalism. None the less the racial discourses on the African continent are also very different from Caribbean society. They are less finely tuned to gradations, tending to distinguish two (African and other) or at most three groups (African, coloured and European). In contrast to many parts of the Caribbean the vast majority of people are and have always been of purely African descent, and the cultural reservoirs of thousands of years of history make colonial racial attitudes more marginal – they tend to be the preserve of the urban élite minority. It is, for example, common for élite families in Nigeria to oppose marriages between their sons and European or mixed-race women, although the latter may be sought after as sexual partners. For the vast majority pale skin is more of an exotic curiosity and difference than a badge of superiority.[7]

Black radical discourse

Black radical discourse has come into its own internationally since the 1960s, when the black power and nationalist movements challenged white supremacy and colonial rule respectively (see Chapter 2). Like colonial-integrationist discourse, black radical discourse has numerous locally specific manifestations, emanating from the various colonial and imperial histories of black people worldwide. In Africa, nationalist movements were about the overthrow of European rule and the emergence of new nation-states, while in the Caribbean there were both nationalist movements for independence (in Jamaica, for example) and black power movements that were peculiarly American in their emphasis on challenging racism. The latter were not necessarily linked to a nationalist project concerned with nation-statehood but were black nationalist in the diasporan sense, which is more about establishing an international racial unity than about nationhood.

The genealogy of black discourses can be traced back to the earliest days of slavery, to the memories and fantasies in the minds of the African slaves. Here they coexisted with colonial discourses, from time to time erupting in rebellions but all the time subverting the white dominated order and sustaining black cultures and a sense of community, which is evident in the oral and written material generated during slavery.

As a modern social movement, however, black radicalism can be traced to Garveyism in the diaspora and to the anti-colonial and nationalist movements across the black world. Garvey gained notoriety and was deported from Jamaica after horrifying the colonial authorities with his call for black people to rise up against 'black and brown oppressors'. Garveyism generally proclaimed the dignity of the black man (*sic*) and after his deportation from Jamaica he founded the Universal Negro Improvement Association in Harlem, New York. His speeches and writings gained a substantial following throughout the 1920s and 1930s, and were accompanied by efforts to secure economic autonomy for the black race, through the founding of the Black Star Line shipping company. Garvey also believed that ultimately the black race should return to Africa (A. J. Garvey 1967, M. Garvey 1983). After his death, Garvey's ideas also gained popularity in the Caribbean, particularly among the Rastafarians whose movement shared many of Garvey's preoccupations (Barrett 1972, Owens 1979, Patterson 1964). Rastafarianism has had a pervasive influence on Caribbean cultural life both in the region and in the Caribbean communities of Europe and North America. Initially a movement that was primarily religious, whose adherents concentrated on reinterpreting the Bible, proclaiming that God was black and insisting that Africans were the true Israelites, Rastafarianism also drew on traditions of rebellion laid down by the Maroons across the Caribbean and called for the liberation of African people and a return to Africa. Popularised and internationalised through the lyrics of leading reggae artists, the movement soon spread widely and has become a central component of Caribbean culture worldwide – one which proclaims and celebrates the African roots of all black people.

Another major source of black radical ideas was the negritude movement that emerged in Paris in the 1950s (see Chapter 2) and which Aime Cesaire, the Martinican poet, is often accredited with founding. Many of these expressions unwittingly echoed the constructions of Africans within colonial discourses, as people of intuition, rhythm and sensuality. What both of these sources had in common was the recasting of the racial characteristics attributed to black people as positive gifts, or even superior attributes, rather than as signs of inferiority. The fact that they were both pan-African in scope is probably due more to their genesis in the remote reaches of the African diaspora than to an understanding of the feasibility of achieving African unity.

Since the 1960s other North American manifestations of black radicalism have developed in response to the extreme racism of North American society (see Chapter 3). North American, African and Caribbean forms of black radicalism have all influenced each other, generating a wide and diverse set of discourses, some of which have found their way into the black communities in Britain.

From examining the sources, we can conclude that black radical discourse is generally about the positive assertion of black identity and culture. It is oppositional to colonial-integrationist discourses that heralded black radicalism, and the two have coexisted unequally since black radical discourses developed into a coherent body of thought. Insofar as it developed as a challenge to white supremacy, black radical discourse can be described as reactive.

However, since it goes beyond opposition, to form and assert alternative views of the world that have frequent recourse to African and Caribbean cultures and their histories of resistance and innovation for inspiration, black radicalism must also be viewed as innovative and creative. It has inspired whole new areas of intellectual work and political struggle, as well as a diverse array of social movements and new identities. The assertion of black British subjectivity and the development of black British culture discussed in Chapter 6 is just one example. Black discursive positions are expressed in the following statements:

MONA: Black but comely.

ANGELA: The blacker the berry the sweeter the juice.

ASHA: It's like the black identity thing – it's only when you establish that black is beautiful that you can go on to do other things. If you're proud in being who you are, then you can go forward in society and demand certain things . . . you don't take sort of half measures – you go with a plan – you know your mind and you know what you want.

The first two extracts are axioms that date back to the 1960s Black Power movement. They indicate the way in which this discourse answers racism back: 'black *but* comely' – comely in spite of being black. Such axioms challenge the idea that black is ugly and reject the white standards of beauty. This is particularly important to young black women who have spent their childhoods in white-dominated societies, longing to have straight hair, blue eyes and boyfriends (as we saw Theresa remarking on page 104). This is a gendered as well as a racialised dynamic because women experience the imperative to be attractive more than men do in a sexist society which circumscribes the possibilities for self-affirmation – pretty, feminine girls are more sought after than intelligent ones (see Chapter 7), and black girls are less likely to be seen as pretty in a racist milieu. Black men may have problems regarding their self-image but face a different situation in patriarchal societies. Black men have the option of 'success' within a masculinist discourse, if they are able or willing to embody the hypersexuality that white society projects on to them and take on the 'stud' identity. Because of sexual inequality, even within racist discourses, black men have a position of prowess not available to women, for whom hypersexuality is a stigma. Within the positioning of black people as hypersexual, black women become 'whores' to be degraded and despised, while men are envied and hated by white men, sought after by white women and so free to exercise sexual choices in a way that black women often cannot. These sexual political legacies have persisted over into some of the early black radical positions which are largely about a vengeful re-assertion of masculinity over women of all colours (see Wallace 1978).

It is apparent from the third extract that the attainment of black identity also has great advantages for women; here it is described as an internal change which is both liberating and enabling. Black women take up positions within black discourse that convey many different positions in gender politics but which share a concern with empowering black women. In finding themselves as black people, black women are able to reject the negative and inferior position afforded to them by colonial-integrationist discourse. This is a process of reflection and recovery which also involves a continuing struggle with the internalised residues of racism which continue to be echoed in a wider society that is still racist. Becoming black means taking a stand against the hegemonic discourse, and this requires drawing on alternative sources for the affirmation not readily available in a white-dominated cultural and political context. This quest has been undertaken by black people in the West at both personal and collective levels. At the collective level there has been an outburst of cultural and political action and creativity, a vigorous interest in pursuing and reconstructing the past as well as changing the present. Black history, black cultural and education projects and black politics are all fundamentally about transformation – about overthrowing white domination and empowering black people psychologically, educationally and politically.

NOTES

1 I made a recent visit to confirm that the dissection report is still available in what was referred to as the 'Venus file' at the Musée de l'Homme. The report

suggests that the size and shape of her buttocks may have been due to a heritable disease or 'contagion' and likens other aspects of her anatomy to those of an Orang Utan.

2 The 1969 Cullingworth Committee, for example, sought to undo the result of racist housing practices by breaking up and dispersing black communities because of the growing fears of ghettoisation.

3 These are documented in a series of publications available from Runnymede Trust, 11 Princelet St, London E1. There has also been a long-standing resistance against these trends: the slogans 'We are here because you were there' and 'Here to stay' both encapsulate the history of the black British subject and assert the right to be 'British'. It is no accident that both of these slogans were produced in anti-deportation struggles, where the right to remain on British soil has been the issue, and there has been confrontation with the authorities responsible for enforcing and extending immigration legislation and its implementation.

4 One may wonder why Angela's mother did not do what so many other abandoned white women did with their part-African children, and put her into state custody to be raised in children's homes. The contradiction is one that many children of mixed parentage are familiar with – her mother probably loved her, despite herself; that is to say, despite her racist positioning.

5 It is worth noting that these categories are gender-biased in that they leave out the possibility of transracial partnerships involving white women.

6 Interestingly contrasted to being a brown woman in Ghanaian society.

7 This is not to imply that African societies are not racist, but that white racism has not the currency that it has had in the Caribbean. The deep and intransigent racism within and between African societies (most apparent of late in Mauritania, Burundi and Southern African countries) has its own multifarious sources and signifiers which cannot be fully explored here.

Chapter 6

Black British subjects

In this chapter I continue to develop the theorisation of subjectivity as being a dynamic process involving the uptake of different discursive positions, positions that become available in the course of the individual's social life. In this and subsequent chapters it becomes clear that this development is no easy process but one of continuous effort, born out of the experience of contradictory incidents and situations. Perhaps it is because subjectivity is dynamic and comprises multiple possibilities that people display a high degree of resilience and are so able to survive existentially difficult or oppressive situations.

Psychological theory has often suggested that contradictory experiences, such as those of racism, are pathogenic. We saw in Chapter 3 that this was true of early black psychology and early civil rights discourses in North America, as well as of mainstream psychology. The problem with the theorisation of black people as damaged by racism is that it pathologises the millions of black people who have lived and continue to live in racist societies.

One of my central themes is to demonstrate that while racism does generate racialised consciousness, this is not necessarily or always pathological. This is not to deny that racism can and does have negative effects but rather to insist that there is a great deal more to black subjectivity than psychological damage. One can just as well argue that experience of racial contradictions (or other kinds of oppression and inferiorisation) can have positive effects, for example as an impetus to artistic, intellectual or personal creativity that is simply not available to those in more powerful positions. If one takes this perspective, then the psychological effects of racism cannot be seen as the source of black disadvantage. Whatever the case, racism clearly produces black subjects who are different from white subjects and who draw on distinctive cultural and historical sources for a sense of themselves. In this sense, racism can be seen as texturing subjectivity, rather than determining black social and emotional life. Put another way, race is only ever one among many dimensions of subjectivity and it never constitutes the totality of an individual's internal life. Even where racial contradictions feature a great deal in people's history and experience, the fact that they are responded to by personal change means that they are not an omnipresent force acting on passive victims. Instead they are responded to collectively by the creation of new discourses and by individual movement between discourses, and individually through psychodynamic processes; these are explored in Chapter 8. Theorised in this way, racism becomes a contradictory collective experience that black individuals respond to in the processes of constructing themselves as subjects. It is therefore both a motor for individual development and a pervasive factor in the production of the particular discourses that I have identified as positioning black people, namely colonial-integrationist and black radical discourses.

If we start with the premiss that people are not rigidly fixed in a single identity, then we can study the ways in which they are able to change, to resist and oppose dominant discourses, either by taking up positions outside these discourses, or by developing alternative ones, or both. When we examine the processes by which women growing up in a racist and sexist milieu constitute themselves as black women, we are also examining how subjectivities that are not necessarily pathological are constituted in oppressive environments.

In this chapter I shall look in more detail at the ways in which different discourses feature in the subjectivities of the participants and in the particular production of that multiple subject who is both black and British.

BLACK AND BRITISH

'I am British. I am black. I therefore exist as that entity – as Black British' (Mona)

To be black and to be British is, when we consider the evidence, nothing new. In the last chapter we saw that this has been the situation of significant numbers of Britain's inhabitants since perhaps as early as Roman times. Why, then, this assertion in the 1980s and 1990s? It tells us that in spite of that long-standing presence, black people are still having to struggle for a recognised place in British society.

In the course of their social relations, black people growing up in Britain during the 1950s, 1960s and 1970s soon learnt that whiteness is very often equated with British-ness, an equation which puts them in an ambiguous and dislocated position. British historiography has long ignored the contributions of black people to the development of the nation (as was discussed in Chapter 5) but for the generation featuring in this study, perhaps the most immediate source has been childhood experience: at school, at home, through the media and through patronising or caricature-like images in some children's books (Fryer 1988: 77–81). The persistent tendency to define non-whites as Other, as foreign, as immigrants, denies their long-term presence in the country and implicitly questions their rights to full citizenship. This has social and subjective consequences for black people which are illustrated below.

SUBJECTIVITY AS A PROCESS OF CONSTRUCTION

Black people living in Britain have developed a number of responses to this situation. Those who do have other countries that they may have some knowledge or direct experience of very often simply answer questions about their origins by stating that they are from Jamaica, St Vincent, St Lucia, Ghana or Sierra Leone. There are, however, a great many who do not have another country, or, if they do, do not have any direct experience or knowledge of it. People brought up in families committed to integrating (as several of the participants in this research were) are particularly unlikely to *feel* Jamaican, or Caribbean or African, or to be convincing in that position. British-raised black people are often:

> young people who are not actually saying they are from a particular island but have created what they think 'Caribbean' culture is. Someone from the Caribbean I was talking to said how insulted they felt to hear a guy on 'Black on Black'[1] talking with a Liverpuddlian accent and a West Indian dialect together. That Caribbean person felt *insulted* – that black people in this country were creating a different language for West Indian people. But that's all we can actually do.
>
> (Priscilla, British-born of Caribbean parents)

For those permanently living in Britain, the experience of being rejected by the society that they were brought up to 'fit into' provokes an inter-rogation of their own identity and, for some, a quest for roots: for a place they can claim as their own without challenge. The accumulated experience of black people is such that they often display a marked reluctance to say they are British or English, even if that is what their upbringing and acculturation has been. The racial divisions of British social life make it difficult and uncomfortable for black people to *feel* British and different individuals find different ways of dealing with this ambivalence:

PRISCILLA: If you ask some black women where they come from, they'll ask if you mean their parents or themselves. And if you ask if they do not relate to the place of their parents, they say 'no, I'm British'.

AMINA: And 'I haven't been there' – which is very realistic.

PRISCILLA: It's realistic. But it's also like . . . well I was born here, but I don't say I'm British. Do you know what I mean?

AMINA: Yes, I know what you mean, but many use the black in front of it – that's what separates them from being just British.

It is in this contradictory context that the assertion of being black *and* British is confrontational. It poses an explicit challenge to the society that they are part of and to the hegemonic racialised discourses which position them as Other. It is also a multiple identity, one which combines national and racial subjectivities and, in so doing, contests the dualistic world order which deems blackness and British-ness to be mutually exclusive. It is an attempt to resolve the existential dilemma of being black in a society that has continuously and irrationally defined itself as white.[2]

The black British subject is therefore born out of an imposed contradiction between blackness and British-ness, British-ness being equated with whiteness in the dominant symbolic order. The black British identity is one of many multiple identities emerging in the post-colonial era, both within the West and in the former colonies, and in the continuous human, cultural and material traffic between the two. The inclusion of blackness in the term asserts difference from other (white) British subjects and enables dignity to be retained since it is also a distance-taking from colonial-integrationist discourses. In what follows, I use the example of black British subjectivity to develop the idea of subjectivity as a dynamic process. Few people started out their lives with fully fledged black identities, or even with the acute race-consciousness that they later develop. Mary talks about what it was like growing up in the small town in the north of England where she was born:

MARY: I called myself black but it was somehow from a different perspective than it is now. I didn't really understand racism. I just thought – you're black – and when you leave school you go home to your own black people, your black community. I didn't really move with white people, whereas in school – I just had my friends – my best friends as they call them. I did notice that all the blacks were in the sort of lower streams. I always remember one black teacher saying 'You're in England now and you don't talk that patois here.' I always remember that, so I think in a way I was aware of racism – I just thought of it as part of life. I do remember certain incidents – in front of white people I used to feel ashamed – of being black. I think that's common to most of us really. Yes, certain things – I used to feel ashamed when Margaret used to come round to my house and I was eating yam and banana.

Now that's actually a lie because *I* never really ate them – we had them kind of thing in our house but my Dad ate them. I mean I used to love dumpling, but I never used to eat yam or cho-cho or anything like that, because going to school you ate white food and, well, our food wasn't as popular as it is now. When my white friends used to come round too I used to think – ooh dear – hide the food – silly little things like that. And like everyone else I used to want long, flowing hair. The same old standard thing – you know – I have this conversation with a lot of people and everybody has moved with the same thing. I used to press my hair with a hot comb, but I never really liked straight hair, I used to just ease it out so that it wasn't too tough, but not really straighten it. The thing that hurts me now the most – is that I used to be ashamed of my parents. Yes it's awful, having to go through all that and think ... I can remember when my white school friends used to come to the house. At that time – 8, 9 years old – I had more respect for them than for my parents who'd done so much. Now I'm so proud of them. It's all reversed.

Mary's speech is changeable – a broad northern English accent, which is periodically interspersed with Jamaican intonation and expressions drawn quite naturally from 'black talk' – the polyglot argot of the contemporary black Londoners among whom she now lives. In this discussion she recalls her emotional states and the values she held before she identified more fully with her non-white (Caribbean) origins and before she was able to assert herself with dignity, because she (like her parents and her school-teacher) was positioned by colonial-integrationist discourse. It was only later in life that Mary was able to identify as a black woman and, by taking a position in black radical discourse, begin to take a sense of pride in herself, her family and her background.

   Building a black identity, or acquiring the ability to secure positions in black discourses, is given impetus by racism. It seems to be something that people work at, once they recover from the initial trauma of realising what racism means for them and begin to be proactive about their blackness. Mona now asserts herself as being both black and British, but before she was able to do this she felt she did not know where she came from:

MONA: I am British. I am black. I therefore exist as that entity – as black British. I felt my parents left me in a situation with no roots as such, no space – nothing to hark back to – which meant that I hit a crisis in my teens at the point when I left home. I had nothing at all. I didn't have any grounding anywhere. What I had in fact was a lot of negative attitudes about blacks – which were turned on myself, because I personify all that is black. Those are the kind of attitudes my brothers and sisters have – the ones that are after me.

The crisis of which Mona speaks manifested itself in violent quarrels with her mother, quarrels which led her to leave home at 17, when her mother threatened to have her placed in state custody. After she left home Mona embarked on a rather lonely quest for identity:

MONA: I spent a year when I was working but living on my own. I actually literally just cut off contact with everybody. I tried to re-establish myself within the black community and found real difficulties. When people started to tell me that in order to be black and cool I had to wear my hair in a certain way, or had to dress in a certain way, I immediately went off in the opposite direction because. . . . It struck me as being a bit stupid. It didn't seem to make any logical sense. I think when it comes down to it, it came to me by my doing a hell of a lot of reading. I'd moved to North London and I was living on my own in a bedsit. I discovered places like the New Beacon bookshop and I started to buy books – and I went crazy – I'd buy 40 or 50 pounds' worth of books – I'd spend all my salary.

THERESA: So who did you read?

MONA: I started – anything that said black!

Different people draw on different sources when they begin to take positions that go against the grain of the dominant ethos of the society they live in. While Mona coped with the contradictions of her childhood in isolation, building herself up by reading, others describe their participation in black organisations as having facilitated a similar process. Several mentioned the importance of their participation in black women's groups at this stage of their lives. Angela, for example, was extremely active in both an African student organisation and the nascent black women's movement. She also describes the changes she went through when she went to visit her father, in Accra:

ANGELA: I was reading this thing about when a black woman asserts her identity it's an expression which represents centuries of struggling against oppression. I couldn't remember the first time when I actually enjoyed being black. I think it was when I went to Ghana. It was in Ghana that I first enjoyed the sun as well, because here I used to really try hard to stay out of the sun. Shit, that used to really bug me because as soon as I was in the sun for half an hour, the pigment just came right up, you know – I had a nice tan. In those days, I remember my Mum being really disgusted when I came back from Ghana and I was so black – 'God what have you done?!' (*laughs heartily*).

In these extracts we see subjectivity emerging as a developmental process, with contradictory experiences leading people to search for alternative discourses within which to position themselves – in this instance for ways of being black people in a white-dominated milieu. The specific reasons for seeking new positions are different for each individual but they always involve retaining a sense of dignity and integrity, a resolution of inner tensions and tensions between oneself and one's social environment. The desire to change and to find new identities appears to be driven or motivated by contradictory experiences.

MULTIPLE SOURCES, MULTIPLE SUBJECTIVITIES

We have seen how different individuals draw on different resources in the course of their personal development – in this study, their development into black womanhood. Here I wish to explore the constitution of subjectivity further and to demonstrate that the subjective process is not a simple, linear evolution in which one moves unidirectionally through successive positions, as the theory of nigrescence suggested (Chapter 3). Instead, it is a process in which various different options are more or less continuously available to the individual. What I wish to draw attention to here is the coexistence of subject positions and the movement of the individual between them in the present – in other words, the multiplicity of subjectivity. One of the participants found words for describing her own multiplicity when she described herself as having 'different expressions of the same personality' (fuller citation below).

Not all the positions we have considered are equally available to particular individuals, however. A number of participants express nostalgia for a culture they have not known, either simply because they have never been there themselves, or because, as noted earlier, the parental desire to integrate meant that knowledge about the Caribbean (or Africa) was suppressed and not readily passed on to their British-born children. Mona (above) described this as a feeling of rootlessness. Mary put it this way:

MARY: I think that's what I miss. I know people go on about identity. I know I don't belong here, but I don't know where I belong. That to me is a really sore point. Because Jamaica couldn't take all these British-born Jamaicans. There's just no way. And I don't know whether – I'd have to go to Jamaica and see. It doesn't sound like that good a place to be really. ... I'd definitely be a foreigner in Jamaica – they call you 'British gal' and all dem sort of thing. It would be like – different – it wouldn't be like growing up there. There's still that difference, so even if I went there now, I don't think I could ever recapture what I've lost. It's changed from my Mum's day, and I haven't really grown up in that society. Yes. That to me is really sad.

AMINA: Well you call yourself black British quite definitely.

MARY: That's what people call me (*laughs*), I'd just say 'black' and done, but you know – if you have to categorise ... I mean I would never call myself 'English'. Never. Because in this society your main focus is that you're black. Not that you're anything else. So that's the reality that I have to live with. I don't know if I'll ever find the day when I can just say 'I'm British' and done. Or if I do say that I'll say 'well, on my passport it says I'm British' (*laughs*).

AMINA: Do you ever call yourself Jamaican?

MARY: Yes. And sometimes I'll say I'm African.

Discussing the tenuous nature of her Jamaican-ness leads Mary to display her multiplicity. At different moments in this extract she refers to herself as 'black', as 'Jamaican' and as 'African'. She retreats from explicitly identifying herself as 'black British' by saying that it is an assignation imposed on her by circumstance rather than one she chooses; she would rather not be pigeon-holed at all. This contrasts with her consistent lack of ambivalence regarding her black identity. While she conveys a deep sense of loss and regret that she cannot really be fully Jamaican, it is in keeping with her down-to-earth style not to romanticise or fantasise about the Caribbean. She is quite well informed regarding the difficulties she would encounter in Jamaica.[3]

Mary also feels differently about each of her identities. Being British is the most problematic (for reasons that must be apparent by now) so that although she does not go so far as to reject it completely, she dissociates herself from it by treating it as a bureaucratic and legalistic fact. She empties her nationality of any emotional or cultural importance when she says 'On my passport it says I'm British.' On the other hand, she is understandably ambivalent about her Jamaican-ness because she lacks real knowledge and experience of being Jamaican, and her restrained remarks probably also stem from her suspicion that she will in any case also be rejected by Jamaicans. Her African identity could be described as a looser cultural affiliation, based on the collective-historical fact that her ancestors came from some unspecifiable location there. Her embrace of African identity is restrained by direct experience of her visit to that continent and her relationships with Africans, both of which have informed her that there is more to being African than being black. In short she displays a multiple identity, the different aspects of which emanate from different elements in her history. All three have different rationales and none of them totally encompasses the person that she is.

Some people make more deliberate choices and therefore narrow down their subjectivity to a particular component. This is most evident when a choice has become collectivised and, therefore, politicised. Rastafarianism is an example of a politicised identification that has grown into a transnational social movement. Below we can see how the identity politics of Rastafarianism differ from the individual cultural affiliation that Mary has, although both involve African identification.

Whereas colonial-integrationist discourse disparages and rejects everything to do with Africa, black discourses include various, generally idealistic relations to the continent. Just as some participants have talked about the process of becoming black, others talk about becoming African. Iscara, a Rastafarian cultural worker of Jamaican extraction, describes developing from being black to being African:

ISCARA: As time went on – I think from around 1980 – I became more aware of my personal identity, more aware of where I was coming from and who I was. I think the change came at the black women's conference. I was working with Angela and organising the conference.

AMINA: A lot of people describe that as a turning point.

ISCARA: Yes, I was very much involved. I think it's because I also had recognition for my poetry there. And because it was dealing with women's issues, and there was a lot of things raised there that made me think, and from then on I started to explore a lot of things . . . from 1980 I would say. Up till then there was awareness of being black but not necessarily associated to being African.

In her case becoming African meant taking up the Rastafarian faith and adopting a different life-style. She is unequivocal and assertive in describing herself as African. She dresses in a style that has been defined by Rastafarians as appropriate for African women: she wears long skirts, keeps her hair covered and has relinquished wearing trousers. She eats only 'Ital' food and does not drink alcohol. The entire change has been expressed outwardly in her changing her original Christian name to an African name, derived from the ancient Egypt beloved by Rastafarians and included in their conception of Ethiopia, the home of all Africans. She expresses her desire to go and live in Africa, since she finds tourist-haven-Jamaica too Americanised for her taste. Her knowledge of Rastafarianism and of Africa (the black man's (*sic*) Israel in Rasta parlance), and the distinctive Jamaican Rastafarian argot that she speaks, have been acquired during her stays in Jamaica. Asked about what she considers African, she says:

ISCARA: The way I dress, the way I talk, when I don't straighten my hair and all dem kin' of things – most time I dress in African dress.

Although Iscara has had personal relationships with African men, these do not appear to have affected her constructions of what is Africa and how to be African. These derive more from the collective imagination of the bredren and sistren than from empirical knowledge of Africa. It is the imaginary, some would say spiritual, Africa that is important to Rastafarianism and which inspires Iscara's poetry. Information which challenges or disputes areas of faith is not taken seriously and Africans who contradict the agreed tenets of that essential 'African-ness' are not considered as 'real Africans' but rather as people who, like their diasporan cousins, have been corrupted by the white-dominated order.

Mary's African identification is not expressed with any of Iscara's flamboyance or imagination. Perhaps it has been tempered by the fact that she has travelled to the African continent and seen for herself how different the reality is from the diasporan dream. This may be why her assertion of her African-ness is more restrained:

MARY: Sometimes I'll say I'm African. But like I say 'African' the word African is used so broadly. It's kind of lost its meaning, I think. I mean I don't go on about England being Europe. It's just all these countries being massed into one as if they're of no importance. But I suppose, as a base ... I mean I don't really know whereabouts I come from – all I can assume is that I come from the West coast somewhere – my ancestors. That's all I can assume. It's such a broad term that I don't really like to use it. . . . My cousins are getting into this thing about Africa. But I don't know if it isn't just a whim. I have to sort of question people. Because if it is really that they're looking for their history, and to understand the ways of people from Ghana or Nigeria or wherever, then there's more behind it than just this 'in thing', 'Back to Africa, Go find Africa'. Style-an-fashion. I don't really want to get into that at all. It's easy to get sucked into that.

She alludes to the problematic historical relationship between Caribbean and African people and has made efforts to address the prejudices that her parents instilled in her:

MARY: I had to get rid of a lot of my misconceptions about African people because of my parents. I remember when I was 16, there was this man called Mr Kojo who lived just down the street, a few doors up. I hadn't seen him many times before. There was this big meeting round at my house. His friend had come round to speak to my Dad. It turned out that Mr Kojo had asked for my hand in marriage! My Mum said 'No, no! Not them African man!' You know the kind of thing between them. I had to get all that kind of rubbish out of my head. It was like I had to go through a whole process of re-educating myself. A lot of black people – Caribbean people – have had that.

Whereas Mary lives with her ambiguities, Iscara has opted to take a more singular route by becoming an adherent to a faith which defines her identity and her code of conduct for her, and which stands as a collective bulwark against the racist order.

DIFFERENT EXPRESSIONS OF THE SAME PERSONALITY

Black people living in Britain often develop the skill of moving in and out of their various subject positions with great alacrity in the course of their social relationships and interactions with a diverse array of groups in their personal, political and working lives. This is a more or less conscious process, one that discussants are exploring in the following discussion between Angela (raised in England with a few brief visits to Africa), Theresa (raised in the Caribbean until her mid-teens) and myself (raised in both Africa and Britain):

ANGELA: I think most black people are schizophrenic though, in that they have to ...

THERESA: I was just about to say that, because I rap in patois when I rap with St Lucians, and I sort of use a different patois when I rap with West Indians who are not St Lucian.

AMINA: And you talk and project yourself very differently – well I do anyway – when I'm with English people compared to being with Caribbean people or West African people.

ANGELA: And what do you become when you're with English people?

AMINA: I become more English. That whole aspect of myself just takes over.

ANGELA: I don't know. I do with certain English people – that's how I get certain jobs and shit like that – because I know I've got to play the game at the interviews, but with other English people I can be what I want. I think I've got so many different personalities – well not personalities – it's the same personality but different ways of expressing that.[4]

This juggling of different identities is sometimes expedient, something that one has to engage in, for example if one wants to get a job. It can also be about sharing a group identity, being from a particular locale (Theresa with people from her particular Caribbean island). None of the identities taken up are 'false' since they are all derived from the person's experience and imbibed knowledge of the various discourses and styles of being. Being multiple in this way would be pathologised within psychological discourse but can be reconceptualised once we view subjectivity as multiple and dynamic. Discussants are describing their own movement between various subjectivities, displaying a skill that is developed in the course of interacting with various groups, just as one may learn various languages.

NOTES

1 One of the early ethnic television programmes run by the BBC.
2 This is what lies behind the title Paul Gilroy chose for his book *There Ain't no Black in the Union Jack*, a book in which he demonstrates the centrality of race in British constructions of national identity and nationhood.
3 Other informants discussing visits to the Caribbean described the difficulty they had in coping with the ridicule and teasing that they received, and with being confronted with the often painful realisation that they were, through no choice of their own, 'more British than anything else'. Jamaicans have a patois word for would-be returnees; they are referred to as 'frosties'.
4 Angela is struggling to express an experience that we are all familiar with but

for which there is no appropriate vocabulary. She ends up adopting two psychological terms, 'schizophrenic' and 'personality', neither of which is satisfactory when one considers their formalised meanings in scientific discourse. Furthermore the dominant significations of these terms are not what she intends to mean. 'Schizophrenic' has pathological connotations, and 'personality' has deterministic and unitary ones. This illustrates the way in which psychological terms filter into and construe lay discourses, even though the dissatisfaction with them eventually leads to the reformulation: 'different ways of expressing the same personality'.

Chapter 7

Psychodynamics of racialised subjectivity

INTRODUCTION

> Resistance to the dominant at the level of the individual subject is
> the first stage in the production of alternative forms of knowledge
> or where such alternatives already exist, of winning individuals over
> to these discourses and gradually increasing their social power.
>
> (Weedon 1987: 111)

For black women, the dominant order is both racially oppressive in
gendered ways and sexually oppressive in racialised ways. In the earlier
chapters we have seen how the history of black women has been one of
collective and individual struggle to overcome these oppressions. Through
political activism, consciousness-raising and cultural action, and through
interpersonal relationships, black women have taken steps to liberate
their hearts and minds from the constraining legacies of their oppressed
position. These legacies intrude upon the present in the form of anachro-
nistic images of black women as wild, sexually licentious, aggressive mat-
riarchs, as dumb domestics, prostitutes and entertainers. I discussed how,
through a collective process of sharing experiences, black women during
the 1980s and 1990s sought to make sense of their social realities and
in so doing generated new discourses about what it means to be black
and female in Britain. With these have come the new, post-colonial
identities that I have conceptualised as new discursive positions, or new
subjectivities.

While I emphasised the importance of the black women's movement in
this process, not all black women were directly involved in the black
women's groups that it comprised. Many worked in black organisations
with men as well as women, or in mainly white women's groups, and a
great many were never involved in any group or organisation, instead
finding their own routes to personal change, through reading, study
groups, or simply by responding to what was happening in and around
them in the course of their early adulthood. In considering the collective
and historical processes of black women's subjectivity, I have left aside

the question of how individuals come to identify themselves in the ways that they do. This applies most obviously to women who have never participated in collectives, yet have still come to take up racialised and gendered positions, as a result of personal experiences.

This chapter addresses the psychodynamic processes through which individuals are constituted. In it I try to unravel the personal circumstances and experiences that might lead a particular person to identify as 'black' or as 'African', while another does not. What conditions lead another not to become black-identified? So far we have focused on social and historical factors: the collective experience of the contradictions of racism in Britain, in particular. We have seen that not all British-raised people with dark skin colour identify as black or African, while, on the other hand, some with very light-coloured skins do. Black identification is evidently not a mathematical function of skin tone. Nor does it appear to depend solely on being exposed to racism, or to black discourses, or even to a combination of these, since there continue to be many black people who are not black-identified.

Furthermore, many of those who do self-identify as black continue to experience contradictions and to behave in ways that appear to be inconsistent with their proclaimed discursive position. People's professed politics are frequently contradicted by their personal practice. The black man who proclaims his love of black skin and black culture yet finds himself sexually drawn to white women is just one example. The black woman who expresses her commitment to the ideal of sisterhood yet undermines another black woman's position in black discourse is another.

To answer some of these questions, it is necessary to consider the role of personal history and personal relations of the individual in the constitution of subjectivity. This requires a more detailed analysis of individual subjects. It will not be possible to do a comprehensive survey of the constitution of all the individual research participants within the scope of this study. What I shall do is illustrate the operation of some of the processes that occur, to initiate an approach which can be used in subsequent work on subjectivity. But first some background to my decision to use conceptual tools borrowed from psychodynamic theory.

PSYCHOANALYSIS, FEMINISM AND POST-STRUCTURALISM

As earlier advocates of post-structuralist psychology have noted, the decentring of the individual that accompanies the theorisation of subjects as discursively produced has many advantages over preceding theories and does succeed in conceptualising subjectivity as multiple, dynamic and discursively (historically and socially) produced. None the less, it leaves certain areas untheorised:

[W]e are left with a number of unresolved problems. First, in this view the subject is composed of, or exists as, a set of multiple and contradictory positionings or subjectivities. But how are such fragments held together? Are we to assume, as some applications of post-structuralism have implied, that the individual subject is simply the sum total of all positions in discourses since birth? If this is the case, what accounts for the continuity of the subject and the subjective experience of identity? What accounts for the predictability of people's actions, as they repeatedly position themselves within particular discourses? Can people's wishes and desires be encompassed in an account of discursive relations?

(Henriques *et al.* 1984: 204)

It is to psychoanalytic theory that both post-structuralist psychologists and feminist theorists of subjectivity have turned for answers to these and other questions. Scholars from both these schools have been highly critical of psychoanalytic theory but have also found much to gain from reconsidering key aspects of Freudian and post-Freudian theory, as my brief discussion will illustrate.

The early indictment of Freudian theory by both feminists and leftist thinkers during the 1960s and 1970s was based on the perceived politics of psychoanalytic theory and practice: politics which were considered to be retrograde and incompatible with the social transformation of capitalist and patriarchal society that leftist and feminists respectively desired. Frosh (1987) has provided us with one of the most lucid accounts of the historical development of psychoanalytic thought.

Briefly put, for leftists, psychoanalytic practice was both bourgeois and conservative, accessible as it was to only a small élite in the society. Psychoanalytic theory's focus on the individual subject also went against the grain of traditional Marxism, which stressed the social and collective over the possessive individual at the heart of capitalist doctrine. None the less there have been numerous attempts to bring Marx and Freud together, particularly when it became clear that the relationship between the individual and society, and between the economic and the ideological-cultural spheres of human reality, demanded theorisation. The Maoist cultural revolution addressed exactly this terrain, by seeking to actively and, where necessary, forcibly, transform the psyche and culture of the Chinese people, once it became clear that psychological and cultural transformation did not simply follow on from political and economic changes. In the West, Wilhelm Reich and Eric Fromm were among several Marxists who attempted to synthesise Freudian and Marxist theory. Reich did so by equating individual repression with social oppression and envisioning sexual liberation as the key to a wider social revolution. Unfortunately he lacked the theoretical tools to advance his project beyond a bizarre form of sex-determinism (Henriques *et al.* 1984, Reich 1970). Several years later a leading structuralist thinker, Louis Althusser, was to use Lacan's rewrite of Freudian theory to conceptualise anew the relationship between what was then referred to as the base and the superstructure of society: namely the economic and ideological-cultural levels of social life (Althusser 1971). It was he who conceptualised the individual as being born into a pre-existing ideological structure with which he comes to identify; Althusser refers to this process of identification as interpellation. His theory is clearly structuralist and has since been challenged for its universalism. Hirst, for example, points out that Althusser fails to achieve his own theoretical goals because he ultimately lapses into an economically deterministic account (Hirst 1976).

Post-structuralists have subsequently drawn attention to the ways in which psychoanalysis has enabled the regulation of sexuality and proscription of homosexuality in particular, through the production of new discourses and sites of intervention (Foucault 1976). As Henriques *et al.* (1984) observed, the work of both Foucault and Donzelot (1980) added fuel to the view of psychoanalysis as a force for conservatism.

Feminists have viewed psychoanalytic practice as normative: aimed at persuading women with legitimate grievances to remain in their allotted place in society. Freudian theory too was initially viewed as irrevocably sexist. The concept of penis envy and the focus on the father in the theorisation of the Oedipal triangle have been roundly condemned, as has Freud's theorisation of femininity as being a direct effect of the anatomical difference between male and female. This biologically determinist aspect of Freudian theory makes gender difference essential and unchangeable, and once behaviour and experience are considered to be determined by psychic structures rooted in anatomical differences, the distinction between what is biological and what is social is lost. Millet (1981) and Firestone (1971) were among the first to take issue with the way in which Freudian theory casts certain social norms as the intractable effect of universal psycho-sexual structures. None the less it is worth noting that different readings of the relationship between biology and gender relations have been made since the earliest days of psychoanalytic theory, mostly by women psychoanalysts. As early as 1917 Karen Horney argued that Freud's theory of female sexual development was one which accurately depicted the psychic costs to women of living in male-dominated society. She went on to consider the possibility that different meanings could be derived from biological sex differences, most notably in her theory of 'womb envy' in which men experience envy of women's reproductive powers (Horney 1939). More recently, another woman psychoanalyst, Melanie Klein, a main theorist within the object relations school of psychoanalysis, developed a theory of human psychic development as being forged out of early relations. For Klein, it is the relationship with the breast and with the mother which are the most fundamental to human psychic development (Klein 1963).

From an anti-imperialist and antiracist perspective as adopted here, Freudian psychoanalysis can be criticised further, for its universalism and ethnocentrism: in taking the concept of the Oedipal triangle as the basis of identity formation, it is the western nuclear family structure that is assumed. A theory which takes sexual repression and taboo as the bedrock of 'civilisation' is also highly culture-bound, most obviously by late-nineteenth-century Victorian values and the longer-term Judaeo-Christian association of sexuality with sin. While Freud himself does not directly address the psychology of black and colonised people, we saw in Chapter 2 that subsequent analysts have done so in ways that are almost wholly objectionable, invariably relying on psychically determined complexes (as Mannoni (1956) did) and reasserting the evolutionary inferiority of 'barbaric races' (as Jung (1928) did). Like Darwinian theory, Freudian ideas often led to exploitative research in which study of so-called primitive races was supposed to provide insights into the early evolution and development of 'civilised' western man.

All these problems notwithstanding, it is to psychoanalytic theory that feminists and post-structuralists alike have increasingly turned during the 1980s and 1990s, in seeking new ways of theorising subjectivity and of comprehending masculinity and femininity. What has been the basis of this return to and reliance on psychoanalytic theory? Why is it that psychoanalysis has defied simply being rejected on the basis of its indisputable anti-feminism, élitism and historical specificity/universalism?

The first reasons must lie in the new reading that has been made of Freud and subsequently of Lacan and others. In 1974, with the publication of *Psychoanalysis and Feminism*, Juliet Mitchell began the rereading of Freud that has opened the way to more progressive appropriations of psychoanalysis. The main argument that Mitchell puts forward is that Freud has been misinterpreted as biologistic and conservative. She argues that in actual fact he offers a theory of how Victorian patriarchy came into being, rather than assuming it as the universal and necessary state of civilisation. For Mitchell, Freud was problematising the production of masculinity and femininity rather than seeing them as inexorable results of 'nature'. She emphasises the symbolic importance of the phallus and the Father, arguing that what Freud does is provide us with an accurate description of the status quo, rather than a universal truth. For Mitchell, the role of the phallus as a signifier of sexual difference is not necessarily tied to the particular patriarchal order that Freud lived in and wrote about.

Mitchell's work initiated radical readings of Freud and subsequently of Lacan's work (Mitchell and Rose 1982). Feminist and radical social theorists now view psychoanalytic theory not as a final and universal account of society as it is and must always be but instead as a historically located account of the production of subjectivity in Western European patriarchal society. Freud's theory has a number of things to offer those seeking to theorise subjectivity.

In contrast to assuming the subject to exist already in a particular form (unitary, rational and fixed), Freud problematised subjectivity as something that had to be theorised and set about developing a theory of how subjects came to be. Freud's theory of the unconscious subverts notions of a unitary rational subject: the Freudian subject is non-rational and multiple, subject to forces that are not always under the control of the conscious mind. His ideas on the development of human sexuality are also subversive, since his theory takes neither masculinity nor femininity for granted. Instead the Freudian infant starts out as sexually undifferentiated (polymorphously perverse) with the potential to develop in any number of directions, and only later develops masculinity or femininity after a complex struggle between contradictory forces.

Psychoanalytic theory is also a truly relational and social account of the history of the individual. The person is constructed in the course of relationships with other people – in Freud's culture, in the nuclear family of child, mother, father. If Marx provided humankind with a theory of history in the large sense of the history of the development of human society, Freud can be viewed as having supplemented this with a theory of the history of the human which theorises the constitution of the individual subject.

THEORISING SUBJECTIVITY THROUGH 'RACE' INSTEAD OF 'SEX'

Freud developed a theory of human psychic development that centres around gender:

> Psychoanalysis offers a universal theory of the *psychic* construction of gender identity on the basis of repression. In doing so, it gives specific answers to the question of what constitutes subjectivity, how we acquire gendered subjectivity and internalize certain norms and values.
>
> (Weedon 1987: 41)

His focus on the construction of gender identity as being central to psychic development may also explain why his work has been so important to feminists, for whom gender is also the key concept. Within contemporary feminist theory too, gender is the foundation stone of all theories of subjectivity. The question of why theorisations of subjectivity have all centred on gender identity appears not to have been posed. But why is this so? More pertinently, must it necessarily be so?

To my mind, this unquestioned focus on gender identity is linked to the problem of universalism and to the persistent recurrence of an ultimately biological explanation of gender difference. Even feminist psychoanalysts appear not to escape fully explanations of gender difference which, in the last instance, rely on notions of essential differences between the sexes, as Hollway (1982) pointed out in her discussion of Chodorow's work. A unitary notion of 'woman' lies at the heart of feminist psychoanalysis as much as a universal male subject lies at the heart of Freud's thinking. The female subject of which feminist psychoanalysis speaks is located in culturally and historically specific notions of femininity which cannot be taken as given for all the many manifestations of femininity and womanhood that exist in a diverse and changing world, and the problem of ethnocentrism and universalism therefore remains. Furthermore, since gender is the one social division which appears in all cultures, classes and groups of human society (albeit in very diverse ways), it is more easily universalised than divisions which are more clearly historically and culturally located. We are all already positioned by gender by the time we come to theorising subjectivity. Other major social divisions which are also central in people's subjectivity include class and caste, religion, politics, age, nationality, ethnicity and, in some contexts, race.

In view of the location of both myself and the research participants as members of a racial minority in contemporary Britain, I decided early on in the research to theorise subjectivity through the trope of race instead of gender. Race has the advantage of being more easily specified and located within particular histories than gender. All societies have men and women, but they do not all categorise their citizens racially. The specifics of racial categories also vary from one racialised society to another, as do the evaluations attached to them.[1] Furthermore, we have seen that the racialisation of subjectivity often occurs later in life, whereas people become gendered much earlier in life, a fact which made the constitution of racialised subjectivity more appropriate to a study of adult subjectivity.

PSYCHODYNAMICS IN ADULT SUBJECTIVITY

A major difference between the approach I develop here and most psychoanalytic accounts of human psychic development is that I do not focus on early infancy but on processes occurring in young adults. Subjectivity is not only dynamically formed but also continually changing and being constituted and reconstituted, from one instant to another, as well as over longer periods of time. Once one has taken this view of subjectivity as being continuously constituted throughout life, then it follows that it can be studied at any point in the life cycle. The women who participated in this study were mostly young adults.

The fact that they were also women, and from particular backgrounds, was also intended to avoid universalism. Subjectivity is treated as being located in history, with specific content, and not as an abstract idea which can be treated as if it were devoid of that content. Even if similar psychodynamic processes occur in all people, the cultural and discursive content will be group specific and historically located. Instead of being about race and gender in 1970s and 1980s Britain, as was the case for participants in this research, the story of their subjectivity may be about changing national identity, conversion to a religion, the acquisition of a professional identity, or any of a potentially infinite number of personal changes. What follows is, in other words, a local and specific process analysis of adult subjectivity. It is not a universal theory of human psychic development.

USING PSYCHODYNAMIC CONCEPTS

The problem of universalism stems from the concern of psychoanalytic theory to provide a grand theory of the human individual in general. Having taken the epistemological position that all knowledge is situated, and that theory will always have cultural and political content, my concern is not to develop a grand theory of the subject, or a general theory of subjectivities. Rather, I am concerned with elucidating some of the processes by which diverse subjectivities are constituted. Having advanced the idea of subjectivity as comprising discursive (culturally and histori-cally generated) positions, I now turn to consider how individuals come to be. In the remainder of this chapter I develop an account of the dynamics through which any given individual comes to be the particular person that he or she is: a person who habitually takes up some positions and not others and exhibits the characteristic reactions and behaviours that enable someone to be known as an individual. I do this by borrowing a number of key concepts from psychodynamic theory and applying them to case material from Mona Smith in which she discusses her relation-ships with other black women in her family and at work. The psycho-dynamic concepts I have found most useful are derived from Kleinian object relations theory. Although these were developed on the basis of work with young infants, Kleinian theory has it that primal processes pave the way for processes that continue throughout adult psychic life.

According to Klein, the human infant starts out undifferentiated, without memory and unable to distinguish between inner and outer worlds. Psychic development occurs through the early splitting between self and object, a split that is fantasised when the infant first experiences separation from the first love-object, the breast. Thereafter he or she can experience relationships with 'objects' in the outer world. During these object relations, the infant goes through a number of defined positions, in the course of which the projective processes are generated. These projective processes then characterise adult psychic life. Splitting is there-fore the first of the projective processes and is considered to be vital to normal development, being the subject's main defence against anxiety and the precursor to repression (Grotstein 1981).

Splitting involves separating an object into good and bad. According to Klein, the primordial experience of good and bad occurs at the breast which is either experienced as benevolent and nurturing, or as rejecting and frustrating. When splitting occurs, the good object is incorporated into the ego – that is to say, it is introjected. The bad object on the other hand is projected – directed outward and away from the ego, on to other people or objects. For Klein these projective processes are intimately bound up with idealisation and denial:

> Idealisation is bound up with the splitting of the object, for the good aspects of the breast are exaggerated as a safeguard against the fear of the persecuting breast. While the idealisation is thus the corollary of persecutory fear, it also springs from the power of the instinctual desires which aim at unlimited gratification and therefore create the picture of an inexhaustible and always bountiful breast – an ideal breast.
>
> (Klein 1986: 182)

Denial of psychic reality, on the other hand, involves the annihilation of the bad object. Annihilation is possible because early mental life is characterised by feelings of omnipotence. When an object is denied, so too is its object relation – that part of the subject that is bound up with the object. Klein sees these two processes of idealisation and denial as occurring together, in what she refers to as the process of hallucinatory gratification. In the case of normal personality development an optimal balance must have been achieved in the early stages. Excessive flight into an idealised internal object, or excessive denial, can result in feelings of disintegration, in the weakening and impoverishment of the young ego.

Projective identification is the process during which the subject first projects an unpalatable aspect of her- or himself on to another person but then identifies with that aspect and therefore with that person. In other words, projective processes are the basis for the human ability to experience empathy or understanding in relationships. However, the side-effect of this ability is the fact that if projection is predominantly dependent or hostile, then real empathy and understanding are impaired.

Klein herself saw the importance of projective processes as a means of understanding adult psychic life:

> [A]n inner world is built up which is partly a reflection of the external one, that is to say, the double process of introjection and projection continues throughout every stage of life. In the same way introjection and projection go on throughout life and become modified in the course of maturation; but they never lose their importance in the individual's relation to the world around him. Even in the adult, therefore, the

judgment of reality is never quite free from the influence of his internal world.

(1963: 5)

The general direction of psychic development is one in which the subject seeks greater integration, moving towards a reduction of the anxiety that produces splitting. In what follows, I take the experience of contradiction as being a source of anxiety or unease, which therefore pushes the individual's psychic development forward as she or he seeks to reduce anxiety. This means that I consider the experience of contradiction to be a major force in the dynamics of subjectivity.

Recall how Mona Smith, in discussing her relationship with her mother, remarked:

What I had in fact was a lot of negative attitudes about blacks – which were therefore turned on myself because I personify all that is black.

As we have seen, Mona also described her mother like this:

MONA: She's very hard on black people. Her own people. She's one of those people who will – her favourite saying used to be 'you don't want to work with black people, 'cause them never do any work'. You know – you can't come out with things like that! . . .
    I think that in parts of her head she doesn't actually see herself as black. If you want she sees herself as 'coloured', as if she can actually see herself as a separate entity. So she can quite justifiably sit there in the house and slag off black people: – 'All the girl dem ever do is getting pregnant' and 'All the boys dem ever do is get into trouble.'

According to the discursive analysis, this was a description of Mrs Smith as being positioned within a colonial discourse that inferiorises black people. Mona was describing it as a way of affirming her distance from all that; she takes up a position that is firmly situated within black radical discourse, a discourse which dismisses Mrs Smith's attitudes to other black people as backward.

Reanalysing this in psychodynamic terms, we can describe Mona as separating from her mother and in so doing, as splitting within herself, as she changed from an earlier position, in which she too had a negative attitude towards black people, to a position in which she recognises herself as a black woman and gives this a positive value. She simultaneously represses her previously negative valuation of blackness and, by projecting it on to her mother, eases the contradiction. Her outraged tone now consolidates her own position within black radical discourse and her commonality with the other two black women she is conversing with. The changes that she has gone through enable her to take this position and distance herself from her mother. None the less, when Mona says of her mother that 'in parts of her head she doesn't see herself as black', she is equally talking about her own, pre-racialised self: it is because she has been in that position herself that she *knows* this. The discursive change, from colonial to black radical discourse, is at the same time a psycho-dynamic movement involving splitting, the repression of the bad, black object and the idealisation of a good black object.

In an apparent paradox, Mona, having been raised by her mother, now uses her mother as a vehicle for her projections: she projects negative ideas about black people that she can no longer identify with on to her mother, and her mother becomes a vehicle for all the things that Mona, who is now a proud-to-be-black woman, must reject. Only by taking distance in this way can Mona really become a person who can feel good about herself and whose life does not resonate with the racist climate of post-colonial Britain and her mother's negative expectations. One con-sequence of these dynamics is that Mona remains emotionally bound to her mother, even though the two of them no longer hold the same views. Now her mother is the reservoir of her projections, a touchstone she defines herself against. By invoking her mother she is better able to express her identification with the other black women with whom she is discussing herself, and we can see that other black women (Theresa in particular) readily empathise: what she describes is something they share and understand.

This theorisation of subjectivity implies that the discursive movements observed in the previous chapter are accompanied by psychodynamic processes within the individual and vice versa: psychodynamic processes have discursive (social and historical) content. In other words, there is a constant resonance between psychodynamics and social experience in the construction and reproduction of the individual's subjectivity. This means that both discourses (theorised as conveyors of history, culture and social meaning) and individual subjects are produced in a continuous dialectic, out of reverberations between historical-cultural and psycho-logical conditions. Here we have a theory which transcends dualism because it conceptualises the individual and the social as being produced simultaneously. This is not to suggest that every individual change gener-ates new discourses but that when individual changes are provoked by conditions that are widely experienced – such as those of race and gender – then these are more likely to become widespread, to gain social power and become discourses that convey culture and social meaning, or collect-ive knowledges. The analysis put forward here is one grounded in the particular experience of black women; that is to say, it has looked at how historical and personal experience of racism (in the dominant culture and in personal relationships) generates black radical discourse and racialised subjectivities. It would seem that a similar analysis could be carried out on other discourses and subjectivities, for example on gendered discourses on femininity or masculinity, or on Islamic discourses and secular or fundamentalist subjectivities, or on any of the new or old nationalisms and their concomitant ethnic or religious identities.

THE PERSISTENCE OF REPRESSED MATERIAL IN THE UNCONSCIOUS

The psychodynamic analysis has so far suggested a series of moves which enable one to take up new positions. These processes seem to occur continuously. In the case of racialised subjects, it is as if the black person is obliged constantly to reaffirm her or his racial identity, which is unstable insofar as there is difficulty in establishing it as a taken-for-granted aspect of oneself. This is very likely due to the fact of living in white-dominated society, an insight derived from the observation that few Africans spend much time consciously 'being black', not so much out of naïvety but because this is redundant when they live in a world in which everyone is black. When black people from the Americas go about proclaiming their blackness (or African-ness) on their pilgrimages to the continent, they tend to arouse bafflement or puzzlement among their African brothers and sisters.[2]

At the intrapsychic level, however, the need for constant reaffirmation can be attributed to the fact that the individual never entirely jettisons earlier positions. Rather it would seem that the individual is in some sense the sum of all the positions (discursive and psychodynamic) that he or she has ever been in. Even if nothing is ever absolutely forgotten – and we are made up of all the former selves we have been in our personal history – clearly not all these positions continuously coexist at the same level of our subjective experience. This is where we need a theory of the unconscious. Subjectivity can then be conceptualised as being multi-layered, with deeper levels that are less accessible to the conscious mind containing material that has been repressed, either with the passage of time and the constant laying down of new material, or because the material is anxiety-provoking, a sense of unease having been the initial cause of its being split off and repressed.

This observation concurs with psychodynamic theory, since according to this, splitting and repression does not eliminate the rejected aspects of one's past object relations. Even the projective processes provide no final solution. Instead, repressed material, particularly when associated with high levels of emotion or anxiety, continues to affect individuals, and this can be observed in the course of their relationships with other people.

In what follows, I use material gathered from discussion of relationships between black women to demonstrate the existence of repressed material, as evidenced by its continuing effects on subjectivity. To illustrate the theory, I use material which demonstrates the existence of persistent insecurities over racial identity, insecurities which black people very easily arouse in the course of their relationships with one another.

In the case of Mona, we can see that other black women are able to undermine her sense of herself as a black women very easily. She describes several occasions on which she has experienced attacks on her identity from her colleagues in the black community organisation where she was working until recently. One example is contained in the following extract:

MONA: Claudette actually in some ways intimidates me. Yes, Claudette does intimidate me – she keeps having a go at my hair and things (*nervous laugh*).

AMINA: She what?

THERESA: How does she do it though?

MONA: Well I don't ... I think she's actually joking – she's not actually attempting to do anything *awful* to me, but I ... when I was working with the black groups and having real problems – it's like seeing that almost brought up again. And so I back off.

AMINA: What sort of things?

MONA: Like the first thing she commented on was ... she said to me ... I didn't have plaits then – she said 'Why do you straighten your hair?' So I said 'I don't straighten my hair'. It's um ... very fine. Anyway. I immediately got paranoid (*laugh*). I immediately thought – Oh shit, here we go again – I'm accused of straightening it – I can't help it – it's the way it stands. [1] I immediately felt my blackness was actually being challenged. That happens quite often, particularly with people who I initially feel, um, whose consciousness level is quite high. [2] Then I will actually back off. I can be quite assertive in certain situations ... (*tails off lamely*).

[1] Mona is familiar with this sort of remark from earlier experiences while she was trying to work with other black community groups, but that does not stop her feeling defensive. Even in describing the incident to others, she says 'I can't help it' in reference to her hair texture. She has never in fact straightened it but now wears it braided with extensions, so the texture of her real hair is not discernible.

[2] It is 'conscious' people – in other words those who 'know' what it is to be black – who make her feel 'paranoid' with remarks of this nature. Mona remarks on this because on the surface it seems to be a contradiction – Mona also considers herself to be conscious but she is not as confident about defining what is and is not on for black people as she might have been, had her personal history not been so fraught with its own racial contradictions. Ironically, one tenet of black consciousness is that of unity – these are 'sisters' and yet Claudette is not supportive towards Mona. Instead she undermines her and it seems that she is exploiting Mona's insecurities to reaffirm her own sense of blackness.

Why should Mona be so easily unsettled, instead of simply correcting Claudette by informing her that she does not in fact straighten her hair? Why should such remarks be experienced as a 'challenge to her blackness', the very thing she has struggled hard to affirm?

A discursive analysis points to the fact that black radical discourse condemns hair-processing, skin-bleaching and other alterations of appearance in the direction of 'whitening'. Within it, black people are encouraged to reject the dominant racial standards of beauty. Mona does not in fact straighten her hair but is accused of doing so, presumably because her skin is so dark that her 'mixed-type' hair texture is assumed to be artificial. It may also be envied. In either case it provokes hostility and rejection from those she calls 'conscious black people'. Light-skinned black-identified women may be more popular with the boys but, when they reject sexual advances, are more likely to be accused of preferring whites than their darker-skinned sisters. Light-skinned women describe similar experiences of rejection from women, in which their light-but-not-white skin colour is despised (and perhaps coveted), so that they talk of being accused of skin-bleaching or 'collaborating with the enemy', or of people assuming they are not 'really black'. These dynamics are probably given impetus because even conscious black people have a tendency to use those around them to display just how conscious they are and to feel empowered by taking a holier than thou stance.[3] Behind this process lie specific, stereotypical prescriptions of what an authentic black or African person should look like. This is somewhat ironic given the facts. A large proportion of the population of Caribbean descent, from whom most of the black people in Britain are descended, are racially mixed and, as those who have visited or come from the continent will be aware, Africans cover a whole spectrum of shades and appearances, most of which do not fit into the 'Negro' type featuring in imperialist anthropology and racist mythology (see Chapter 2).

Discourses are not, in other words, always rational. Nor are they a direct reflection of social reality. What we are seeing here is a manifestation of an identity politics of racial nationalism, in which race politics are linked to physical characteristics, an identity politics that has had a pervasive influence on black radical discourses internationally (see Chapter 5). In psychodynamic terms, it also suggests a high level of denial. What is being denied is the disturbingly contradictory history of inter-racial relations in which collaboration and collusion coexisted alongside the more easily glorified history of resistance and rebellion. Racial 'impurity' signifies the denied history of collusion and the fact that people's inner desires and emotional lives all too often continue to contradict the professed politics of the black radical position. Within the limited space opened up by black radical discourse the power relations of the pigmentocracy appear to be reversed, so that the 'blacker' a person is, the better. Mona looks to other black people for what it means to be black in a positive sense, because, like many of this age group, she was not raised to be black and has had to seek out the necessary information for herself (see Chapter 6).

The psychodynamic explanation of these processes suggests that a great many black people are not as sure of their blackness as they might appear. Many continue to have a need to project their own inner racial insecurities on to others. The most likely vehicles for these projections are people like Mona – black people who are susceptible because their physical attributes do not conform to the black ideal that has been constructed in reaction to the white ideal and who are perceived to be vulnerable. There are a great many of them available in the British context, where black people with 'white' personal histories abound. For those black people who do not opt to remain 'whitified' or to conform to what can become a stifling discursive regime, life involves a continuous confrontation with the contradictory realities of race and their own multiplicity.[4]

Mona is easily undermined by her colleagues because of her personal relational history. The repressed aspects of the 'whitified' childhood engineered by her mother lie just beneath the surface of her black self-assurance, so Claudette has no difficulty in stirring these up. Mona's anxieties during this and other similar incidents stem from her fear that she has been exposed, not for what she now is but for what she used to be, became uncomfortable with and has engaged in a psychic struggle against.

This interpretation of Mona's vulnerability is supported by the fact that she experiences some guilt about the way she is, admitting that in some ways she has taken on all the 'advantages' that her mother drummed into her:

MONA: ... [W]e were sitting having a discussion about job prospects and how racism works. And of course I'm very aware that in a white society, if they are going to employ black people they're going to employ black people they feel they can deal with. And all they actually work on is things like the way you talk, the way you look. And they'll attempt to match, 'cause like goes for like and that sort of stuff. And if people assume that my features [1] look European and that helps in job prospects ... I'm very aware of how that works but the thing for me – what hurts is that knowing how that dynamic works there is nothing I can do about it. That's the way it is. I can't help the way white people relate to me at all. But to then have black people using the same thing against me. ... Then you don't have anywhere to move back to for solidarity. You can't move back because they say 'that's not fair'. I know it's not fair but that isn't my fault. I can't do anything about that. [2] I can't alter my features. [1]

[1] Mona here attributes her experience to her 'features', which she cannot change. In the previously cited extract it was her hair, while at

other moments it was her dress style that was being attacked. It seems most likely that what she describes is the result of the total effect of her physical appearance, dress style and behaviour. Perhaps this, like the tone and hesitation in this quotation, is a further indicator of the anxiety and defensiveness that this situation arouses. Mona's features, like those of many black people, contradict the stereotypes of 'Negro' that prevail in and outside the black community: thick lips, wide nose, woolly hair, black skin, and she makes no compensatory attempts to 'dress black'.

[2] Mona feels she is being wrongly accused by the black people who reject her. In fact what she describes is an in-group effect of racism. It shows how black people often take out the frustrations and stresses of racism and discrimination on one another, because they still live within and under white domination. In other words, becoming conscious does not solve the problem. Subjects do not change from one thing into another without some residual effects remaining, and black people do not make it easy for each other.

At the level of discourse analysis, we can see from these extracts that black discourse means different practices (behaviour, ways of speaking and dress style to be precise) to different people. Claudette (like Iscara, Chapter 5) is a Rastafarian who has a particular view on how black women should be. In a separate discussion Theresa points out that both Claudette and another of Mona's black colleagues do in fact describe Mona as 'white', which shows that Mona has correctly interpreted their behaviour towards her. In her emotional responses, Mona arrogates to others the right to define what is and is not black, even though at a conscious level she challenges the idea of anyone having that right as being 'silly'.

Dress, hair style and skin colour are still important signifiers of status and, more importantly, attitude. The valuations attached to 'whiteness' by black people have changed, thanks to the development of black radical discourse. Although Mona's hair is not straight in European terms, it still conjures up the white other for her colleagues, perhaps because it is combined with other powerful signifiers of class (dress and speech style).

FURTHER ANALYSIS

In a different extract from the same discussion group, Mona describes another instance in which her colleague Claudette attacks her:

MONA: Just before I left we had a situation over lunch. I was sitting – I was smoking, so I moved back from the table where people were eating, so I sat back a bit so I wasn't actually blowing smoke in people's faces, and Claudette suddenly swung round and said, '*why is it you have to dress like that?!*' And I just went ... eek!

AMINA: What were you wearing?

MONA: I was wearing a three-piece suit or something and a tie.

AMINA: Oh, I see.

MONA: Yes, and knowing me I probably had a trilby hat and an over-coat. I – I do overdo it at times. [1]

THERESA: No, you're just trendy.

MONA: Anyway, I just freaked. I was not able to come back at all. It was Winston who bailed me out. He turned round and said to Claudette, 'Fuck off. Leave her alone.' I felt quite bad about it really, because I should have turned round and said, 'Come on Claudette don't be so stupid girl – I'm not going to sit here and comment on your clothing so don't comment on mine.' But I immediately backed off and thought 'Oh Jesus'. [2] I think it's still the continuing thing to do with me needing to sort out my relationships with ... not black women – certain black women. Black women coming from a partic-ular place. [3]

[1] Mona sounds almost as apologetic about her dress style as she was about her hair texture. In practice, however, she has maintained her right to dress as she pleases over the years. In the same discussion she says with a little laugh, 'I suspect that what I present in terms of an image is pretty odd.' Later Mona argues that it is not in fact her dress style that is producing this sort of reaction from 'conscious' black people but attributes it to her physical features, which of course she cannot in any case change. Her dress style consists of an assortment of styles and fashions. She tall, slim and attractive, and evidently enjoys dressing.

[2] Anxiety/unease: Mona is undermined by Claudette's attack and unable to respond in her own defence.

[3] Once again it emerges in the discussion that it is a particular type of black woman to whom she is unable to respond. Mona refers to 'certain' black women and, as we have already noted, elsewhere she describes them as 'conscious' black women – women to whom she arro-gates the right to define what is and is not 'black'. As a Rastafarian, Claudette is probably a great deal more dedicated to being rootsy.

As the discussion continues this last point is reaffirmed as a dynamic that can only happen between black women:

THERESA: Had it been one of the white workers you would have come back wouldn't you?

MONA: Oh no problem – I'd have slapped her (*laughs*).

THERESA: Well – it's ... you know – because it's Claudette or Jean.

MONA: Yes – it's one of my own. Because rejection from white people I expect. [1]

THERESA: But not from your own.

MONA: That is what causes me problems. Because what I do is turn it on myself – I must be wrong – not they. [2]

THERESA: I think we have all done that for a long time, until you suddenly ask yourself (*clicks her fingers*) – why should I?

AMINA: But we're still susceptible to it, is that what you're saying? (*to Mona*). I recognise that in me.

[1] She has (correctly) felt rejected by black women. As we have seen, it is an old sinking feeling she is familiar with from her past.

[2] Because this is coming from black people Mona takes this on instead of dismissing it (in psychoanalytic terms she introjects it).

But why should Claudette spend so much energy attacking Mona, often (as during the pub luncheon scene described above) when they are the only two black women present? A consideration of the power dynamics of the situation suggests why she is not more generous. Mona's account describes her own disempowerment and does not explicitly consider the possibility that she may not appear as weak and vulnerable as she feels, although the way she describes what she was wearing and doing when Claudette attacked her suggests that at some level she is aware that she provoked Claudette. A power analysis suggests that Mona's posture and style has been read as superior, or perhaps even arrogant, by Claudette. The style Mona has displayed is a sophisticated European one signifying confidence and cosmopolitanism, compounded by the fact that she was leaning back and smoking a cigarette. All this may be Mona's natural personal style but Claudette sees her as a poser and is not impressed; as a Rastafarian she does not smoke cigarettes or drink, an English pub is not her kind of territory, and she would probably not be seen dead in a three-piece suit. Mona appears to be quite at ease and is (albeit unintentionally) displaying various characteristics that align her with the white, middle-class status quo and surroundings and distance her from Claudette, a distance all the more irritating to Claudette because they actually come from very similar backgrounds: they are both from working-class Jamaican families settled in London. In attacking Mona in the way she does, Claudette cuts Mona down to size and strongly asserts her own distance from Mona's perceived position. By knocking Mona off her pedestal, she also succeeds in reversing the power dynamic. The psychodynamic pay-off is that Claudette, perhaps unsettled by her own inner racial insecurities, vents her irritation and, by projecting 'whiteness' on to Mona, reaffirms herself in her own position within black discourse. If Mona had been more secure in her own position as a black woman, Claudette would not have succeeded in unsettling her in this manner but by this time it is a familiar dynamic between them, which Mona falls for repeatedly.

I have pointed out that it is common for black people to describe other black people as 'white' and suggested that this is a direct result of the persisting hegemony of racist discourses in the British context – a hegemony which means that there are in fact many people of African and Caribbean descent who are not positioned within black discourses, or have not developed black subjectivity. In Britain, a great many people of Caribbean and African descent have not lived or grown up in strong communities of black people but in isolation from one another. This explains why, for many, black identity is a preoccupation of early adulthood – a process embarked upon when they move away from childhood homes, or to large towns where there are significant concentrations of black people and there is a 'black culture' to speak of. Those raised in all-white environments (suburbia, care institutions, boarding schools, foster families) do not have black discursive positions readily available to them. One consequence of this is that they may be 'unable' to perceive and respond to racism, even though it is part of their experience. Such people will have subjectivities that are racialised, but in ways that differ from those who have become part of the collective change heralded by black radicalism, because they will have been subjected to racism without having access to any of the real or imaginary alternative referents which we have seen the women in this study make use of. To cite an extreme example, black children raised in children's homes commonly develop a habit called 'skin-scratching' in which they compulsively scratch away at their skin, as if to exfoliate themselves. Black children raised in white homes often have the less dramatic skin and hair problems that stem from unintentional neglect, since in temperate climates both often require extra care. These and other visible markers can be seen as the result of internalisation of the derogatory images of black people that continue to prevail wherever they have not been sufficiently challenged. None the less it is worth pointing out that even isolated, individuals can withstand such images and carve out positive subjectivities, as the creativity of women such as Jackie Kay (a poet who was adopted and raised by a Scottish family in Edinburgh) demonstrates.

When we come to consider relations among black people, here too there is, in psychodynamic terms, a vested interest in having surrogate whites in any black group. These individuals can be used to serve as vehicles for every other black person's projections of those unacceptable 'white' parts of themselves. According to the theorisation put forward here, these dynamics are likely to continue to characterise black social relations for as long as racist discourses pervade black experience.

Individuals with the kind of background that Mona has described experience a high level of stress in their relationships with their black peers, peers who often undermine rather than affirm their racial identification. Some (Mona and Dot in this study) formed relationships with men who did not pull them over the barrel of race, perhaps because they were white. Others find expression in creative work, as artists, singers, poets and writers, either on a full-time basis or whenever they make time for themselves. Perhaps as a result of these repeated rejections from those whom Mona still refers to as her own people, many multiply-identified women are strongly individualistic and in many ways put themselves beyond the reach of black identity politics in their professional and social lives. At a superficial level, and as seen by many 'conscious' black people, Mona appears to fulfil Fanon's sardonic conclusion that 'The black man wants to be like the white man. For the black man there is only one destiny. And it is white' (Fanon 1967: 228). However, the analysis put forward in this chapter takes us some way beyond this because within it, people are not simply either black *or* white but rather complex, multi-layered beings, with a capacity to move between positions, create new ones, and constantly negotiate and renegotiate their identities as they struggle to make sense of a world in which fixed categories are constantly subverted and changed.

This application of psychodynamic theory has taken our theorisation of subjectivity far beyond its discursive aspect. Subjectivity is now not only a dynamic social process emanating from the collective history of the people under consideration but also an intrapsychic process in which positions and changes are constituted out of the personal relational history of the individual. But how has this use of psychoanalytic theory avoided the shortcomings of earlier applications?

In the first place it is a theorisation that looks at identity as a continuous dynamic process and does not postulate the development of fixed psychic structures. This enables us not to be deterministic. It may be recalled that earlier social theorists of colonial psychology, who did not have the benefit of post-structuralist thought to draw on, suggested that the coloniser and the colonised had complexes which had negative consequences for both but especially for the colonised (see Chapter 2). Even Fanon's (1967) theory of 'lactification', according to which black people desperately desire to become white, also implicitly pathologised black people. By developing a discursive and psychodynamic theory of subjectivity, I have tried to avoid reducing racial identifications to static complexes which have pathological consequences for black people. Instead, racialised subjectivity is viewed as being merely one dimension of subjective processes which involve constant negotiation and change in the course of social relations. Theorising subjectivity as dynamic and multi-layered opens up the possibility that experiences of contradiction, and the unease they generate, may also give impetus to cultural creativity and self-development.

This analysis has avoided the gender politics that have dogged psycho-analytic theory by taking race as the main analytic trope through which to theorise subjectivity. Although, as in many women's studies, I chose to have a subject group comprised solely of women, this was not because I wanted to theorise femininity, as has been the case in other feminist psychological studies. And although I focused on the production of racialised subjectivity, I have not used this as a basis to develop a grand or universal theory of subjectivity in the way that psychoanalysts have used gender but rather to develop a grounded theoretical approach and methodology for theorising the potentially infinite number of human subjectivities.

This approach has had the added advantage of avoiding the universalism of many psychoanalytic accounts. Because not all societies are racialised in the same ways, and because current thinking on European anti-black racism has elucidated its links to the specific histories of slavery and colonialism, race is more clearly contextual than sex or gender. This has made it easier to develop concepts grounded in the specific history of the research group, rather than free-floating universals. In the next chapter I further explore the subjectivities of the research participants, but shifting from an emphasis on race to consider the ways in which the racialised subjectivities already identified are also gendered.

NOTES

1 My own categorisation changes as I travel between Africa (where I am relatively light skinned and described as 'half-caste' or 'fair' and nationality is in any case afforded more significance), the Caribbean (where I am described as 'red') and Europe (where I am categorised and identify myself as black). I am less comfortable with the significations of my appearance among black Southern Africans (as 'coloured') than among West African or Caribbean people. In other words, race has a clear historicity and contextuality that is harder to delineate for gender. I am a woman, whichever part of the globe I may be on, and however I am racially identified or misidentified.

2 Wole Soyinka, the Nigerian writer, summed this up when he responded to negritude in the 1960s by asking whether tigers find it necessary to proclaim their 'tigritude'. For their part, diasporan blacks often view their African counterparts as naïvely lacking in race-consciousness.

3 Cross (whose work is discussed in Chapter 3) has observed 'holier than thou' attitudes in black Americans, but he locates these as characterising one of the stages of nigrescence, rather than being a continuous aspect of racialised subjectivity.

4 One of the derogatory terms deployed in black discourse for a black person who does not know how to be black is 'coconut', defined as someone who is black only on the outside and white on the inside. Given the fact that a growing majority of black people in contemporary Britain have been raised in a white-dominated world, the possibilities for being black all the way through are remote enough to be a common source of anxiety.

Chapter 8

Black femininity

Unforgiving as the course of justice
Inerasable as my scars and fate
I am here
a woman ... with all my lives strung out like beads
                    before me

It isn't privilege or pity
that I seek
It isn't reverence or safety
quick happiness or purity
                    but
the power to be what I am – a woman
charting my own future – a woman
holding my beads in my hand

(Grace Nichols)

INTRODUCTION

We have been considering the processes through which racialised subjectivities are constituted. I now propose to look at the ways in which these
racialised aspects of black women's subjectivity are also gendered. This is
appropriate in view of the fact that, as the black women's movement
realised, black women's lives are structured not only by class divisions of
late capitalist society but also by the combined effects of race and gender
oppression. The idea of 'triple oppression' is an attempt to theorise and
respond to the multiply oppressive dynamics of exclusion and marginalisation, and to explain the poor economic and political status of black
women in British (and North American) society. Deriving from dualistic
structuralist and Marxist traditions of social theory, the idea of triple
oppression conjures up the notion of a monolithic social structure bearing
down on all oppressed groups but especially on black women. It is
perhaps at its least effective in considering the psychology of black women,

because of the way in which it has tended to imply accumulated pathologies, or black women as ultimate victims. It fails to account for the dynamic
and creative manifestations of black women's subjectivity, their resilience
and their profound capacity to come up with innovative ways of living and
being. None the less, it is logical to assume that if subjectivity is racialised
in racially divided contexts, it will also be gendered in patriarchal societies.
But what does it mean to say that subjectivity is gendered?   Are all
the positions that women, or for that matter men, take up gendered; that
is to say, specifically 'feminine' or 'masculine'?   Or are femininity and
masculinity aspects of subjectivity that are not always manifest?   How
does black femininity differ from white or other femininities in the wider
society?   Not all these questions can be fully addressed here, but having
already put forward a non-pathogenic approach to theorising racialised
subjectivities, I now propose to develop this further to consider how these
are gendered.

Recent feminist theorists view subjectivity as something that is
produced, therefore not an immutable fact of life but something that
is changeable. This understanding has been central to feminist social
theory ever since the early distinction was made between sex and gender.
According to this early theorisation, individuals were born with a biological sex (which was unchangeable) and then developed gender through
the process of socialisation. Conceptualised within the dualistic paradigm,
socialisation involved the idea of a unitary society impacting on a blank-
slate individual in the course of his or her upbringing and education. Here
I have developed an understanding of subjective processes as being much
more active and complex than has been implied by socialisation theory,
during which people take up and move through different positions
that are discursively and psychodynamically generated in the course of
collective and individual social relations.   Extending this approach to
consider the production of black femininity leads us to pose the question differently, to consider just what it is about black women's racialised
subjectivity that is gendered.

Ever since Freud, it has been clear that notions of masculinity and
femininity are themselves problematic. Anthropological research has also
demonstrated that these are not universal, whereas historical evidence
suggests that they vary over time as well as between cultures, races and
classes. This means that before we can even ask whether people can take
up the discursive positions of the opposite sex, we have to consider anew
what we mean by masculinity and femininity.

It seems to me that race and gender are both concepts which bridge the
different levels of social life, concepts which are produced and reproduced
in the course of intrapsychic, socio-cultural, economic and historical
relations. In the preceding chapters I have concentrated on the black
subjectivities emerging in the context of a racially divided world. In view

of the fact that the subject group also lives in a world divided by gender, it is appropriate to consider the gendering of black women's subjectivity. My consideration of black femininity is also grounded in the specific history and experience of the subject group of black women living in Britain, even though, as we shall see, black femininity has a much wider reach than that afforded by the British Isles and the multiply oppressive legacies bequeathed to black women living within its shores.

In the earlier chapters we saw research participants talking a great deal about what it means to be black. Much of the material generated in discussions is implicitly or explicitly gendered, in that it clearly comes from women and not from men. In what follows, I identify some of the discourses positioning black women as women and how black women, who have been subjected to the combined negative legacies of racism and sexism, are continuously struggling against and transcending these. In other words, our main concern here is to explore how black women are constructing and projecting themselves as feminine subjects, out of the past and into the future.

But what have earlier studies had to say about black femininity? There is now a growing body of research literature on black masculinity (e.g. Segal 1990, Staples 1982) but black femininity remains largely unexplored within the social sciences. In Chapter 2, it became apparent that black women have hardly featured in psychological discourses about colonised peoples.[1] Mannoni (1956) had little to say about Malagasy women, noting only anecdotes about their alleged mystical hold over French men. Fanon, for his part, typified the black women he encountered in France and the Antilles as obsessed with becoming white, or at least with attracting white partners and bearing children whiter than themselves (Fanon 1967). In the Algerian women he saw a revolutionary phoenix arising from the ashes of colonialism, a combatant and heroine who wears the haik not because tradition obliges her to but instrumentally – because it is a shrewd disguise for a freedom fighter (see Fanon 1980: 14–45, 77–98; Perinbram 1977). His greatest insights into colonial subjectivity are not those concerning women but rather those derived from his observation of French men, whom he noticed to have violent sexual obsessions with the inaccessible Algerian women, and Algerian men, who found it difficult to continue their relations with wives who had been raped by the French and to cope with the changes in gender relations that the war conditions required.[2]

Nor has the work of North American black psychologists seriously considered the possibility that gender might play a part in the process of racial identity formation (Chapter 3). At most we have observations concerning slight differences between men and women's test scores (Cross 1991). It is important to reiterate that the American-based research on black psychology has really centred on the black male, leaving gender unproblematised and untheorised. Psychologists of nigrescence, for example, have so far assumed that men and women 'nigresce' in the same way. This neglect of gender by black American psychologists is all the more surprising because gender has been a hotbed of controversy ever since the notion of the black matriarch was first put forward to explain the disadvantaged position of black people in the United States (see Chapter 3). As early as the 1970s Wallace (1978) was able to detail the vested interests of both the white establishment and black men in this stereotyped construction of black womanhood. Her polemic paved the way for a great deal of rethinking on the history of black gender relations and a new generation of ideas on black womanhood has blossomed (for example, Davis 1981, hooks 1982). Even so, the field of racial identity theory has evaded the entire debate on sexual politics, with researchers making little or no reference to questions of gender and sexuality.

The neglect of gender within black psychology may be partly attributed to simplistic conceptualisations of race and racism, as well as to the general tendency of psychologists to treat race as if it affected all black people in a uniform manner. A similar point may be made in relation to theorisations of gender. In focusing on a universalised idea of woman, psychoanalytic and psychological theories of gender development have ignored the role of race and other social divisions, and how these might be involved in the production and reproduction of gender (see, for example, Chodorow 1978, Gilligan 1982). It is therefore incumbent upon us to deconstruct the categories 'woman' and 'black' in our consideration of black femininity, to resist setting up what hooks aptly describes as a new 'totalising telos' (hooks 1991). I therefore deliberately do not spell out what black femininity is. Instead I merely sketch some of its manifestations in discussions between black women, supplementing this with reference to the creative expression of femininity found in black women's poetry.

Paving the way for the study of black femininity is the work undertaken on the other side of the Atlantic by African-American women scholars who have taken issue with the pervasive masculinism of black social and intellectual life, mostly doing battle in the broad arena of cultural studies. bel hooks's work on the cultural representations of black people in North American society challenges the manner in which both white and black cultural production have reproduced sexism (hooks 1992). In her essays on race, gender and cultural politics, hooks carries the earlier critiques of black sexism forward to argue that only a truly radical black subjectivity – by which she means one informed by feminism as well as anti-racism – will further the aims and goals of the black liberation struggle.

In what follows I look at the discursive production of black femininity in the British context and at the manner in which black women are reaching beyond the immediate conditions of their everyday lives to forge new ways of being black and female. In the extracts below we can see how femininity often comes up during discussions in which women recall their adolescent experiences as young black women. We can see how the racialised subjectivities of young black women are also inscribed with gender and sexuality. One of the sites at which these are most discernible is in the feminine preoccupation with notions of attractiveness.

COLOURISM, ATTRACTIVENESS AND FEMININITY

I hate dat ironed hair
And dat bleaching skin
Hate dat ironed hair
And dat bleaching skin.
But I'll be all alone
If I don't fall in.

(Louise Bennet, cited in Cobham and Collins (eds) 1987)

The concern with being physically and sexually attractive is also a useful site at which to examine the emergence of femininity. In the case of heterosexual women, this is primarily a desire to be attractive to men, although lesbians, and men too, can be highly concerned about their sexual attractiveness. Attractiveness also has other wide-ranging social consequences, best understood from the testimonies of those deemed to be unattractive. An earlier study of the gendering of subjectivity also draws attention to the feminine preoccupation with being attractive to members of the opposite sex, locating this within a dominant discourse (Hollway 1982). This 'have-hold' discourse makes getting and keeping a man a key site in the production of femininity. Although Hollway's study may only have involved white, middle-class subjects, the material which follows clearly indicates that a concern with being attractive features strongly in black women's femininity, probably all the more so because racist discourses have historically defined black women as 'ugly' and their sexuality in negative terms. If white women were supposed to incarnate an asexual purity and beauty, black women were supposed to be pornographically sexual and crudely featured. The fascination that the European public had with women such as Saartje Baartman (Chapter 5) was a perverse one, which was part of a dynamic in which black women were endowed with all the taboo fantasies of the sexually repressed European psyche. The success of the superstars Josephine Baker, who would appear in a banana tutu during the 1920s, and today's Grace Jones, photographed scantily clad and caged, owes much to these constructions of black femininity.

During the 1970s, black girls growing up in Britain were by and large subjected to the dominant society's notions of female 'attractiveness':

notions which appear in their desire for long, flowing hair, lighter skin and aquiline features. The content of 'attractiveness' is invariably racialised, indicating that many black women's early experience of their femininity is structured by the racist aesthetics which derive from colonial-integrationist discourses. To be acceptable, black women were expected to look as white as possible and to repress their sexuality. Several of those raised by white or white-identified mothers or mother-figures recall being cautioned against wearing bright colours, displaying their bodies, or in any way drawing attention to themselves, lest they be viewed as sexually loose. In any case, various degrees of sexual assault and insult are part of the daily experience of young black women in racist societies, however frumpily they may have been dressed. A great many grew up feeling unattractive:

DOT: I might have felt inferior physically, but it wasn't because I was black necessarily, because the sort of problems that I had was because of black people. It wasn't because I was black that I felt inferior – it was because I was black and . . . I was an *ugly* black. I used to get called 'Blackie' – Joe Smith, the guy who lived next door – we went to primary school together, and I was saying to him recently, 'Remember when you used to tease me at school?' They wouldn't play with me. And if the guys wouldn't play with you, then the girls wouldn't either.

AMINA: Who used to call you Blackie – the other black kids?

DOT: Yes.

AMINA: What – because you were darker than them?

DOT: Yes. And 'flat-nose' (*laughs*). I grew up with a thing about my nose. I always said that when I was 25 I'd change it. That was my uncle's fault – his favourite name for me was 'Big-nose-ugly' – and he still calls me it. I don't think I ever was really ugly.

It is noteworthy that in this case it was primarily black boys (Joe Smith) and men (her uncle) who defined Dot as 'ugly', although, as she notes, the girls at school followed the boys' lead and also ostracised her. This extract illustrates male dominance in setting the standards for girls' appearances and the influence that they have on how young black women feel about themselves. Dot responds to the taunts of her schoolmates and her uncle's teasing in a predictable way:

DOT: There's this cream called Venus de Milo which was meant to get rid of spots – I mean I only bought it for the spots but then I realised that I was getting lighter and lighter, and I liked it at the time. Yes, I wanted to be lighter, but then one day, I was about 18 or 19 then, I looked at my face good in the mirror and I thought – there's nothing wrong with your face at all. I thought to myself, well you're never going to be light, light – you're not going to be white – there's nothing wrong with your colour, and I had started to see some really good-looking black people around. I also noticed that fair skin doesn't necessarily mean you're good-looking. That's when I started to pull myself together. None of it had really worried me until we moved next door to this family – Joe Smith who I told you about who used to call me Blackie – his sisters and the whole family were really fair. I think I'd just been going through that sort of phase – wondering why I couldn't have a boyfriend.

There is a certain ambivalence in Dot's admission to having used skin-bleaching products. She seems to imply that it was not a fully deliberate, conscious act on her part but rather something with an accidental conse-quence which she happened to like. Dot is now positioned by different discourses and would not bleach her skin, so the idea that she once did is a little too embarrassing to admit fully. It is also possible that only part of her wanted to be lighter; in other words, this was only one of her posi-tions, rather than an all-pervasive characteristic of her subjectivity. Mary displays the same ambivalence when she talks of 'not really straightening' her hair but using the hot comb 'just to ease it out a little', although she also admits that she and her friends did share the childhood fantasy of having long, flowing hair (Chapter 6). The significant male figures in Dot's life are black men but their attitudes towards her are remarkably similar to those of the white men Angela is referring to when she describes how she was never fancied. This indicates that men of all colours share the dominant racialised notions of female attractiveness which few black women can ever hope to attain. Skin bleaching and hair-straightening are therefore less about black women wanting to be white than about black women wanting to be attractive, especially to men in a patriarchal world that assumes beauty to be blonde and blue-eyed, and makes it impera-tive for women to be attractive enough to succeed with men.

It is not only in Britain that black women found it hard to perceive them-selves as attractive in any positive sense of the word. Dark-complexioned women who recall Caribbean childhoods have similar memories, but here lighter-skinned black women were more likely to have a different story from those raised in Britain where the subtler gradations of colour are ignored. Theresa's memory of her nearly-white grandmother tugging and exclaiming at her 'nigger hair' and her feeling that she was ugly (Chapter 5) is not an isolated experience. Claudette Williams recalls her Jamaican childhood in the small community of Heartease in the district of St Thomas, where contact with white people was minimal. There she describes the warmth and love of community life but also the pervasive 'colourism'.

I suffered whenever anything went wrong in the house... I grew up doubting my abilities, and because reprimand would be associated with my colour I simply linked being Black with being unable to do anything correctly. I was the darkest of the children in the household, and colourism featured strongly in Jamaican life. My inability to believe in myself took me many years to recognize and attempt to correct.

(Williams 1988: 148–9)

We can see from this quote that she experienced colourism through the domestic role she was allocated as a dark-skinned girl. She goes on to describe how her later experience of British schools worked in the same direction, since here too black girls, who were not expected to be high achievers, were consistently placed in the lowest streams. The colonial/racial legacy was not challenged in South London until the black power movement took root there in the 1970s. Since groups such as the Black Panthers did not address gender, it is not surprising that it was not until her subsequent involvement with the black women's movement that she was able to reconstruct her femininity.

The examples I have given indicate that black women, like white women, are positioned by a concern with attracting the opposite sex. The statistical evidence showing that a larger proportion of black women than white are single parents has often been misinterpreted as supporting a stereotypical image of black women as powerful, independent and aggressive, and therefore not in need of any form of social or personal support. This version of the myth of the black matriarch operates to isolate many black women. Elsewhere I have documented how the desire to attract and hold on to a male partner is so powerful that it leads many black women to tolerate unsatisfactory relational situations (Mama 1989b).

It is worth noting that this racial myth resonates with black feminist discourses insofar as these too often suggest that men are unimportant to black women. While it may be true that many black women can and do live satisfactory existences without male partners, the fact is that, with the exception of black lesbians, most black women are as keen to be part of a heterosexual couple as anyone else, even though they may have their own ideas regarding the terms of their relationships with men. To my mind, the disproportionate number of black women living singly is not because black women do not need and desire male support so much as other factors, be these social or material.[3]

Faced with a discursive regime whose prescriptions are so often unattainable, it is not surprising to find that many black women have begun to reject the prescriptions of colonial-integrationist discourses and create new discourses which enrich black radicalism with feminist themes.

CHANGING BLACK FEMININITY

The collective response to the contradictions of race and gender is succinctly expressed in a poem by Veronica Williams:

I am a woman and I'm angry
With a world that pigeon-holed me
into stereotyped roles that I do not fit into.
                    (Cobham and Collins 1987: 21)

Black women have not accepted the patriarchal prescriptions for femininity without challenge. The Jamaican poet Louise Bennet's skilful satire on the theme of black women's appearances dates back to the 1950s. The fact that we find black women rejecting the same discursive regime – that of white supremacy – in the 1980s suggests that resistance to the oppressive prescriptions of the white and male-dominated order is being repeated down the generations. Presumably there have always been women who resisted uncomfortable discursive positions because they found them either unattainable or contradictory, or undesirable. However, the coming together of black women as a movement only became apparent in Britain in the 1980s. It happened because they were driven by shared emotional and intellectual reactions to a dominant order which inferiorised them along the two dimensions of race and gender. With this movement came the articulation of black feminism and the creation of new discourses on black femininity.

The emergence of an explicitly feminist movement within the communities of the African diaspora must also be seen as a contemporary manifestation of the long traditions of both female autonomy and black resistance: traditions which can be traced to disparate sources in Africa, the Caribbean and on both sides of the Atlantic, as well as in the imagination of black poets, writers and film-makers. Women of the generation who were in their twenties and thirties during the 1980s contributed to and were influenced by the resurgent western feminist discourses which challenged the whole focus on women as sex-objects. Out of these different sources emerges the black feminism apparent in conversations between black women, as well as in the poetry generated within the black women's movement, some of which expresses not only anger, pain and bitterness but also their rejection of the more macho aspects of black radical discourse:

You call me 'Sister' Brother,
yet I know
that it is simply a psychological lever to prise apart my legs.
'Sister make coffee for the movement,
Sister, make babies for the struggle'
You raped my consciousness with your body
my body with reason.
                    (Iyamide Hazeley, cited in Busby 1993: 907–9)

Many of today's black women want a different, less exploitative kind of relationship with black men. In rejecting male oppression and exploitation, black women often find their relationships with one another to be of particular importance. One outcome of this woman-to-woman focus has been the emergence of black lesbianism. For others it has been enough simply to recognise the importance of women in their lives. Iscara, the Rastafarian poet who participated in the discussion sessions used in this study, acknowledges Queen Mother Moore, the American pan-Africanist, as having had a major influence on her decision to identify as African. Others cite Angela Davis, Michelle Wallace, Audre Lorde and bel hooks, and the creators of a new fictional genre such as Toni Morrison, Paule Marshall, Toni Cade Bambara, Maya Angelou, Alice Walker and others. What these activists and writers have in common is that they articulate the collective challenge to the male-domination of the black liberation movement which black women have mounted on either side of the Atlantic.

While most of the literary figures embraced by black women in Britain are African-American, there is none the less an emergent black feminist culture accompanying the increased gender awareness that has characterised black politics in Britain since the 1980s. With the empowerment derived from these diverse expressions of black womanhood come alternative definitions of femininity: new aesthetics reaching out to all the women who have found that they will probably never be slim or blonde or blue-eyed or long-haired enough for the world they live in. So it is that Nichols can boldly proclaim:

Beauty
is a fat black woman
walking in the fields
pressing a breezed
hibiscus
to her cheek
while the sun lights up
her feet
   (Grace Nichols 1984)

Nichols, a British-based poet originally from Guyana, turns to the tropical world for her imagery: images which could come from anywhere in the African world and which she derives from her African-Caribbean heritage. Lorna Goodison has also found a following in the British communities of black women:

Great grandmother
was a Guinea woman
wide eyes turning
the corners of her face
could see behind her
her cheeks dusted with

a fine rash of jet-bead warts
that itched when the rain set up.
        (Lorna Goodison 1986)

Goodison is Jamaican by birth but we see her use of African referents in her innovative constructions of black womanhood. The frequency of references to other times and places in black women's poetry and discussions demonstrates a willingness to reach across the seas and centuries in their creative effort to forge positive identifications: new subjectivities which invoke subaltern images of female heroism, a heroism which can be used to combat and shake off the oppressive legacies of centuries. From Nanny the Maroon to Nzinga of Angola, from the Caribbean Mary Seacole to Queen Amina of Zazzau, black women in Britain are no longer as short of heroines as they once seemed to be. Thus we see the emergence and development of a transnational, pan-African discourse that is discernible not just in poetry but also in the subjectivities and styles of individual women.

In addition to drawing on available historical information, black women also come from diverse experiences. We have seen how Caribbean experience features in the racialisation of the subjectivity of women such as Claudette Williams. For some this is actual experience, while for others, like Mona and Mary (Chapters 5 and 6), the Caribbean features through the lens of parental recollection, whether this is romanticised or suppressed, taken literally or enriched with a bit of imagination. References to African sources too range from real to imaginary (Chapter 6). They also vary a great deal, ranging from the earnest and religiously inspired dreams of Rastafarians to the profoundly commercialised and commoditised displays and sales of Kente-clad rap musicians.

Women of African parentage have similar recollections of the undermining effects that racism in British schools had on them, whether this was manifest in the discriminatory attitudes of their teachers, or in the ignorance displayed by white children raised by a declining imperial culture still refusing to recognise its own demise. One of my informants recalls having her skin scratched 'to see if the dirt will come off'; another describes being asked the colour of her blood and whether her family still lived in trees. Because many of those with African parentage have either visited the African continent themselves, or been informed by a regular flow of relatives and friends moving between Africa and Britain, they tend to have been buffered from extreme feelings of alienation and rootlessness. Those who have visited their African source appear to have been either enriched or traumatised by the experience. Several describe an initial sense of relief at finding themselves surrounded by other black people and suddenly ceasing to be 'other', an experience which is as true of people of mixed descent as it is of those with two African parents.

Angela, for example, pointed out that it was when she first visited Ghana that she suddenly found herself much in demand, as a woman.[4] Other women with African parentage speak of undergoing a change from feeling unattractive and awkward in Europe to becoming more confident in Africa, where they discover new ways of being feminine and are thus able to 'come out' as women.[5] Olivette Cole-Wilson describes how, on a visit to her parents' homeland, she was inspired by West African women:

> Many so-called men's jobs are daily undertaken by women in Sierra Leone, lifting, carrying and pounding, to name but a few. ... There are more women choosing not to marry even though the financial implications may be daunting, and more women entering into all areas of employment with confidence and determination.
>
> (Grewal *et al.* 1988: 162-3)

This diversity of real and imaginary sources opens up numerous possibilities for black femininities, a diversity reflected in the cultural productions and styles displayed by black women in Britain as well as on the other side of the Atlantic.

This richness is not without its problems. While black women found it relatively easy to identify with one another's experiences of racism and sexism during the formative years of the black feminist movement, I noted in Chapter 1 that this diversity became problematic when, having recognised this commonality, the articulation of new collective identities began. A competitive identity politics often came into play, with black women competing over degrees of authenticity, often with recourse to foreclosed and essentialist constructions of black womanhood, constructions which often owed more to a preoccupation with rebuffing racism than to the diversity of sources I have outlined. In the last chapter I addressed the psychodynamics of this process. In emphasising the need for unity in the face of a multiplicity of oppressive forces, black people risk creating a new discursive regime, namely a set of prescriptions for how to be black and a set of sanctions and epithets for those daring to differ (Chapter 7). bel hooks (1991: 28–9) makes a useful distinction between the easier and safer option of embracing the idea of a black essence and the more challenging recognition of the way black identity has been specifically constituted in the experiences of exile and struggle. Identity politics may be a necessary rejoinder to the tyranny of homogenised and universal paradigms but to be progressive this game must be played in a manner that embraces diversity and change rather than promoting the stifling essentialisms that narrow the discursive space opened up by the struggles for black and women's liberation.

NOTES

1 Vaughan, in her work on colonial medicine (1991), however, provides some useful information on the colonisers' view of African women – largely as defective mothers.
2 In his essay 'Algeria Unveiled', Fanon cautions against the proliferation of French-run women's organisations which he saw as a form of imperial feminism; that is to say, a guise for penetrating and undermining the last bastions of Algerian resistance in order to advance imperial interests (Fanon 1980: 13–45).
3 Social factors include the high education levels of black women, the shortage of eligible black men, black men's perceived preference for white women and, at least until recently, the reluctance of black women to engage in transracial relationships. Material factors include the economically weak position and high rates of homelessness among black men.
4 Although other black women describe the same experience of suddenly feeling good about themselves in a black social milieu, it is true to say that in Angela's case she may have been particularly sought after as a 'half-caste' woman about whom West Africans have their own myths of hypersexuality and availability.
5 In my own case, regular travelling between Nigeria and a series of English schools meant constant changes, and led me to experiment with a great many modes of self-expression as I learnt to perceive and respond to the various forms of racism and colourism in both societies.

Chapter 9

Charting post-colonial subjectivities

DECONSTRUCTING SUBJECTS, THEORISING SUBJECTIVITIES

It is now time to bring this book to an end. But how does one end the beginning of something? In developing a new approach to theorising the production and reproduction of subjectivity I have raised at least as many questions as I have answered. Furthermore, at the very heart of the approach advocated here is a feeling of perpetual change and move-ment: movement and change of cultures, of individuals and of scientific theories. This in itself makes the idea of closure somewhat inappropriate. This is not a neat story ending with all capillaries cauterised and stitched with surgical precision but one which makes a small opening through which, it is hoped, many new ideas and arguments may flow. For this reason I shall end with a brief appraisal of how far we have come and what future work may gainfully do. The question of the extent to which I have met and honoured all the commitments set out in the early parts of this work I leave for the reader to decide, instead of going into an over-detailed reiteration and appraisal of the preceding pages. A brief thematic review of the central ideas put forward will suffice, before concluding with a brief consideration of the applicability of this approach to other contemporary subjectivities.

I began by outlining the parameters of an approach to theorising sub-jectivity which viewed subjects, whether self-defining or constructed by dominant others, as being organically generated out of social conditions prevailing at the time of their emergence. Having decided to theorise the particular subjectivities of black women in post-colonial Britain, I then detailed the social and political context of the study I carried out with other black women in the London of the early 1980s and identified the main intellectual influences on my approach: black political activism and the black women's movement, feminist politics and theory, psychodynamic theory and, subsequently, the broad philosophical shift now known as post-structuralism. I take the view that post-structuralism, in decentring the intellectual universe, also cracks open the hegemony of western-centred grand theories and offers not just new theories but new ways of theorising.

I then set out to deconstruct the historical representation of black subjects within the scientific discourses of psychological theory, looking at the construction of African slaves, colonial subjects and finally black people living in the West. I argued that psychology has generated scientific discourses which construe the Other in ways that have reproduced and legitimised white supremacy. I also argued that scientific discourses do more than underwrite existing regimes of truth, since they are also productive. Academic production and political power are intimately related in such a way that intellectuals can also generate new theories and facts to meet the changing institutional and intellectual needs of a dominant regime. Slaves were not just constructed as suited to slavery but pathologised when they resisted it. Psychological constructions of 'the African' in the colonies and 'the Negro' in Britain and North America also tell us more about the subjectivity of Europeans than about what it meant to be black and Other under a colonial or racist order. Psychological research findings and theories which collude with the taken-for-granted assumptions of dominant regimes of truth apparently tend to prevail over those which challenge the status quo. I put forward a conceptualisation of the relationship between scientific discourses and wider societal discourses which is complex and dynamic, and which defies the laws of linear causality. The two can be viewed as locked into a recursive relation to one another, in which there is constant resonance between the social and the scientific, with slight changes in either occurring with each repercussion. Major discursive shifts are more occasional, emanating from the less frequent and more dramatic changes, such as those heralded by grand historical events such as the abolition of transatlantic slave-trading, or the defeat of colonial regimes by nationalist movements. This recursive relationship between academic discourses and social conditions, in which each continuously produces and is produced by the other in complex ways, can only be studied retrospectively and requires the kind of detailed historical mapping that has characterised deconstructionism.

A consideration of the power relations under which discursive regimes rise and fall from ascendance is also required. The repeated resurgence of scientific racism down through the ages (after abolition, after the North American civil rights struggle and in post-colonial Europe) suggests that old knowledges are seldom entirely dispensed with but can be reactivated and brought into play long after they appear to have been made a nonsense of. In Chapter 2 my analysis suggests that even when a dominant regime has been overthrown, as was the case with the institution of slavery, the associated scientific discourses may continue to exist in a subaltern manner, resurging whenever conditions permit. Since the intentionality of scientists is not at issue in this formulation, it should be clear that I do not attribute the persistence of scientific racism solely to conspiracy theory – although there have certainly been racist conspirators in the scientific establishment. Instead I point to the methodological constraints of scientific psychology as having acted alongside discursive regimes to ensure a certain conservatism in social science production. It is in this vein that I argue that the production of psychological discourses has also been constrained by the post-Enlightenment philosophical assumptions under-pinning the discipline as a whole, in particular the notion of man as a universal, unitary, rational subject, and the adherence to empiricist scientific methods. Psychology has, on the whole, been limited by its adherence to narrow empiricist methods that have only allowed the emergence of theories based on the assumption of the subject as a unitary, rationalistic individual, within yet separate from a social structure. The emphasis on measurable and observable external behaviour and the retention of experimental and quantitative methods have precluded a fuller theorising of subjectivity. On the other hand, grand and universal theories of man and society have been unable to take on the dynamism of social and psychological existence, or the internal multiplicity and complexity of subjectivities that must always be historically and personally specific.

In Chapter 3, I note that black psychology, despite its emergence dur-ing the 1970s and 1980s as a reaction to the racism of western psychology, has in the main retained orthodox methods and assumptions. Consequently, despite the changed conditions and their antiracist intentions, those engaging in black psychology have often continued to reproduce the prevailing ideas about black people. In other words, empiricist paradigms have only allowed the subject to be conceptualised in certain ways and so slowed the emergence of more radical theories that would be better able to capture the diversity and dynamism of post-colonial realities.

None the less, I deem black academic psychology to be of great interest because it has not developed just in relation to the dominant (i.e. white) society but is also a derivative of black social, cultural and political life. I make this point using the example of the construction of the self-hating Negro, a notion which featured in some early black literature but which was reproduced and given scientific credence by white psychologists, subsequently taken up by the civil rights movement and then further authenticated by the black psychologists who were to become famous for it. Black psychology too has had a unitary subject at its heart – and one who is not accidentally masculine. The difference lies in the fact that whereas the black lobby argues that racism must be ended because it damages black folk, racists argue that it is because black people are damaged that they do not make progress.

The most recent North American theories about black identity make major advances insofar as they link identity formation to social changes.

Initially a simple-stages model in which the black individual moves in a linear fashion from a negative self-hating state to a more integrated, mature and racialised identity, the psychology of nigrescence has more recently been developed to include the possibility of continuous recycling through the various stages. In this way it now includes the idea that there are various 'shades of black', in acknowledgement of the observed diversity of African-American subjectivity. However, while the theory of nigrescence and the scientific testing of it on predefined populations may provide a useful description of the development of black identity, it does not actually theorise subjectivity. Within it the black individual is still assumed to be a unitary subject (albeit a black one) devoid of gender, class or other central aspects of social life. I attribute these limitations to the paradigmatic conservatism of black psychology. The psychology of nigrescence effectively reiterates the post-1960s black discourse on race consciousness in scientific jargon, complete with calibrated measuring devices – questionnaires aimed at assessing just 'how black' an individual is. The observed relationship between the black individual and the black social movements of the 1960s and 1970s is not actually theorised. Is it, for example, a correlation? Does the individual reflect the social or vice versa? Is it perhaps a product of interaction between the individual and white society, or black society? The fact that these questions are not addressed or answered means that however useful the descriptions of nigrescence may be, they remain descriptions, limiting the conceptual contribution of nigrescence theory.

Some black psychologists have realised the limiting effect of the empiricist paradigm on the possibilities for theorising black mental life and have therefore sought alternative referents in African philosophy. Here too it has been assumed that it is possible to speak of a unitary body of thought and values – an African world-view – out of which black psychology can emerge. The fact is that the very idea of there being a single 'African' philosophy is hotly contested, embraced mainly by the diaspora-based Afrocentric school of black intellectuals, for whom Afrocentrism is the logical answer to Eurocentrism and racism. Overall, it becomes clear that Afrocentric and Eurocentric philosophies share the assumption of a racially divided philosophical universe. They therefore fail to acknowledge the breakdown of the old categories heralded by the irreversible exchanges of culture, genes, geographical location and a great many other things besides. These exchanges have created a post-colonial world of flux and diversity, in which the fabric of contemporary Europe (or of Africa, of Asia, etc.) is woven out of cultural and psychological threads from the rest of the world.

It is no accident that post-structuralism has emerged in this context, moving us away from the tyranny of the grand theories spawned by an imperialist world order, offering instead new ways of addressing the complexities of contemporary social reality. I take the view that neither Eurocentric nor Afrocentric philosophies – or for that matter any other racial or ethnic philosophy – can withstand the paradigm shift heralded by post-structuralism and by the demise of the grand old frames of reference, a demise that heralds our entry into the post-colonial era that will end the twentieth century.

The psychological discourses on the Other discussed in the early chapters can best be grasped through an understanding of their historical location: their embeddedness in the conditions of slavery, colonialism and racism and the discourses and practices of these three regimes. The discursive conditions of psychological theory have, in other words, been both modernist and pre-feminist.

To carry theory beyond this location, I move on from looking at psychological constructions of the black subject to develop a theory of subjectivity that seeks to utilise some of the insights of feminist and post-structuralist thought. To do this I use extracts of discussions among British-based black women in order to generate theory. I cite moments of social interaction between black women and use these to argue that individual consciousness emerges out of the resonances between collective history and personal experience; that subjectivity is in fact a process of movement through various discursive positions whose availability is determined by the experience, exposure and imagination of the individual.

The method I deploy is not one of the orthodox psychological research methods. Instead of claiming distance and objectivity, I state my commitments as a researcher and as an involved member of the social group under study. And rather than denying my personal characteristics, I use similarities to and differences between myself and those who are participating in the research process, both in generating conversations and subsequently in analysing them. My first level of analysis involves identifying and describing discourses and locating moments of individual subjectivity within them. This enables me to meet the theoretical goals of theorising subjectivity as dynamic, as multiple and as socially and historically produced. More specifically, I demonstrate through a series of sketches how black women in Britain have been uncomfortably positioned by the legacies of colonial and racist discourses, which they are now rejecting in favour of black radical and feminist ones.

It is this shift in consciousness that the fledgling black feminist movement sought to articulate and propagate, and it is a movement that has greatly influenced my conceptualisation of research and the subjectivities of the participants, myself included. In my first chapter I introduce this movement as providing the social context of this study. My examination of the changing subjectivities of black women demonstrates that it was a movement that involved the coalescence of individual and social changes. Changes in individuals resulted from experiences of contradiction and injustice, and social changes have accompanied the demise of the colonial order and the emergence of various expressions of nationalism and black radicalism.

After developing and applying this method of discourse analysis as a means of demonstrating the socio-historical construction of subjectivity, I then turn to consider the role that individual history and relationships play in the production of individual subjects. To do this I analyse Mona's account of her life and relationships, and her personal identity. Having already theorised this as being about changing from her positioning within colonial-integrationist discourse to one within black radical discourse, in Chapter 7 I consider the role of personal relationships in her identity in order to theorise some of the psychodynamics of racialised subjectivity. Here the emotional consequences of being subjected to contradictory and oppressive regimes become more apparent, with the anxieties and discomforts of being black and female making individuals seek and take up new positions. I advance the idea that subjectivity is psychodynamic as well as discursive.

I conclude that psychodynamic processes and the movements from one discursive position to another can best be understood as occurring simultaneously and inseparably. In this way subjective processes are conceptualised as being at once socio-historical and intrapsychic. This is a difficult idea to grasp, which can perhaps be made easier by reference to certain bridging concepts. These are described as such not because they bridge a gap between two separate levels – the individual and the social – but because they enable us to move from one way of thinking to another. By placing these two concepts at the centre of our conceptual apparatus, we can make them the keys to an understanding which transcends dualism by making it redundant.

Positionality is the first such concept. I have developed the idea of subjectivity as being the sum of all the positions available to an individual: positions which are both psychodynamic and discursive. The study of subjectivity can be undertaken by charting the various positions that any individual occupies, with reference to his or her personal and collective history. In this study I chart the movement of a number of black women from colonial-integrationist discursive positions to black radical ones, and then look in detail at the corresponding psychodynamic processes occurring in an individual.

The second bridging concept is that of movement, which I have used to refer both to the intrapsychic changes that result from projective processes and to social movements and cultural changes that result from the changing discursive positionings of individuals. New discourses are created when many individuals experience similar changes, so that they become collective experiences. Any given discourse gains in social power as growing numbers of people take it up and position themselves within it; in other words, as visions become shared. Alternatively, discourses may decrease in significance and fade from relevance simply because they lack meaning for people and are not therefore taken up and collectivised. In this particular study we see black women abandoning colonial-integrationist for black radical positions, infusing and enriching these with new notions of femininity.

According to this approach, personal and social change occur in consonance, as psychic and discursive events resonate with one another. When such resonances occur they are experienced as sudden flashes of insight, or as primordial events which then reshape the subjectivity and experience of the individual. In this way we are able to understand subjectivity non-dualistically, as recursive rather than as resulting from interactions between two ostensibly separate levels of being.

OTHER POST-COLONIAL SUBJECTIVITIES

I see no reason why the methodology and approach developed here can not be applied to the investigation of other social groups and subjectivities. Whereas race and gender have been the main tropes of this particular analysis, one could equally take class, sexuality, nationality, religion or any other main vectors of difference as starting points for researching the subjectivities generated in any part of the world. Within Western Europe, for example, one could apply a similar approach to theorising black masculinity, or white femininity. More currently, the emergence of pan-Europeanism and the concomitant resurgence of micro-nationalisms and racism could be studied in the context of the political changes accompanying the constitution of the European Community, now appropriately dubbed 'Fortress Europe'.

In the former colonies too there is no shortage of subject matter. The earlier nationalist movements and the radical ideas encapsulated in the concept of an African personality or the new men and women citizens of independent nations have either been abandoned or have undergone profound changes in African social and political contexts. What subjectivities have emerged in post-colonial African or Caribbean (or, for that matter, other) countries? To what extent have the tropes of race and gender persisted or been replaced by other divisions? Are today's Nigerians, for example, primarily nationalised subjects, or primarily Islamised and Christianised, or does the 'tribal paradigm' favoured by colonial analysts still find currency in contemporary social and political life?

In the Caribbean it may be fruitful to chart the emergence of regional as opposed to island subjectivities and to examine the extent to which colourism has been overcome, changed, or continues to pervade people's consciousness, decades after the departure of the European colonialists.

In every conceivable context, the gendering of subjectivity merits research and documentation. One may pose new questions regarding gendered subjectivities. What does it mean to be feminine in the context of multi-partyism as compared to military dictatorship? Or how does militarisation affect the masculinity of a nation's population? To what extent has independence, or even democratisation, been accompanied by radical changes in the conditions of women and their gendered sub- jectivities? If there are new African women, are there also 'new men'? How do we ensure that the tyrannies of the past can successfully be broken down to create discursive space for the emergence of new subjects, new social movements and new social orders?

In short, there are now as many questions as before but we have at our fingertips a new language in which to ask them, one which one hopes will generate new insights into and understandings of ourselves and our positioning in the world.

Appendix

A Where did you grow up? Were you born here first of all?

M Yes, I was born here – Munfield.

A And both your parents – where are they from?

M From St Elizabeth, Jamaica.

A Both of them – same village – same town?

M Yes, both of them. They're sort of like – I think distantly related or summat – some sort of cousins far removed or something like that.

A So they came here – long before you were born?

M Not really –

A What sort of – brought them over?

M They came . . . well to work and . . .

A . . . the usual things?

M Yes, the usual things. They came over . . . was it – my sister was born in '57 [so they came about] '54 – I can't remember.

A Oh – that generation.

M Yes (*laughs*) – you know.

A It is fairly standard. . . . How old are you? – about my age?

M 26.

A Same. OK, so you grew up in Munfield, went to school and everything there.

M I left there when I was 19.

A And that's when you came to London?

M London, yes.

A And you've been in London since then?

M Mm-mh. Seven years.

A So what made you move to London?

M Well it's . . . (*sighs*). Well, it was my cousin really. She was going to come to London to do 'em. . . . She was going to come to North London Poly, but this was depending on whether she got her A levels or not, right?

A Mm.

M And then, she mentioned it to me, and I said – yeh, I'll come up with you – you know, like I was really bored.

A Mm.

M (*sighs*) I wouldn't kind of say it was depression . . . but . . . well I suppose in a way it was really. I used to kind of go around saying I might as well be dead than live the life I'm living now, you know.

M Mm.

M I used to go to work and come home from work and watch the telly and get up in the morning and go to work – the same kind of thing, you know?

A   Yeh.

M   And um – anyway when she said she was going to come to London, I thought – I just said – Yeh – you know – I'll come with you.

A   Mm.

M   But then what happened – she didn't get her A levels, so she couldn't come to college, and she met this man, and then she decided to just stay with this man. I thought well – I just wanted to come then. Because once the idea was in my head, I said, no, I don't want to stay in Munfield any more. So I came down here.

A   On your own?

M   Yes.

A   So what's Munfield like? My granny's from North Yorkshire – from that area – so what's Munfield like? Fairly small – is there a black community there?

M   Yes, there's a large black community there . . .

A   Mm.

M   A lot of people from the same district of Jamaica, you know – there's a lot of – mainly Jamaicans I think – and um – It's sort of quiet – I mean it's changing a bit now. It's like a city now – it was a community then, and a strong Asian community as well.

A   Mm.

M   And it's – you know – pretty dull. There's not much to do there. It's a good place to kind of bring up kids.

A   Mm.

M   That's what I always say about Munfield because you know – people are friendly – like I say it's changing a bit now, as it's growing, it's become more citified, but – it's – I dunno – what to say about it really. It's just a bit dead, there's not really that much there for young people to do – y'know – in terms of politics I don't think it's anywhere – I think I've learnt a lot since I come to London.

A   Yes.

M   Because I wasn't really very political at all – um –

A   Sounds a bit like me, because I was born here – well I went to Nigeria when I was quite young, but I grew up in Kent – but in Kent there wasn't a black community at all, so I lived with – well I boarded, but my grandmother – English grandmother – looked after me. So um – would you say you grew up in a black community?

M   Yes, I did. Yes – mainly – like my home life was all black. If course – when I went to school there was a lot of white people there – white children, but I was – like I mean – what – are you talking about junior school or secondary school or whatever?

A   Yes – secondary school more.

M   Secondary school. It was funny 'cause when I went to um – 'cause I didn't pass my 11-plus right?

A   Mm.

M   So – but I was in the top band of the people that didn't pass their 11-plus, and then our school went comprehensive – um – it was kind of difficult because in my class there weren't many black kids really. Y'know I mean we were sort of like – geared towards CSE which to me was just a waste of time because – unless you get a Grade 1 – and everybody can't get a Grade 1, then you know – it wasn't worth that much really.

A   Mm.

M   Um – but like at school – my best friend was Indian – Manjit Singh, and I always remember her and Margaret Bailey and Beverly Jones. Margaret Bailey – she was black – she is black I should say, and Beverly Jones, who was white.

A   Mm.

M   So my two close friends were black really – y'know – one white one – and she was more like a black girl, really, in terms of – y'know – she always went out with black men and was in contact with black people, even though her parents didn't like it – but – you know.

A   So when you were sort of growing up there, did you think of your – did you have an idea about race and think of yourself as black and call yourself black and that kind of thing?

M   Yes – I called myself black, but it was like in a different perspective than it is now, if you see what I mean.

M   Mm.

M   Because I always knew I was black, right? But um – I didn't really understand racism, really. I just thought, you know, well you're black – it's like y'know – when you leave school you automatically go to your – the black people, your black community. I didn't really move with white people, whereas in school . . . Mind you I never really moved that much with the white people in the school really, because – I don't really know why that was. I just had my friends – you know – my best friends as they call them then. Um –

A   So you were never sort of – the only black in a situation?

M   Oh no. No. I did notice that all the blacks were in the lower streams.

A   Yes.

M   I always remember one black teacher saying – um, 'You're in England now, and you don't talk that patois here' (*mimicking*). And I always remember that, so I think in a way I was aware of racism, but at the time I didn't really sort of –

A   It wasn't sort of called that. Sounds like me. I didn't really think of it as a political thing at all. It was just – well my mother used to say 'prejudice' – which means they're ignorant – they [her parents] did not sort of feel that you had to deal with it particularly. It was just – part of life.

M   No. Yes – I just thought of it as part of life. I know – I do remember certain instances like. I think in front of white people I used to feel ashamed – of being black. I think that's common, really.

A   Yes, I think most of us.

M   Yeh. Certain things that I used to feel ashamed of. Like when Margaret used to come round to my house, if I was eating my yam and banana. Now actually that's a lie, because I never really ate – I mean we had them kind of things in our house, right, but my Dad really ate it. I mean, I used to love dumpling and them kind of thing, but I never used to eat yam and banana or cho-cho, or anything like that, because going to school you ate white food and in a way it's . . . you know – our food wasn't as popular as it is now.

A   Yes.

M   And in a way, when my white friends used to come round I used to – Ooh dear, hide the food! You know – silly little things like that. And like you know – everyone used to want long, flowing hair and that kind of thing (*laughs*)!

A   Yes.

M   The same old standard things. I mean, I have this conversation with a lot of people and everybody's moved with the same thing.

A   So did you ever straighten your hair and that kind of thing?

M   Yes, I used to press it with a hot comb. But I never really liked straight hair. It's funny that. I used to sort of ease it out so it wasn't too tough, but not *straighten* it. I never really liked that.

A   Mm. And your parents – Did you ever go back to Jamaica at all?

M   Never been.

A   Never been.

M   I hope to go when I get some money.

A   You still – you haven't been yet?

M   Never been.

A   Do your parents sort of talk about it a lot, or – ?

M   No. Not really. Only when people come round, they'll sort of reminisce and talk about Duggenhill and Morant Bay, but if I try to talk to them – about it, it's like – they're just not. . . . They don't want me to know for some reason. I don't know why. Even just lately since I've got more political – as time goes on – and I really want to know.

A   Mm.

M   I don't want to – I mean not about things – I don't really want to know all that much about the political side, right?

A   Mm.

M   Just about basic things, like what they did when they went out, and – you know, just simple things that you can learn a lot from. You know – the nursery rhymes they used to sing to the children, y'know – just those kind of things – just basic things that I think I've missed out on. Old proverbs and folk tales and things like that.

A   So why do you think your parents weren't that keen on bringing you up as Jamaicans? Are they planning to stay here, or do they have an idea about going back?

M   I know now they don't want to go back. But I don't know – like I said, they don't really want to talk about it. It's funny. I think they've been so white-washed, and they think that white is good and all those kind of things. It's kind – leave all that behind.

A   So they want you to grow up as British.

M   Well this is it. I just don't. . . . I mean I try to talk to them about it, but it's as though they don't really want to know. They just keep saying to me, 'Mary what's all this black thing you keep going on about?' That's what I get. I mean it's really frustrating. It's frustrating because I really want to know. But I've tried so many times in the last. . . . Even this past Christmas – just a few weeks ago when I went home. My Dad just said, 'Oh Mary, you're out of that now, you know – just move with the times.' And they still talk in terms of 'coloured'. And no matter what I say to them, they still use the word 'coloured'.

A   Mm.

M   They've got negative images of young black youth and all this kind of thing. They think Rasta is disgusting – the same old thing that a lot of –

A   Yes, I think it's true of a lot of people's parents. Some are not like that, but quite a lot of people say that their parents don't develop – they don't take it on. It's because they haven't moved in any sort of –

M   I think they just think in terms of like – Jamaica was struggle, they came over here for a better life for their kids and they want to leave that kind of thing behind. Because they think that I'm going backwards, kind of regressing. But at the same time they wouldn't want me to be involved with – well my Mum once said to me that if I married a white man they would disown me. So it's like a contradiction. I can – in many ways I've been living a contra-dictory life.

A   Yes.

M   It's like one thing at home and one thing when you go out there. (*door bell*) (*coming back into the room*) Sorry.

A   Yes. So when – you reckon that coming down to London changed your outlook on things a lot.

M   Not immediately, But yes, after about – a couple of years I would say.

A   Mm. What do you think that was – because of the people you met or moved around with or – ?

M   Mm.

A   Or the situation, or – ?

M   Yes. Mainly the people. I've been influenced by people in sort of – the job I do now. When I first came – I got transferred from Munfield to London, and I was working for the GPO.

A   Mm.

M   And I was in data-processing, right.

A   Mm.

M   And like the kind of people. The kind of people I used to move with were sort of like – I used to hate women at one time.

A   Mm-mh.

M   I really used to hate them. They used to get on my nerves something bad! I'm telling you, because all they used to do was gossip, gossip, gossip (*laughs*). You know?

A   Mm.

M   I remember when I was working in Munfield I used to work in this office, and there must have been at least 200 women.

A   Mm.

M   I used to tear my hair out sometimes! Gossip all the time. And then when I came down to London – I was working in – like I used to work in an open-plan office in Munfield, so there was all these women surrounding me, right? And the man was the boss.

A   Mm.

M   Typical, right? And um – then when I came to London I was working in a smaller office, right, I was working in a registry office, and dealing with people's personnel files and there was two women in the office and I took over from another – and there were people – there were the postmen – and they were gossipy too! You know, it was like – I'm not a person for gossip, right? I think I get that from my Mum.

A   Mm.

M   I'll gossip with my friends – but you know, personal friends – but not anybody's gossip. So, yeh – they used to drive you mad. Then one day I just said I was going because I'd just had enough. Because like – I knew – I didn't know what I wanted, but I knew it wasn't that.

A   Mm.

M   Because those people, I mean – they were a lot older than me as well. Because I was 19 and they were sort of – I mean I think Sarah was the youngest, or one of them anyway – one was 28. But she was more like 38 to me, because they were really old in their outlook.

A   What, married and settled?

M   Yes, married and settled, and that's all they could see really. And – I wasn't really into that. Now I don't say they particularly influenced me – those people, except that I didn't really want to be there and so I just – one day something just snapped in me, right, and so I just went in there and said, 'Look, I'm leaving today.' Because I had – because I was getting paid weekly, right? And I knew I had one week's leave left, so – because you only had to give one week's notice, I said to them, 'It's today I'm going.'

A   Mm-mh.

M And they all. . . . What happened was that – I mean I'd been working in the Post Office for five years and I never got promoted. In Munfield I could understand it, because the opportunities weren't there. But when I moved to London there was all these promises about – you know – I'd get promoted and this, that and the other. I did this test and I passed it – because I was a clerical assistant, and I did this test and I passed it and I was a clerical officer. But there was no job to give me. So I was still doing the same old boring thing and I just – you know – like I stuck it for a year and a half in London and then I decided, nah, there must be more to life than this.

A The same thing.

M Because I wasn't under this illusion like a lot of other people from Munfield or wherever, right? I can only speak for Munfield because that's what I really know –

A Mm.

M You know, they sort of think, 'Oh London, the big city – bright lights and you go out and rave, and this sort of thing. It's funny but I didn't – that just didn't enter my head really. You know, because I'd been working in my uncle's club since I was 13, 14, so all this club life – I was used to it from a long time ago, because I'd had that.

A Mm.

M So it wasn't any big deal at all.

A So what did you do when you left?

M (*sighs and laughs*) I was unemployed. No, then I went to um – well I wasn't unemployed because I didn't have no job to go to, right?

A Mm.

M I used to live dangerously then time, boy. Then I just went to the job agencies and you know, sort of sold myself.

A Which part of London did you live in then?

M Well. That's sort of a long story. When I first came to London I used to live just down the road – just down off Southfield Lane, right?

A Mm.

M That was a next story in itself, right? Because um – like when I – I got the place – it was in this woman's place – Mrs Bunton. I don't know how I survived the first six months. It was just pride. From I'm so proud, right, I won't sort of say . . . Me and my parents didn't have any sort of disagreement.

A Mm.

M I mean – it was – it was OK. My Mum couldn't believe that I was going to really go. She didn't talk to me for about three months before because she didn't want me to go. But you know – we've got a good relationship. And then I came to stay with Mrs Bunton, whose . . . there's a guy in the house. I can't remember his name – he was a really nice guy – he's about 65 – he's the only one that kept me sane. We used to drink rum and whatever, and he used to tell me all these stories.

A What – English? Jamaican?

M No, Jamaican man – Missa Bill (*claps*)! That's what he's called. And he's an uncle or a cousin – some relation to another cousin of mine 'cause I've got two sets of cousins – well, three sets of cousins, living in London, but I don't really know 'em – they're like strangers to me but through that contact, I got into that house.

A That house, yes.

M And my Mum and my sister came down with me first day, right – this was a Saturday – and they were supposed to stay until the Monday, right? But when they saw where I was living they went back the next day (*laughter*). I couldn't believe it, because I was living in this one room and the woman – it was a black household right, and Mrs Bunton was black and she had this daughter called – Carol.

A Mm.

M Was it Carol? And she used to drive me mad. Every single day she used to shout my name – but I think because I was young – she was 12 and I was 19, and like – her Mum was in her forties and I was quite young to her.

A Mm.

M And she always used to want to talk to me. At first it was nice, because I didn't really know anybody, so that was OK but then it sort of got – on my nerves a bit. And like I had to be in at 9 o'clock, you know? Like – all those kind of things. I couldn't have the electric kettle in my room, because it would steam off the wallpaper. She left the plastic on the bed, so the sheets . . .

A Oh God!

M It was really bad for the first six months.

A Yes.

M And I remember when my Mum put the phone in, boy! Jesus did I ball. . . . Because my Mum wouldn't have a phone you see. And then because I went away, she decided to get the phone in. The first time I heard my Mum's voice boy – I cried for about three hours, I was so (*laughter*) – it was really bad, because there was just me – I didn't know anybody really.

A Phoning up home and sobbing!

M Yeh well – this is it. It was me and like – sort of one room. I was more free at home!

A Yes.

M I mean – 19 years old and I was coming in at 9 o'clock.

A God. Sounds like school.

M It was awful. 'Cause like I mean, in Munfield I was – like I said I worked at my uncle's club when I was 14, you know, I worked there for a few years and I was used to coming in at 2 and them kinda hours – well after 2 because the club finished at 2 – by the time we had cleared up and everything. And then I used to go out on the town. It was just totally different. And to come back to that –

A Mm.

M It was like I was going backwards. And I was spending a whole heap of money trying to find somewhere else to live. That was funny because I bumped upon a friend of mine Jean Bailey, whose sister was my best friend at school – remember when I said there was a black girl called Margaret? Well, that was her sister, that used to be in the same class as my sister, and I know Jean from when I was 8 years old. So I went back to Munfield, y'know, just to visit and I met up with Jean and she said to me, 'Oh, you know I'm living in London', so I asked her where she lived and she said she lived in Wandsworth, and I said I live in Balham, just off Balham Road, and she said, 'Well that's just nearby!' I was so glad! She was sharing this flat with three other people, so every weekend, like – I have to say thank God for Jean, because if it wasn't for Jean I think I would have cracked up by now. Every weekend I used to go and stay with her, which was really good.

A Mm-mh.

M So that sort of kept my sanity a bit, until I found somewhere to live. And then – well what happened was that two of the people who were sharing her flat moved out, so I moved in with her. Then we got evic – (*laughs*) – well we didn't get evicted, but we was on this thing called a licence and they just said the licence was up.

A   Mm.

M   So we had to find somewhere else to go. While I was at the Post Office I was advised to put my name down on the council waiting list, so I went to the council and I harassed them. Even then I knew how to harass people (*laughs*).

A   Mm.

M   And I got a council flat. I stayed there for five years and then I moved here.

A   Mm.

M   But that wasn't the original question you asked me. I think – um – well – when can I say I really got influenced? I think I got influenced through Jean in a way.

A   Mm.

M   When I came to London, right? She was at college – and, like her friends became my friends, right?

A   Mm.

M   Because I didn't really know anybody.

A   Sure.

M   'Cause, although I am pretty outgoing still – 'cause I sort of went next door and said y'know, 'I'm Mary, who are you?' and sort of got talking like that. But for a while I was sort of living off Jean's friends really. And I felt that there was something missing.

A   Mm.

M   Because they weren't really my friends. I mean – y'know they were sort of like second-hand friends, although a lot of them I'll still sort of see now – but um, yeh – that time there were a lot of white people in my life. Because like Jean's friends, being at college there weren't that many black students, so – a lot of her friends were white and they became my friends, right?

A   Mm.

M   So – I think – I became more liberal towards white people. Because I came from a really strong black community, where white people didn't figure much in my social life, right? In my working life, yeh, but that was all. I didn't see them after work, or anything. And then to come to London – 'cause Jean was always sort of a bit white anyway.

A   Mm.

M   I don't know if you sort of use the same term – like we used to call them whitified black people.

A   Yes, yeh.

M   Like her sister Grace – I just can't relate to her any more, she's married this white man – I'm not saying that it's – just that in itself, but you know it's like – she's different from the person I used to know and I can't . . .

A   Mm.

M   Or maybe I'm different. I think more likely it's me that's different. So I was influenced in that way, y'know – the people that I was moving with then – they were really sort of – I thought at the time – quite bright – and I sort of looked up to them, right?

A   Mm.

M   And I sort of realised that – maybe I could do something a bit better. Also I started getting involved in voluntary work – basically I didn't have any money and I couldn't really rave.

A   Mm.

M   At one point (*sighs*) – I had this babysitting job. I used to get up at 6 o'clock in the morning and go all the way over to Stepney for half past 8, then come back – get back in about quarter to 7, then this guy would be on the doorstep to pick me up to do babysitting. I'd come back about 3 o'clock in the morning sometimes, and then the next morning I'd do the same again – get up at 6 o'clock – just to make ends meet. It was really rough. I've got it *easy* now compared to then. It was really rough at first. Just to pay the money ... because obviously being a clerical assistant – I was a clerical assistant in Stepney – you hardly get any money. I used to spend five pounds travelling, which seven years ago was a lot of money. Plus the wages ... I can't even remember how much I was getting but it wasn't very much. Plus then I had to pay forty-odd pounds a month for rent. This was when I was in the flat – plus my heating bills and everything else.

A   Mmm.

M   So – I don't think I really had that much time to be influenced by people more than so.

A   Yeh.

M   But like Paul – I think Paul sort of influenced me a lot. Marlene and Ernest – there were two Marlenes – big Marl and little Marl. They sort of influenced me in a way.

A   Mm.

M   But then at the same time I was getting to know these other people who used to live next door to me – and they were white too. They –

A   Were most of that crowd white?

M   Yes. And so – in a way I was sort of – know what I mean – I understood the *basics* of racism, like I knew black people couldn't get jobs because of dem black and the housing, and all them kind of things. But I didn't realise how deep it was at that time and I just thought, well these are my friends and I ain't got anybody else, and anybody's better than nobody, you know?

A   Mm.

M   That's how I felt at the time ... I think even then I realised that. Because when you're in London and alone, it's not easy, you know?

A   Yes. Mm.

M   I mean, I'm not excusing myself but that's the way it was. Um – so – So I don't know how much they influenced me – I think they just made me a bit more liberal towards white people.

A   Mm.

M   And they sort of like kept me away from – the realities, because they were my friends and they were OK. That's as far as I could see ...

A   So when did the reality slip through to you?

M   Actually it wasn't that long ago really – I don't think. Through talking to Errol, like, who is a black guy – one of Jean's friends – it started to hit me. But when it really, really, really hit me with its intensity was when I was setting up the black women's group. And I got so much overt racism then.

A   What, the one in Clapham?

M   Yes – which is what – about – ?

A   Yes. OK – that's when I first sort of met you.

M   That's right. You know, because. ... When I first set up the group – I mean I wanted to set up a women's group, right?

A   Mm.

M   No, I tell a lie – let me get back to – a bit further back – I think I was influenced before that. That was when it really struck home but I was becoming aware before that. When I was working at the volunteer bureau.

A   What sort of voluntary work was that?

M   Well, I was actually a paid worker and what you do is you get volunteers to help certain sections of the community – help out in children's homes and disabled homes – those kind of things – do work for old age pensioners and stuff like that. And there was a woman there called Jan, and she was my boss, and she was very, very political.

A Mm.

M Particularly up on women's issues.

A What – an English woman?

M Yes. And we used to talk about – about black things and. . . . Hang on, I'm trying to remember – let's get these things in sequence. There was a whole heap of things that I was doing at the time. I'm just trying to remember, 'cause I used to do my voluntary work and on top of that I used to do youth work and I was doing this thing with kids out of care – all kinds of things I was doing at the time. I'm just trying to get it in sequence. . . . Um – yeh, I think even – actually, even before then actually. God – I never really thought about it! But even before that I was – Yes! –

A Yes, it's only when you start tracing things back that they all start to fit in.

M That's the truth! Because even before that I was doing this thing with kids out of care. And it was two mixed-race kids, right?

A Mm-mh.

M And one in particular thought that he was white. He didn't *look* white but because he was brought up in a children's home – he really – he wouldn't even call himself black. And he didn't even like black people except for me, right? Because he –

A Yes – I did the same, when I was at school we went to do voluntary stuff at children's homes and that's where it hit me.

M Yes.

A Because I went to this kids' home in Bexley Heath and there were these mixed kids, and of course I'm mixed, so . . . but they were completely different, you know, they'd like scratch their skin and stuff, and not know they were black, or where they were from –

M Yes!

A And that's what took me by surprise.

M Yes that was when – I think I was about 20. Four, coming on for five years ago. That's when I sort of realised. It was Pete mainly – Pete as opposed to David. He was so anti-black –

A Mm.

M He always used to say to me that black people are so miserable. If you tread on their toes they would turn round and stab you – all this kind of thing.

A Mm.

M And from then, I was trying to sort of say, y'know – black people are good, you have to have a positive identity about yourself – you're black no matter what you say.

A What was this guy? What was Peter?

M Peter was mixed. Half English and half – what was he – I don't even think he knew his Dad, come to that. I'm not sure if he was half Jamaican or half Nigerian. I think it was either Nigerian or – I think it was probably Nigerian.

A And was he in one of those children's homes?

M Yes. He was in a children's home from when he was 2. And they had this scheme that when they reach a certain age they would . . . 'cause what they used to do was once you reached 18 they would stick you in bed and break-fast – which he was in. Or they just say bye-bye and there was no support that was given then. I mean you grew up in a children's home and nothing – they don't teach you anything, right?

A Mm.

M So then the council had this scheme where like – a few kids were given flat shares. But because of the situation they were brought up in, they needed support. That was where I came in. I took 'em round the shops. They had this really – unrealistic view of life.

A Mm. Mm.

M Because they've got so much money – I think it was 200-odd pounds, like to furnish and stuff – and they'd say, 'Yea man, I'm going to have a deep pile carpet and all these fantastic things.'

A (*laughs*)

M And I said, 'Look, life doesn't go that way', you know.

A Yes.

M You've got to realise that money doesn't stretch, so . . . They wouldn't believe me at all, so I got me pencil and me paper and I took them just window shopping – and they were so depressed when they came back.

A Oh.

M You know?

A Yes.

M But it's just – that kind of reality hit me, and in lots of ways, in respect to children's homes, you know. They should teach them more just about basic life. And also about – you know, Pete, in particular, about his identity. Because the guy (*laughs*). I mean you'd look at him – and you could see he was black. But he just wanted to deny it totally. He didn't want to live the lot of black people and this, that and the other.

A Mm.

M So I think it was from then that I became aware of how deep it was. Because like, in Munfield I didn't even know any social workers. You know, and like now, I could reel off so many off the top of my head but I mean – I just heard the name. It's like a lot of things in Munfield, you sort of hear the name but – I mean I had respect for police – in Munfield! Because you know, I was in such a closed community, things were so – more subtle.

A They were probably different.

M Yes, right.

A Yes, with me it was coming to London, because I was in Kent and I was in Scotland, and I came to London at about the same age and did some of the same kind of thing, living in South London. I was living in a house, sharing with other white people – English people, but it was in the middle of Brixton, so I met all these people around in passing and that's when I started checking things.

M Mm-mh.

A Because I certainly didn't get it from my family. I mean I was told I was Nigerian and there was nothing wrong with that, but my Mum said you are English – not black. She used the word 'coloured'. My grandmother certainly did – the Yorkshire woman – 'all these coloured people' – she was a real racist, but you know – I was different – I was her daughter's child . . .

M Yes, well, this is it.

A I was the granddaughter, so we got on well and we still do. But her attitudes are typically racist attitudes.

M Really. Have they changed much?

A No, not really. So I didn't grow up thinking – I am black and proud – I wasn't brought up to see race, or see it as a problem.

M This is it.

A It was only when I came here . . . so it's the same kind of – very similar . . .

M Yes – same thing I went through. And what happened then. . . . Yes, I think I was – when I started to think about it. . . . Oh yes, of course! Then I met this other black guy who was doing this thing on black kids in care. I'd forgotten all these things you know! It's amazing how it just comes back to me. Yes – I was going to get involved with that book. By the time I was doing so many different things, you know like ... I was doing my youth club and doing the scheme, plus work and my – what else was I doing? – my baby-sitting – I still didn't have any money. And so I suppose in a way I was influenced by that – what I – I don't think I realised at the time.

A Mm. Mm.

M I think it's only just now I realised that you know – that it did influence me. Then I went to work at the volunteer bureau. I think I got more interested in women's issues then.

A Mm.

M Because of the woman. She was really political. She used to get on my nerves a bit.

A What? A classical feminist?

M Yes. A very staunch feminist.

A Mm.

M But I mean – I remember sometimes she used to get on my nerves, like it was always 'these men! (*huff*)'. And like I was never anti-men. Like I knew my capabilities as a woman.

A Mm.

M It's just that I never put the label 'feminist' on it.

A Mm-mh.

M I mean I still don't call myself a feminist now.

A Mm-mh.

M I don't know – there's something about the term. I don't feel it really suits black people. I don't think it was ever designed for black people, although a lot of people would argue against that.

A Mm.

M But that's how I personally feel. So I don't really use the term for myself. Well, I mean, I was all –

A Why don't you think it's. ... What makes you think that about the word?

M I think it was designed by white, middle-class feminists. White middle-class women, right?

A Mm-mh.

M And they've already made all the standards for it – all their guidelines for it, without even thinking of us.

A Mm-mh.

M You know? So I think that, unless we were there from the actual beginning, taking part in the like – sort of formation of the ideologies and policies and whatever –

A Mm. And the few black women that were involved in it weren't sort of – black identified or whatever, they –

M Well this is it. So I can't be bothered with that. Although I agree with a lot of their principles, but I don't want to label myself that.

A Mm.

M And I think black women's experiences are different anyway. Because I was always brought up to be strong.

A Mm.

M Like I said, I couldn't stand women (*laughs*). Well, not that I couldn't stand women, because to me they were all – well it's white women that I'm really talking about.

A Mm-mh.

M   Because they were always simpering and all I ever heard about was their flip-ping boyfriends. Every bloody word that their boyfriend told them the night before they would come and tell me, and this kind of thing. They used to just drive me mad!.

A   Mm.

M   So a lot of my friends were men, through that.

A   Mm.

M   But then I didn't realise at the time that men were so sexist (*laughter*). So – you know – I was influenced. . . . Yes, I was influenced, but by men I suppose.

A   Mm.

M   But I must admit that a lot of the men that I was then around with. . . . Like when I came to London, through Jean's friends – they were thinking about sexism. And they would talk – not so much in a derogatory way as – a lot of black men I've met.

A   Right. They were mostly white men?

M   Yes.

A   Yes. They're different (*laughter*). Their sexism is different (*laughter*).

M   Yes, so Jan – I can't remember what her surname was now – she influenced me a lot in terms of women.

A   Mm.

M   Or . . . I think it just sort of made me realise what type of person I was anyway.

A   Mm.

M   Because I always knew – nothing could stop me really – if I wanted to do some-thing – that was me. You know, but I didn't sort of think of it in terms of feminism. Like, you know, having a right to choose, 'cause I just did it anyway.

A   Mm.

M   Like I came to London, and pack up my job when I feel like it and . . . you know – I was doing my own thing. But I think black women are sort of brought up to be strong and self-sufficient, right. Because, coming to London – a lot of people would have fears . . . like white people have said to me, 'You were good to come here on your own.' But to me it was like nothing.

A   Mm.

M   I knew how to look after myself. I knew how to manage money – at least I did then – I don't know about now (*laughs*)! Um – you know . . . so that to me wasn't a worry. And like my parents were always going on about, 'Get a career for yourself.' I mean, admittedly, they didn't say go and try bricklaying, right?

A   Mm.

M   They was more thinking in terms of teacher, nurse and all them kind of things. At the same time they really wanted me to earn a living, you know, and be self-sufficient.

A   Earn a living. Yes.

M   I always remember my Mum saying that, you know, 'Have kids when you're ready', you know?

A   Mm.

M   Not just go and do it. So I think really my Mum and Dad influenced me – well I mean they always do – a lot.

A   Do you have brother and sisters? You said you've got a sister?

M   Yes, I've got five sisters and two brothers.

A   Five sisters. I haven't got one (*laughs*).

M   Really? I love coming from a big family. Throughout we'd have problems but I just couldn't imagine being the only child. I mean, at least like – if there's nobody else there's always your sisters.

A   Yes.

M   I mean that's one thing I do miss – about London. I do feel homesick some –

A   None of them are down here?

M   Not one of them.

A   All still in Munfield?

M   No, I've got one in Zimbabwe – um –

A   Yes?

M   Yes, she just went out there in May. She's got a three-year contract. Before that she was in Mozambique for two years, so she sort of travels about . . . and then I've got – the rest are in Derby now. Um. . . . One sister was married to a guy in the army, so she was travelling around with him, right, but she's got divorced now so she's back in Munfield.

A   Oh. Where was he from?

M   He was from Jamaica – well his Dad was African and his Mum was Jamaican, but I don't know which part of Africa. I think – was his Dad – half African. I don't know. I hate to just say African because it makes it sound just like a country and it's not. But I don't know which part. So that's all I can really say. Ernest was his name – Ernest Robinson. . . . A right bloody womaniser. Anyway, they've sort of split up now. He lives in Southfield now, he lives in London. I tend to see him at Notting Hill Carnival (*laughs*).

A   Yes. Mm. So you got into the woman thing – what shall we call it? So what. . . . After. . . . Round then you set up the women's group?

M   No, that was after –

A   After.

M   Yes, when I went to work at the Hadson Lane Community Centre. Then it was like – I was a proper community worker then, I'd consider, like –

A   Mm.

M   Before then I'd done a lot of community work but – because I'm not qualified even now I don't even feel – I say to people I've met I'm a community worker, but in a way I would feel better saying it if I was qualified. I know that experience counts for a lot and all that but it's like this thing I've got instilled inside me – It's nice to have the piece of paper and then – I can really say. . . . But um – yes, that's when I'd sort of consider myself a community worker. I'd wanted to set up a women's group, an' like – to tell you the truth – I have to be really honest here, right? It was like a little fanciful notion of having a black women's group. Not really thinking about the politics, right?

A   Yes. You wanted to set up a black women's group?

M   Yes, I did. But I don't think it was for the right reasons.

A   Why do you think you did?

M   Because like I said it was more like a fanciful notion, rather than, yeah, the politics of racism and this and that and the other. It was more like – oh yes, wouldn't it be nice – that's the honest truth.

A   What – just to like – get a group of black women together?

M   Yes, mm. Without really thinking about all the implications of the idea. Although I did know – I did – I had an idea of what I wanted it to be about. But it was after doing a bit of research, like going to talk to various people, like Rose and those kind of people. And then all the stick I got, because. . . . Oh I – Oh I had so much trouble!

A   Mm-mh?

M   That's why I said that that's when it really hit me. I was bombarded with overt racism then – and I – the management committee wouldn't support me – they couldn't understand why I wanted to call it a black women's group, when I should call it an Afro-Caribbean-Asian women's group. All this kind of thing.

I had posters returned to me, I had people ringing up and saying that if – oh – I put an ad in the newsletter, and I really made it stand out right? Because I used to do the newsletter, and I really sort of fancied it up – everything was plain, right, except for this – so everybody would look at it, you know?

A Mm.

M I had people ringing up saying, 'If you don't withdraw that from the newsletter I'm going to sue you!'

A Mm-mh?

M Yes – a whole heap of trouble that you just can't believe. I tell you, my head was just pounding. It was just too much, because I was getting no support, literally. The people in the office were so sort of – yeah, but – they were all ready to appease, nobody – I had –

A I can remember you talking about it.

M Yes!

A When we first met.

M A whole heap of trouble!

A At the black women's centre. I suppose that's what took you down there.

M Yes, right – that's why I went down there you see. To go and get some more information about how to set up groups, and about other groups, and how they did it. To know what kind of things they were focusing on, you know. I always knew then that I wanted it to be for local women on the estate. I didn't want it to be sort of – high political thing like that. I didn't want to alienate anybody. Because like what I said to you now – even now I've a lot of respect for that group, because you can see people – the women in the group – like their opinions are changing.

A Which – in Brixton you mean?

M No, in Hadson Lane – although I haven't been there – but I saw Susan and Yvette last week, so you know – it's – it's like I have seen them and like – they've changed, right, in their attitudes. Like myself too, right?

A Mm.

M And I think that's really good. And. . . . Yes, I had a whole heap of trouble. And I even had um – the director from the Town Hall come down to see me. I mean I created history (*laughs*)!

A What – in Hadson (*laughter*)?

M Yes, 'cause normally –

A Is there – a lot of black people live there?

M Yes – you know? I mean look at Pinton Estate.

A Yes. I missed that sort of experience because the first black women's group I contacted was the Brixton one. Well, I went to a white women's group first, very briefly.

M Yes.

A And they asked me why I hadn't gone to a black women's group, so I thought – Yes, why haven't I (*laughs*)? It was funny because the one that asked me was Jewish. So that was when – I saw the black women's centre – and I thought, yes, I'll check this out – so that was the first one I met, so this business about setting one up and all the flack you get – the first time I heard about it was from you really.

M Yes.

A I mean people there talked about that struggle, but it had been ten years before – setting it up.

M Yes. And I'm glad I was there, because that taught me a lot. I mean at the time . . . I really felt like I was having a hard time. Because I know when I went home – it was just before Christmas, because the group started in –

November. I started work in October and the group was set up in November. And – when I went home for Christmas, I just slept.

A   Mm.

M   I was just so tired! Through it all, you know – and like I had to sort of be confronted by the management committee. Then we got the grant. And that was even worse (*laughs*)! That was terrible! We had all kinds of things. Women used to come – white women used to come and interrupt the group, coming to sell knickers from some catalogue – all this kind of thing. Like in the middle of a session, you know – a whole heap of complaints. I had to go and I had to talk to people, and I had to sort of pacify them. Like even now, if I'm dealing with authority, I get annoyed – like if I'm dealing with the local community I will sit down and I will explain the reasons why, right?

A   Mm.

M   So even then I was like that, and I still do it now. Like when the summons came down from the Town Hall and all them kind of things – I was just vex! It was like I could hardly be bothered to talk to them. And like um – that was one of the reasons I left, actually.

A   Hadson Lane? Oh.

M   Yes, because after a year of that I couldn't take their racism.

A   What – were you still getting it all the time?

M   Not as badly, but I mean. ... In certain ways – like they didn't really have any respect for me as a woman, as a black person – nothing.

A   Mm.

M   You know? And I was just like the little token there. I don't really know why I was appointed. Well, partly I do – because I used to run the girls' night there – just on Wednesday evenings – so they sort of knew the type of work that I did, and they thought I would be – the actual centre co-ordinator. John, who was fairly liberal, you know? He thought that I was good. And I think – I think I did a lot of good to that centre, if I say so myself. They needed shaking up. You know?

A   Mm.

M   But I mean I just – after over a year – I just couldn't take it any more, you know. Because it was like me alone. I mean I had support from the black women's group, but we only used to meet once, on a Monday. And it wasn't enough. Although we got one of the women on the management committee, to give me that support, but even then. ... I mean every day working. Plus there was a whole heap of black youths, you know, that were being flipping whitewashed by these co-ordinators. 'Cause they couldn't understand – you know – what I was going on with. They couldn't understand women being alone anyway.

A   Mm-mh. Mm.

M   And they used to – it was like they were living a contradiction – I could see them – I was like that in a way – not as bad as – well I shouldn't say bad. But not as strong as that. I mean they were really black in one sense.

A   Mm.

M   But they didn't really want to face the realities of it. I mean – I used to get quite a lot of abuse from them as well. So I felt really isolated.

A   Mm.

M   But it made me stronger. I've got so much pride, that come hell or come shine, whatever happen – if anybody starts with that – if I have to die, I will continue, you know.

A   So, setting up a women's group – you said about the feminist who you thought had some sort of influence. What about your own experiences of sexism – did they come into it? Or not really. Because what you said – it doesn't seem like there was any particular thing –

M I think in my job as a whole it came into it a lot – because I was the only woman.

A Oh.

M Well there was only four staff anyway – wait – I tell a lie – there was two women, but one was the secretary, right. But sort of co-ordinating and assistant co-ordinators – there was three of them. And I was the only black person and I was the only woman. And like I really used to notice it a lot when – like when people used to come into the centre to book the hall.

A Mm.

M They'd go straight to the caretaker. You know – they couldn't – I mean – partly because I was young as well – I mean – how old was I then – 24, 23, 23 going on 24 – summat like that anyway. And – um – partly because I was young. They probably couldn't believe that someone so young could be in charge of a building, 'cause like – when the co-ordinator went out – I was in charge, so there used to be myself and the caretaker. So I mean, but I mainly think it was to do with being black – I think the number one reason was being black, woman and then being young as well. And there was Ed, sort of like middle-aged white man. He obviously looked like the person to go and see about anything. And like he used to be so funny sometimes! I had to laugh sometimes, because Ed used to say – 'Well, there's the boss' (*laughs*) – and I used to see their face drop! And even then they wouldn't want to come and – they couldn't believe it – they wouldn't even want to talk to me really. So. . . . Yes, so I mean through that I really experienced it. You know.

A Mm.

M I would say that – I think because – like what I said before – about the volunteer bureau . . . and also the office where I used to work – there was four . . . charity organisations – voluntary organisations – they were really strong feminists too. I mean they were the ones that introduced me to my first women-only disco (*laughs*)!

A Oh, really. Which one was that?

M It was the Spare Rib tenth anniversary. And I was scared to death to go.

A Yes, how did you feel about these only-women discos?

M Well, there's a lot of them now. But the first time – it was funny, now that I think about it. First time – I remember – I can't even remember their names – really bad – Ingrid and – can't remember, anyway it doesn't matter – and they said to me, 'Well there's this' – it was Friday – 'there's this disco tomorrow – Spare Rib tenth anniversary and it's women only.' And I said wha . . ?! (*laughter*) 'Cause I never used – me never hear of this before in my entire life!

A So?

M They said to me, 'Don't be so stupid – nothing's going to happen – just come, you'll have a good time.' So I went home to my flat, and I said to Jean, who was sharing the flat with me at the time – and I said to Jean, 'Jean! These 'oman invite me to a ' 'oman only disco' (*loud laughter*)! I was really going on stupid! Now, when I check it out I was so stupid (*continuing laughter*)! Eh?

A Well, it's not something we grew up with.

M Well, this is it. And so I said to Jean, 'Please come, I-beg-you-I-beg-you. Please – 'cause they're saying that I'm stupid, and I don't wanna look stupid in front of them,' right? Because I'd said to them – I left it – that I would phone them up the next day. I told them I'd phone them and tell them whether I was coming or not. So I said to Jean, 'Please come, because I don't know what

I'm going to find in that place' (*laughs*).

A (*laughs*) What did you think you would find?

M (*shriek*) I dunno! Well, I obviously thought there was going to be a whole heap of lesbians that were going to jump on me, yes?

A Like me (*laughs*)!

M Right, so that was in my mind. And then I said 'Ooh, well I'm a bit curious.' But she had something else doing. So I thought, well I would go!

A What, you went on your own?

M Yeh, but I rang up the people, and said 'Meet me outside' (*laughter*)! Because I don't want to walk in there, right? Well, I walked in there and – had a good time! I mean it wasn't like – sort of like – a heavy session, right, but it was OK, I mean I didn't really mind it, but ... I always remember going into the toilet – I went in to the toilet, and I came out, and I was just about to wash my hands and this woman – she only smiled – that's all she did, I swear to God – she just smiled. Me wash my 'ands so fast and through the door (*laughter*)! I mean I feel shame now, when I check it, right? I feel shame now, because obviously it was really stupid.

A Mm.

M But that was my first.

References

Adebimpe, V. (1981) 'Overview: white norms in psychiatric diagnosis of black patients', *American Journal of Psychiatry* 138 (3), pp. 279–85.

Adlam, D., Henriques, J., Rose, N., Salfield, A., Venn, C. and Walkerdine, V. (1977) 'Psychology, ideology and the human subject', *Ideology and Consciousness* 1, pp. 5–56.

Adorno, T. W., Frenkel-Brunswick, E., Levinson, D. J. and Sanford, R. N. (1950) *The Authoritarian Personality*, New York, Harper.

Ake, C. (1979) *Social Science as Imperialism: the Theory of Political Development*, Ibadan, Ibadan University Press.

Alcoff, L. (1988) 'Cultural feminism versus post-structuralism: the identity crisis in feminist theory', *Signs* 13(3), pp. 405–36.

Alexander, Z. and Dewjee, S. (eds) (1984) *Wonderful Adventures of Mary Seacole in Many Lands*, Bristol, Falling Wall Press.

Allier, R. (1929) *The Mind of the Savage*, London, G. Bell & Sons.

Allport, G. W. (1979) *The Nature of Prejudice*, Reading, Massachusetts, Addison-Wesley.

Althusser, L. (1963) *For Marx*, London, Allen Lane.

—— (1971) *Lenin and Philosophy and Other Essays*, London, New Left Books.

Amos, V. and Parmar, P. (1984) 'Challenging Imperial Feminism', *Feminist Review* 17, pp. 3–20.

Appiah, K. (1992) *In My Father's House: Africa in the Philosophy of Culture*, London, Methuen.

Baldwin, J. L. (1986) 'African (black) psychology: issues and synthesis', *Journal of Black Studies* 16, pp. 235–49.

Banks, J. A. and Grambs, J. D. (eds) (1972) *The Black Self-Concept: Implications for Education and Social Science*, New York, McGraw-Hill.

Banks, W. C. (1976) 'White-preference in blacks: a paradigm in search of two phenomena', *Psychological Bulletin* 83(b), pp. 1179–86.

Baratz, S. S. and Baratz, J. C. (1970) 'Early childhood intervention: the social science basis of institutional racism', *Harvard Educational Review* 40, pp. 29–50.

Barnes, E. J. (1980) 'The black community as the source of positive self-concept for black children: a theoretical perspective', in R. L. Jones (ed.) *Black Psychology*, New York, Harper & Row.

Barret, L. (1972) *Rastafarianism in Jamaica*, Kingston, Sangsters.

Barret, M. (1980) *Women's Oppression Today: Problems in Marxist Feminist Analysis*, London, Verso.

Barret, M. and MacIntosh, M. (1982) *The Anti-Social Family*, London, Verso.

—— (1985) 'Ethnocentrism and feminist theory', *Feminist Review* 20, pp. 23–48.

Bastide, R. (1972) *African Civilization in the New World*, New York, Harper Torchbooks.

Becker, H. S. (1970) 'Problems of inference and proof in participant observation', in W. J. Filstead (ed.) *Qualitative Methodology: Firsthand Involvement in the Social World*, Chicago, Rand McNally College Press.

Becker, H. S. and Greer, B. (1970) 'Participant observation and interviewing: a comparison', in W. J. Filstead (ed.) *Qualitative Methodology: Firsthand Involvement in the Social World*, Chicago, Rand McNally College Press.

Beechey, V. and Donald, J. (eds) (1985) *Subjectivity and Social Relations*, Milton Keynes, Open University Press.

Benedict, R. (1942) *Race and Racism*, London, RKP.

Bhabha, H. K. (1983) 'The other question . . .', *Screen* 24(6), pp. 18–36.

—— (1991) *Nation and Narration*, London, Routledge.

Bhaskar, R. (1979) *On the Possibility of Naturalism*, Brighton, Harvester.

Bhavnani, K. (1990) 'What's power got to do with it? Empowerment and social research', in *Deconstructing Social Psychology*, London, Routledge.

Bilby, K. and Steady, F. C. (1981) 'Black women and survival: a maroon case', in F. C. Steady (ed.) *The Black Woman Cross-Culturally*, Cambridge, Mass., Schenkman.

Billig, M. (1976) *Social Psychology and Intergroup Relations*, European Monograghs in Social Psychology No. 9, London, Academic Press.

—— (1982) *Ideology and Social Psychology*, Oxford, Blackwell.

Billingsley, A. (1968) *Black Families in White America*, Englewood Cliffs, NJ, Prentice Hall.

—— (1970) 'Black families in white social science', *Journal of Social Issues* 26, pp. 127–42.

Black Patients and Health Workers Group (1983) 'Psychiatry and the corporate state', *Race and Class* 25(2), pp. 49–64.

Black, J. (1961) *Family Structure in Jamaica*, New York, Glencoe Free Press.

Blackler, F. (ed.) (1983) *Social Psychology and Developing Countries*, Chichester, Wiley.

Block, N. and Dworkin, G. (eds) (1977) *The IQ Controversy*, London, Quartet Books.

Boahen, A. (ed.) (1985) *UNESCO General History of Africa*, vol.7, *Africa Under Colonial Domination*, London, Heinemann.

Boas, F. (1911) *The Mind of Primitive Man*, London.

Boykin, A. W. (1979a) 'Black psychology and the research process: keeping the baby but throwing out the bath water', in A. W. Boykin, A. J. Franklin and J. F. Yates (eds) *Research Directions for Black Psychologists*, New York, Sage.

—— (1979b) 'Work notes on empirical research in black psychology', in A. W. Boykin, A. J. Franklin and J. F. Yates (eds) *Research Directions for Black Psychologists*, New York, Sage.

Boykin, A. W., Franklin, A. J. and Yates, J. F. (1979) *Research Directions for Black Psychologists*, New York, Sage.

Braithwaite, E. K. (1974) 'The African presence in Caribbean literature', in S. W. Mintz (ed.) *Slavery, Colonialism and Racism*, New York, Norton.

Brand, E. S., Reiz, R. A. and Padilla, A. M. (1974) 'Ethnic identification and preference: a review', *Psychological Bulletin* 11, pp. 860–90.

BBWG (Brixton Black Women's Group) (1981) *Speak Out* 4.

—— (1984a) 'Black women organising', *Feminist Review* 17, pp. 83–9.

—— (1984b) Statement (author's files).

Brovermann, I. K., Brovermann, D. M., Clarkson, F. E., Rosencrantz, P. S. and Vogel, S. R. (1970) 'Sex role stereotypes and clinical judgements of mental health', *Journal of Consulting and Clinical Psychology* 34, pp. 1–7.

Bryan, B., Dadzie, S. and Scafe, S. (1985) *The Heart of the Race*, London, Virago.

Bulhan, H. A. (1981) 'Psychological research in Africa: genesis and function', *Race and Class* 23(1), pp. 25–41.

Burman, E. (ed.) (1990) *Feminists and Psychological Practice*, London, Sage.

Burt, C. L. (1909) 'Experimental tests of general intelligence', *British Journal of Psychology* 3, pp. 94–177.

Busby, M. (ed.) (1993) *Daughters of Africa*, London, Vintage.

Butler, J. (1990) *Gender Trouble: Feminism and the Subversion of Identity*, London, Routledge.

Cabral, A. (1980) *Unity and Struggle*, London and Ibadan, PAIGC/Heinemann.

Carasco, B. (1983) 'Participatory research: a means towards collective community action', ISS Seminar, The Hague, July 4–15.

Carby, H. (1982) 'White women listen: black feminism and the boundaries of sisterhood', in *The Empire Strikes Back*, Birmingham, CCCS.

Carothers, J. C. (1953) 'The African mind in health and disease: a study in ethnopsychiatry', *WHO Monograph* Series No. 17, Geneva, WHO.

—— 1954) *The Mind of Mau Mau*, Nairobi.

—— (1972) *The Mind of Man in Africa*, London, Tom Stacey.

Cattell, R. B. (1946) *Description and Measurement of Personality*, London, Harrap.

Centre for Contemporary Cultural Studies (CCCS) (1977) *On Ideology*, Birmingham, CCCS.

—— (1980) *Culture, Media, Language*, Birmingham, CCCS.

—— (1982) *The Empire Strikes Back*, Birmingham, CCCS.

Cesaire, A. (1950) *Discours sur le colonialisme*, Paris, Editions Reclame/Presence Africain.

Chesler, P. (1972) *Women and Madness*, New York, Doubleday.

Chinweizu (1975) *The West and the Rest of Us: White Predators, Black Slavers and the African Elite*, New York, Vintage Books.

Chodorow, N. (1978) *The Reproduction of Mothering*, Berkeley, Calif., University of California Press.

Clark, R. and Clark, M. (1947) 'Racial identification and preferences in Negro children', in T. M. Newcomb and E. L. Hartley (eds) *Readings in Social Psychology*, New York, Rhinehart & Winston.

Cleaver, E. (1965) *Soul on Ice*, New York, McGraw-Hill.

Cobham, R. and Collins, M. (eds) (1987) *Watchers and Seekers: Creative Writing by Black Women in Britain*, London, The Women's Press.

Collard, J. (1937) *Caste and Class in a Southern Town*, New York, Harper.

Collignon, R. (1982) 'Social psychiatry in French-speaking Africa', in O. A. Erinosho and N. W. Bell (eds) *Mental Health in Africa*, Ibadan, Ibadan University Press.

Coopersmith, S. (1967) *The Antecedents of Self-Esteem*, San Francisco, Freeman.

—— (1975) 'Self-concept, race and class', in G. Verma and C. Bagley (eds) *Race and Education across Cultures*, London, Heinemann.

Cronbach, L. (1957) 'The two disciplines of scientific psychology', *American Psychology* 12, pp. 671–84.

Cronon, E. D. (1968) *Black Moses*, Madison, Wis., University of Wisconsin Press.

Cross, W. E. (1971) 'The Negro to black conversion experience: towards a psychology of black liberation', *Black World* 20(9), pp. 13–37.

—— (1974) 'Empirical analysis of the Negro–black conversion experience', paper presented at the 5th Annual Conference on Empirical Research in Black Psychology, University of Michigan, Ann Arbor, Mich.

—— (1980) 'Models of psychological nigrescence', in R. L. Jones (ed.) *Black Psychology*, New York, Harper & Row.

Cross, W. E. (1991) *Shades of Black: Diversity in African-American Identity*, Philadelphia, Pa., Temple University Press.

Curtin, P. (1969) *The Atlantic Slave Trade: a Census*, Madison, Wis., University of Wisconsin Press.

—— (1974) 'The black experience of colonialism and imperialism', in S. W. Mintz (ed.) *Slavery, Colonialism and Racism*, New York, Norton.

Daly, M. (1979) *Gyn/Ecology*, London, The Women's Press.

Davidson, J. P. (1974) 'Empirical development of a measure of black student identity', unpublished Doctoral dissertation, University of Maryland.

Davis, A. Y. (1975) *An Autobiography*, London, Hutchinson.

—— (1982) *Women, Race and Class*, London, The Women's Press.

—— (1990) *Women, Culture and Politics*, London, The Women's Press.

Deutsch, M. (1960) 'Minority group and class status as related to social and personality factors in scholastic achievement', *Monograph No. 2*, Society for Applied Anthropology, Ithaca, NY, Cornell University Press.

Dinnerstein, D. (1978) *The Rocking of the Cradle and the Ruling of the World*, London, Souvenir Press.

Donzelot, M. (1980) *The Policing of Families*, London, Hutchinson.

Dubois, W. E. B. (1903)*The Souls of Black Folk: Essays and Sketches*, Chicago, A. C. McClurg.

—— (1920) *Darkwater*, New York.

Easlea, B. (1981) *Science and Sexual Oppression: Patriarchy's Confrontation with Woman and Nature*, London, Weidenfeld & Nicolson.

Eysenck, H. J. (1971) *Race, Intelligence and Education*, London, Temple Smith.

Fanon, F. (1967a) *Black Skin, White Masks*, New York, Grove Press.

—— (1967b) *The Wretched of the Earth*, Harmondsworth, Penguin Books.

—— (1970) *Towards the African Revolution*, Harmondsworth, Penguin Books.

—— (1980) *A Dying Colonialism*, London, Writers and Readers Co-op.

Filstead, W. J. (ed.) (1970) *Qualitative Methodology: Firsthand Involvement in the Social World*, Chicago, Rand McNally College Press.

Firestone, S. (1971) *The Dialectic of Sex*, London, Cape.

Flax, J. (1990) *Thinking Fragments: Psychoanalysis, Feminism and Postmodernism in the Contemporary West*, Berkeley, Calif., University of California Press.

Foner, N. (1979) *Jamaica Farewell: Jamaican Immigrants in London*, London, RKP.

Foucault, M. (1967) *Madness and Civilisation*, London, Tavistock.

—— (1972) *The Archeoloqy of Knowledge*, London, Tavistock.

—— (1976) *The History of Sexuality*, vol. I, Harmondsworth, Penguin Books.

—— (1979) *Discipline and Punish*, London, Peregrine Books.

Fox Keller, E. (1983) 'Gender and science', in S. Harding and M. Hintikka (eds) *Discovering Reality: Feminist Perspectives on Epistemology, Metaphysics, Methodology and the Philosophy of Science*, Dordrecht, The Netherlands, D. Reidel.

Frazier, E. F. (1939) *The Negro Family in the United States*, Chicago, University of Chicago Press

—— (1949) *The Negro in the United States*, Macmillan.

Freud, S. [1910] (1976) *Two Short Accounts of Psychoanalysis*, Harmondsworth, Penguin Books.

—— (1970) *Beyond the Pleasure Principle*, New York, Liveright.

—— [1970] (1973a) *The Crisis of Psychoanalysis*, Harmondsworth, Penguin Books.

—— (1973b) *New Introductory Lectures on Psychoanalysis*, The Pelican Freud Library, vol. 2, Harmondsworth, Penguin Books.

—— (1976) *The Interpretation Of Dreams*, The Pelican Freud Library, vol. 4, Harmondsworth, Penguin Books.

Freud, S. (1977) *On Sexuality*, The Pelican Freud Library, vol. 7, Harmondsworth, Penguin Books.

Frosh, S. (1987) *The Politics of Psychoanalysis*, Basingstoke, Macmillan.

Fryer, P. (1984) *Staying Power: the History of Black People in Britain*, London, Pluto Press.

—— (1988) *Black People in the British Empire: an Introduction*, London, Pluto Press.

Garvey, A. J. (1967) *The Philosophy and Opinions of Marcus Garvey, or Africa for the Africans*, New York, Frank Cass.

Garvey, M. (1983) *The Marcus Garvey and Universal Negro Improvement Association Papers*, Berkeley, Calif., University of California Press.

Gendzier, I. L. (1973) *Frantz Fanon: a Critical Study*, London, Wildwood House.

Genovese, E. O. (1979) *From Rebellion to Revolution: Afro-American Slave Revolts in the New World*, New York, Vintage Books.

Gerber, S. N. (ed.) (1968) *The Family in the Caribbean*, Proceedings of the First Conference on the Family in the Caribbean, Institute for Caribbean Studies, University of Puerto Rico.

Giddens, A. (1976) *New Rules of Sociological Method: a Positive Critique of Interpretative Sociologies*, New York, Basic Books.

Gilligan, C. (1982) *In a Different Voice*, Cambridge, Mass., Harvard University Press.

Gilroy, P. (1987) *There Ain't No Black in the Union Jack*, London, Hutchinson.

Glaser, B. G. and Strauss, A. L. (1967) *The Discovery of Grounded Theory: Strategies for Qualitative Research*, Chicago, Ill., Aldine.

Glass, R. (1961) *London's Newcomers: the West Indian Migrants*, Cambridge, Mass., Harvard University Press.

Goodison, L. (1986) *I Am Becoming My Mother*, London and Port of Spain, New Beacon Books.

—— (1988) *Heartease*, London and Port of Spain, New Beacon Books.

Gordon, C. (ed.) (1980) *Michel Foucault: Power/Knowledge*, Brighton, Harvester Press.

Gramsci, A. (1971) *Selections From the Prison Notebooks*, London, Lawrence & Wishart.

Grewal, S., Kay, J., Landor, L., Lewis, G. and Parmar, P. (eds) (1988) *Charting the Journey: Writings by Black and Third World Women*, London, Sheba Feminist Publishers.

Griffin, S. (1984) *Woman and Nature: the Roaring Inside Her*, London, The Women's Press.

Grotstein, J. S. (1981) *Splitting and Projective Identification*, Northvale, NJ and London, Jason Aronson.

Guntrip, H. (1968) *Schizoid Phenomena, Object Relations and the Self*, London, Hogarth.

Guthrie, R.V. (1976) *Even the Rat was White*, New York, Harper & Row.

—— (1980) 'The psychology of black Americans: an historical perspective', in R. L. Jones (ed.) *Black Psychology*, New York, Harper & Row.

Gutman, H. G. (1976) *The Black Family in Slavery and Freedom, 1750–1925*, Oxford, Blackwell.

Gutzmore, C. (1993) 'Carnival, the state and the black masses in the United Kingdom', in W. James and C. Harris (eds) *Inside Babylon: the Caribbean Diaspora in Britain*, London and New York, Verso.

Hall, G. S. (1904) *Adolescence*, New York, Appleton.

—— (1905) 'The Negro in Africa and America', *Pedagogical Seminary* 2, pp. 350–68.

Hall, S., Lumley, B. and McLennan, G. (1978) 'Politics and ideology: Gramsci', in *On Ideology*, Birmingham, CCCS.

Hall, W. S., Cross, W. E. and Freedle, R. (1980) 'Stages in development of black awareness: an exploratory investigation', in R. L. Jones (ed.) *Black Psychology*, New York, Harper & Row.

Haraway, D. (1989) *Primate Visions: Gender, Race and Nature*, New York, Routledge.

—— (1990) 'A manifesto for Cyborgs: science, technology and socialist feminism in the 1980s', in L. J. Nicholson (ed.) *Feminism/Postmodernism*, New York, Routledge.

Harding, S. G. (1979) *Social Being*, Oxford, Blackwell.

—— (1986) *The Science Question in Feminism*, Ithaca, NY, Cornell University Press.

—— (ed.) (1987) *Feminism and Methodology*, Bloomington, Ind., Indiana University Press.

—— (1990) 'Feminism, science and the anti-Enlightenment critiques', in L. J. Nicholson (ed.) *Feminism/Postmodernism*, New York, Routledge.

—— (1991) *Whose Science? Whose Knowledges: Thinking from Women's Lives*, Milton Keynes, Open University Press.

Harding, S. G. and Hintikka, M. (eds) (1983) *Discovering Reality: Feminist Perspectives on Epistemology, Metaphysics, Methodology and the Philosophy of Science*, Dordrecht, The Netherlands, D. Reidel.

Harding, S. G. and O'Barr, J. F. (eds) (1987) *Sex and Scientific Enquiry*, Chicago, University of Chicago Press.

Hartsock, N. (1983) 'The feminist standpoint: developing the ground for a specifically feminist historical materialism', in S. Harding and M. Hintikka (eds) *Discovering Reality: Feminist Perspectives on Epistemology, Metaphysics, Methodology and the Philosophy of Science*, Dordrecht, The Netherlands, D. Reidel.

—— (1990) 'Foucault on power: a theory for women?', in L. J. Nicholson (ed.) *Feminism/Postmodernism*, New York, Routledge.

Hayes, W. (1980) 'Radical black behaviourism', in R. L. Jones (ed.) *Black Psychology*, New York, Harper & Row.

Heckman, S. J. (1990) *Gender and Knowledge: Elements of a Postmodern Feminism*, Oxford, Polity Press/Blackwell.

Helms, J. E. (1990) *Black and White Racial Identity: Theory, Research and Practise*, Conn., Greenwood Press.

Henriques, J., Hollway, W., Urwin, C., Venn, C. and Walkerdine, V. (1984) *Changing the Subject: Psychology, Social Regulation and Subjectivity*, London, Methuen.

Hirst, P. Q. (1976) 'Althusser and the Theory of Ideology', *Economy and Society* 4(5), pp. 385–412.

Hirst, P. Q. and Woolley, P. (1982) *Social Relations and Human Attributes*, London, Tavistock.

Hollway, W. (1982) 'Identity and gender difference in adult social relations', unpublished Ph.D. thesis, University of London.

—— (1989) *Subjectivity and Method in Psychology: Gender, Meaning and Science*, London, Sage.

hooks, b. (1982) *Ain't I a Woman: Black Women and Feminism*, London, Pluto Press.

—— (1991) *Yearning: Race, Gender and Cultural Politics*, London, Turnaround.

—— (1992) *Black Looks: Race and Representation*, Between the Lines, Toronto.

Horney, K. (1939) *New Ways in Psychoanalysis*, New York, Norton.

Horowitz, E. (1936) 'The development of attitude toward the Negro', *Archives of Psychology* 104, Columbia University.

Horowitz, E. and Horowitz, R. (1938) 'Development of social attitudes in children', *Sociometry* 1, pp. 301–38.

Horowitz, R. (1939) 'Racial aspects of self-identification in nursery school children', *Journal of Psychology* 4(1), pp. 91–9.

Hountoundji, P. J. (1983) *African Philosophy: Myth and Reality*, London, Hutchinson.

Huizer, G. and Mannheim, B. (eds) (1979) *The Politics of Anthropology: From Colonialism and Sexism Towards a View from Below*, New York, Mouton.

Jackson, G. (1971) *Soledad Brother: The Prison Letters of George Jackson*, New York, Bantam Books.

Jackson, J. J. (1973) 'Black women in a racist society', in C. V. Willie, B. M. Kramer and B. S. Brown (eds) *Racism and Mental Health: Essays*, Pittsburgh, Pa., University of Pittsburgh Press.

Jaggar, A. and Bordo, S. (eds) (1989) *Gender/Body/Knowledge: Feminist Reconstructions of Being and Knowing*, New Brunswick, NJ, Rutgers University Press.

James, W. (1993) 'Migration, racism and identity formation: the Caribbean experience in Britain', in W. James and C. Harris (eds) *Inside Babylon: the Caribbean Diaspora in Britain*, London and New York, Verso.

James, W. and Harris, C. (eds) (1993) *Inside Babylon: the Caribbean Diaspora in Britain*, London and New York, Verso.

Jayawardena, K. (1986) *Feminism and Nationalism in the Third World*, London, Zed Books.

Jensen, A. R. (1969) 'How much can we boost IQ and scholastic achievement?', *Harvard Educational Review* 39, pp. 1–123.

Johnson, B. (1985) *I Think of My Mother: Notes on the Life and Times of Claudia Jones*, London, Karia Press.

Jordan, W. (1977) *White Over Black: American Attitudes Towards the Negro, 1550–1812*, The Norton Library, New York, Norton.

Jung, C. G. (1928) *Contributions to Analytical Psychology*, New York, Harcourt Brace.

—— (1930) 'Your Negroid and Indian behaviour', *Forum* 83, pp. 193–9.

Kagame, A. (1956) *La Philosophie Bantu-Rwandaise de l'etre*, Brussels.

Kamin, L. (1974) *The Science and Politics of IQ*, Potomac, Erlbaum.

—— (1977) 'Heredity, intelligence, politics and psychology', in N. Block and Dworkin (eds) *The IQ Controversy*, London, Quartet Books.

Kardiner, A. and Ovesey, L. (1962) *The Mark of Oppression*, New York, Norton.

Kielstra, N. (1979) 'Is useful action research possible?', in G. Huizer and B. Mannheim (eds) *The Politics of Anthropology: From Colonialism and Sexism Towards a View From Below*, New York, Mouton.

Klein, M. (1963) *Our Adult World and its Roots in Infancy*, London, Heinemann.

—— (1986) *The Selected Melanie Klein*, (ed.) J. Mitchell, Harmondsworth, Penguin Books.

Klein, M. and Rivière, J. (1964) *Love, Hate and Reparation*, New York, Norton.

Klineberg, O. (1956) 'Race and psychology', in L. Kuper (ed.) *Race, Science and Society*, UNESCO, Paris, Allen and Unwin.

Kramer, J. (1972) *Unsettling Europe*, New York, Random House.

Krate, R. Leventhal, G. and Silverstein, B. (1974) 'Self-perceived transformation of Negro-to-black identity', *Psychological Reports* 35, pp. 1071–5.

Kuhn, T. (1962) *The Structure of Scientific Revolutions*, Chicago, University of Chicago Press.

Kuhn, T. (1976) *Changing Jamaica*, London, RKP.

Lacan, J. (1977a) *Ecrits: a Selection*, London, Tavistock.

—— (1977b) *The Four Fundamental Concepts of Psychoanalysis*, Harmondsworth, Penguin Books.

Ladner, J. (ed.) (1973) *The Death of White Sociology*, New York, Vintage Books.

Lanternari, V. (1963) *Religions of the Oppressed: a Study of Modern Messianic Cults*, London, MacGibbon & Kee.

Lather, P. (1988) 'Feminist perspectives on empowering research methodologies', *Women's Studies International Forum* 11(6), pp. 569–81.

Lawrence, E. (1982a) 'In the abundance of water the fool is thirsty: sociology and black pathology', in CCCS, *The Empire Strikes Back*, Birmingham, CCCS.

—— (1982b) 'Just plain common sense: the "roots" of racism', in CCCS, *The Empire Strikes Back*, Birmingham, CCCS.

Leighton *et al.* (1963) *Psychiatric Disorders Amongst the Yoruba*, New York, Cornell University Press.

Lemaire, A. (1977) *Jacques Lacan*, London, RKP.

Lerner, G. (ed.) (1973) *Black Women in White America*, New York, Vintage Books.

Levene, L. W. (1977) *Black Culture and Black Consciousness: Afro-American Folk Thought from Slavery to Freedom*, Oxford, Oxford University Press.

Levi-Strauss, C. (1966) *The Savage Mind*, London, Weidenfeld.

Lewis, G. (1993) 'Black women's employment and the British economy', in W. James and C. Harris (eds) *Inside Babylon: the Caribbean Diaspora in Britain*, London and New York, Verso.

Lorde, A. (1984) *Sister Outsider: Essays and Speeches By Audre Lorde*, Trumansburg, Calif., The Crossing Press.

Malcolm X (1965) *The Autobiography of Malcolm X*, Harmondsworth, Penguin Books.

Mama, A. (1984) 'Black women and the economic crisis', *Feminist Review* 17, pp. 21–36.

—— (1987) 'Race and subjectivity: a study of black women', unpublished Ph.D. thesis, University of London.

—— (1989a) 'Violence against black women: race, gender and state responses', *Feminist Review* 32, pp. 30–48.

—— (1989b) *The Hidden Struggle: Statutory and Voluntary Sector Responses to Violence Against Black Women*, London, London Race and Housing Research Unit/Runnymede Trust.

—— (1991) 'Shedding the masks and tearing the veils', *Gender Analysis and African Social Science Seminar Papers*, Dakar, Senegal, CODESRIA.

—— (1994) 'Heroes and villains: conceptualising colonial and contemporary violence against African women', in C. Mohanty and J. Alexander (eds) *Third World Feminisms*, London, Routledge.

Mama, A., Mars, M. and Stevens, P. (1986) 'Breaking the silence: women's imprisonment', Policy Report, Greater London Council.

Mannoni, O. (1956) *Prospero and Caliban: the Psychology of Colonisation*, London, Clay & Co.

—— (1966) 'Towards the decolonisation of myself', *Race and Class* 7(4), April 1966.

Marcuse, H. (1962) *Eros and Civilization: a Philosophical Enquiry into Freud*, New York, Vintage Books.

—— (1970) *Five Lectures*, Boston, Mass., Beacon Press.

Marks, E. and de Courtivron, I. (eds) (1981) *New French Feminisms: An Anthology*, Brighton, Harvester.

Marx, K. (1974) *Political Writings*, London, New Left Review and The Pelican Marx Library, Harmondsworth, Penguin Books.

Marx, K. (1977) *Selected Writings of Karl Marx*, ed. D. McClelland, Oxford, Oxford University Press.

Marx, K. and Engels, F. (1973) *Manifesto of the Communist Party*, Moscow, Foreign Languages Press.

Mathurin, L. (1975) *The Rebel Woman in the British West Indies*, Institute of Jamaica, Kingston, Jamaica.

Mbiti, J. S. (1969) *African Religions and Philosophies*, London, Heinemann.

Memmi, A. (1965) *The Coloniser and the Colonised*, New York, Orion.

Mies, M. (1979) 'Towards a methodology of women's studies', Institute of Social Studies, Working Paper 77, The Hague, The Netherlands.

Miller, C. L. (1986) *Blank Darkness: Africanist Discourses in French*, Chicago, University of Chicago Press.

Miller, J. B. (1973) *Psychoanalysis and Women*, Harmondsworth, Penguin Books.

—— (1976) *Towards a New Psychology of Women*, Harmondsworth, Penguin Books.

Millet, K. (1981) *Sexual Politics*, London, Virago.

Milliones, J. (1973) 'Construction of the developmental inventory of black consciousness', doctoral dissertation, University of Pittsburgh.

—— (1980) 'Construction of a black consciousness measure: psychotherapeutic implications of psychotherapy', *Theory and Practice* 17(2), pp. 175–82.

Milner, D. (1981) 'Racial prejudice', in J. Turner and H. Giles (eds) *Intergroup Behaviour*, Oxford, Blackwell.

Mintz, S. (ed.) (1974a) *Slavery, Colonialism and Racism*, New York, Norton.

—— (1974b) 'The Caribbean region', in S. W. Mintz (ed.) *Slavery, Colonialism and Racism*, New York, Norton.

—— (1981) 'Economic role and cultural tradition', in F. C. Steady (ed.) *The Black Woman Cross-Culturally*, Cambridge, Mass., Schenkman.

Mitchell, J. (1971) *Woman's Estate*, Harmondsworth, Penguin Books.

—— (1974) *Feminism and Psychoanalysis*, London, Allen Lane.

Mitchell, J. and Rose, J. (eds) (1982) *Feminine Sexuality: Jacques Lacan and the Ecole Freudienne*, London, Macmillan.

Mohanty, C. (1988) 'Under Western eyes: feminist scholarship and colonial discourse', *Feminist Review* 30, pp. 61–88.

Moore, R. (1975) *Racism and Black Resistance in Britain*, London, Pluto Press.

Morrison, T. (1987) *Beloved*, London, Chatto & Windus.

—— (1992) *Jazz*, London, Chatto & Windus.

Moses, Y. T. (1981) 'Female status, the family and male dominance in a West Indian Community', in F. C. Steady (ed.) *The Black Woman Cross-Culturally*, Cambridge, Mass., Schenkman.

Moynihan, D. P. (1965) *The Negro Family: the Case for National Action* (the Moynihan Report), Washington DC, US Department of Labor, Office of Planning and Research.

Mullard, C. (1973) *Black Britain*, London, George Allen & Unwin.

Muse, B. (1968) *The American Negro Revolution: from Non-Violence to Black Power 1963–1967*, Bloomington, Ind., Indiana University Press.

Myrdal, G. (1944) *An American Dilemma*, New York, Harper.

Narayan, U. (1989) 'The project of feminist epistemology: perspectives from a non-western feminist', in A. Jaggar and S. Bordo (eds) *Gender/Body/Knowledge: Feminist Reconstructions of Being and Knowing*, New Brunswick, NJ, Rutgers University Press.

Nettleford, R. M. (1970) *Mirror, Mirror: Identity, Race and Protest in Jamaica*, Kingston, Jamaica, Collins/Sangster.

Nichols, G. (1983) *I is a Long Memoried Woman*, London, Karnak House.
—— (1984) *The Fat Black Woman's Poems*, London, Virago.
Nicholson, L. J. (ed.) (1990) *Feminism/Postmodernism*, New York, Routledge.
Nkrumah, K. (1964) *Consciencism: Philosophy and Ideology for Decolonisation and Development with Particular Reference to the African Revolution*, London, Heinemann.
Nobles, W. W. (1973) 'Psychological research and the black self-concept: a critical review', *Journal of Social Issues* 29(1), pp. 11–29.
—— (1978) 'Towards an empirical and theoretical framework for defining black families', *Journal of Marriage and the Family*, November 1978, pp. 675–88.
—— (1980a) 'African philosophy: foundations for black psychology', in R. L. Jones (ed.) *Black Psychology*, New York, Harper & Row.
—— (1980b) 'Extended self: rethinking the so-called Negro self-concept', in R. L. Jones (ed.) *Black Psychology*, New York, Harper & Row.
Norris, K. (1962) *Jamaica, a Search for Identity*, Milton Keynes, Open University Press.
Oakley, A. (1981) 'Interviewing women: a contradiction in terms?', in H. Roberts (ed.) *Doing Feminist Research*, London, Routledge.
Okpara, E. (1985) *Psychological Strategies for National Development*, Ibadan, Nigerian Psychological Association.
Opitz, M., Oguntoye, K. and Schultz, D. (eds) (1992) *Showing our Colours: Afro-German Women Speak Out*, London, Open Letters.
Otaala, B. (1971) 'Performance of Ugandan African children on some Piagetian conservation tasks: an exploratory investigation', in H. A. El Abd (ed.) *Readings in Educational Psychology in East Africa, Book Two*, Kampala, Makerere University.
Owens, J. (1979) *Dread: the Rastafarians of Jamaica*, London, Heinemann.
Padmore, G. (1956) *Pan-Africanism or Communism?*, London, D. Dobson.
Parham, T. (1989) 'Cycles of psychological nigrescence', *The Counselling Psychologist* 17(2), pp. 187–226.
Patterson, O. (1964) 'Rastafari: cult of outcasts', *New Society* 4(3), pp. 15–17.
—— (1967) *The Sociology of Slavery: an Analysis of the Origins, Development and Structure of Negro Slave Society in Jamaica*, London, MacGibbon.
Patterson, S. (1965) *Dark Strangers*, Harmondsworth, Penguin Books.
Peach, C. (1968) *West Indian Migration: a Social Geography*, Oxford, Oxford University Press.
Perinbram, B. M. (1977) 'The parrot and the phoenix: Fanon's view of the West Indian and the Algerian woman', *Savacou* 13, pp. 7–13.
Pettigrew, T. (1964) *A Profile of the Negro in America*, New York, Van Nostrand.
—— (1973) 'Racism and the mental health of white Americans: a social psychological view', in C. V. Willie, B M. Kramer and B. S. Brown (eds) *Racism and Mental Health: Essays*, Pittsburgh, Pa., University of Pittsburgh Press.
Philips, C. (1991) *Cambridge*, London, Bloomsbury.
Phinney, J. S. (1990) 'Ethnic identity in adolescents and adults: review of research', *Pyschological Bulletin* 108(3), pp. 499–514.
Poster, M. (1984) *Foucault, Marxism and History*, Cambridge, Polity Press.
Potter, J. and Wetherall, M. (1987) *Discourse and Social Psychology*, London, Sage.
Powell, G. J. (1973) 'Self-concept in white and black children', in C. V. Willie, B. M. Kramer and B. S. Brown (eds) *Racism and Mental Health: Essays*, Pittsburgh, Pa., University of Pittsburgh Press.
Price, H. D. (1957) *The Negro and Southern Politics*, New York, New York University Press.

Price, R. (ed.) (1973) *Maroon Societies: Rebel Slave Communities in the Americas*, New York, Anchor Books.

Prince, M. (1831) *The History of Mary Prince, a West Indian Slave, Related By Herself*, London and Edinburgh.

Proshansky, H. and Newton, P. (1974) 'Colour: the nature and meaning of Negro self-identity', in P. Watson (ed.) *Psychology and Race*, Chicago, Aldine.

Prudhomme, C. and Musto, D. F. (1973) 'Historical perspectives on mental health and racism in the United States', in C. V. Willie, B. M. Kramer and B. S. Brown (eds) *Racism and Mental Health: Essays*, Pittsburgh, Pa., University of Pittsburgh Press.

Pugh, R. W. (1972) *Psychology and the Black Experience*, Monterey, Calif., Brooks/Cole.

Rainwater, L. (1967) 'Crucible of identity: the Negro lower-class family', in T. Parsons and K. B. Clark (eds) *The Negro American*, Boston, Beacon Press.

Reason, P. and Rowan, J. (eds) (1981) *Human Inquiry: a Sourcebook of New Paradigm Research*, Chichester, J. Wiley & Sons.

Reich, W. (1970) *The Mass Psychology of Facism*, Harmondsworth, Penguin Books.

Roberts, H. (ed.) (1981) *Doing Feminist Research*, London, Routledge.

Rodgers-Rose, L. A. (ed.) (1980) *The Black Woman*, London, Sage.

Rodney, W. (1969) *The Groundings with My Brothers*, London, Bogle-L'Ouverture.

—— (1974) *How Europe Underdeveloped Africa*, Washington DC, Howard University Press.

Rogers, J. A. (1967) *Sex and Race*, vol. 1, New York, H. M. Rogers.

Rose, N. (1979) 'The psychological complex: mental measurement and social administration', *Ideology and Consciousness* 5, pp. 5–70.

—— (1985) *The Psychological Complex: Psychology, Politics and Society in England 1869–1939*, London, RKP.

—— (1990) *Governing the Soul: the Shaping of the Private Self*, London and New York, Routledge.

Rose, S. (1976) 'Scientific racism and IQ', in H. Rose and S. Rose (eds) *The Political Economy of Science*, Macmillan.

Rose, S. and Rose, R. (1971) 'The myth of neutrality in science', in W. Fuller (ed.) *The Social Impact of Modern Biology*, London, RKP.

Rosenburg, M. (1972) 'Society and the adolescent self-image', in J. A. Banks and J. D. Grambs (eds) *The Black Self-Concept*, MacGraw-Hill.

Rosenthal, R. (1966) *Experimenter Effects in Behavioral Research*, Appleton, NY, Century Crafts.

Runnymede Trust Statistics Group (1982) *Britain's Black Population*, London, Runnymede Trust.

Said, E. (1978) *Orientalism*, London, RKP.

Sartre, J.-P. (1963) *Black Orpheus*, Paris, Presence Africain.

Sayers, J. (1982) *Biological Politics: Feminist and Anti-Feminist Perspectives*, London, Tavistock.

Segal, L. (1990) *Slow Motion: Changing Masculinities, Changing Men*, London, Virago.

Senghor, L. S. (1971) 'The foundations of "Africanite", "Negritude", "Arabite"', Paris, Presence Africain.

Sharpe, S. (1976) *Just Like a Girl: How Girls Learn to be Women*, Harmondsworth, Penguin Books.

Sherwood, R. (1980) *The Psychodynamics of Race*, Brighton, Harvester.

Shyllon, F. (1974) *Black Slaves in Britain*, Oxford, Institute of Race Relations.

Sinha, D. (1977) 'Orientation and attitude of the social psychologist in a developing country: the Indian case', *International Review of Applied Psychology* 26(1), pp. 1–10.

Smith, D. (1981) *Unemployment and Racial Minorities*, London, Policy Studies Institute no. 594.

Smith, M. G. (1965) *The Plural Society in the British West Indies*, Berkeley, Calif., University of California Press.

Spivak, G. C. (1990) *The Post-Colonial Critic: Interviews, Strategies, Dialogues*, ed. Sarah Harasym, New York and London, Routledge.

Squire, C. (1989) *Significant Differences: Feminism and Psychology*, New York and London, Routledge.

Stanley, L. and Wise, S. (1983) *Breaking Out: Feminist Consciousness and Feminist Research*, London, RKP.

Staples, R. (1982) *Black Masculinity: The Black Male's Role in American Society*, San Francisco, The Black Scholar Press.

Steady, F. C. (ed.) (1981) *The Black Woman Cross-Culturally*, Cambridge, Mass., Schenkman.

Stephan, N. (1982) *The Idea of Race in Science: Great Britain 1800–1960*, London, Macmillan.

Stone, M. (1980) *The Education of the Black Child in Britain: the Myth of Multiracial Education*, London, Fontana.

Stott, R. (1989) 'The dark continent: Africa as female body in Haggard's adventure fiction', *Feminist Review* 32, pp. 69–89.

Sutton, C. and Makiesky-Barrow, S. (1981) 'Social inequality and sexual status in Barbados', in F. C. Steady (ed.) *The Black Woman Cross-Culturally*, Cambridge, Mass., Schenkman.

Tajfel, H. (1973) 'The roots of prejudice: cognitive aspects', in P. Watson (ed.) *Psychology and Race*, Chicago, Aldine.

—— (1978) 'The structure of our views about society', in H. Tajfel and C. Fraser (eds) *Introducing Social Psychology*, Harmondsworth, Penguin Books.

—— (ed.) (1982) *Social Identity and Intergroup Relations*, Cambridge, Cambridge University Press.

—— and Fraser, C. (eds) (1978) *Introducing Social Psychology*, Harmondsworth, Penguin Books.

Tempels, P. (1959) *Bantu Philosophy*, Paris, Presence Africain.

Thomas, A. and Sillen, S. (1974) *Racism and Psychiatry*, New York, Bruner-Mazel.

Thomas, C. (1970) 'Different strokes for different folks', *Psychology Today* 4, September 1970.

Tomlinson, T. M. (1970) 'Determinants of black politics: riots and the growth of militancy', *Psychiatry* 33.

Towa, M. (1971) *L'Idée d'une Philosophie Negro-Africain*, Yaounde, Editions Cle.

Turner, T. C. and Giles, H. (eds) (1981) *Intergroup Behaviour*, Oxford, Blackwell.

Vaughan, M. (1991) *Curing Their Ills: Colonial Power and African Illness*, Cambridge, Polity Press.

Venn, C. (1984) 'The subject of psychology', in J. Henriques, W. Hollway, C. Urwin, C. Venn and V. Walkerdine, *Changing the Subject: Psychology, Social Regulation and Subjectivity*, London, Methuen.

Verma, G. K. and Bagley, C. (eds) (1979) *Race, Education and Identity*, London, Macmillan.

Walden, R. and Walkerdine, V. (1981) 'Girls and mathematics: the early years', *Bedford Way Papers* 8, London, Heinemann.

Walkerdine, V. (1981) 'Sex, power and pedagogy', *Screen Education* 38, pp. 14–21.

Walkerdine, V. and Lucey, H. (1989) *Democracy in the Kitchen: Regulating Mothers and Socialising Daughters*, London, Virago.

Wallace, M. (1978) *Black Macho and the Myth of the Superwoman*, London, Calder.

Walvin, J. (1973) *Black and White: the Negro in English Society 1555–1945*, Harmondsworth, Penguin Books.

Watson, P. (ed.) (1973) *Psychology and Race*, Chicago, Aldine.

Weedon, C. (1987) *Feminist Practice and Poststructuralist Theory*, Oxford, Blackwell.

White, J. L. *et al.* (1980) 'Black psychology: the Afro-American tradition as a unifying force for traditional psychology', in R. L. Jones (ed.) *Black Psychology*, New York, Harper & Row.

Wilcox, R. C. (ed.) (1971) *The Psychological Consequences of Being Black American: a Collection of Research by Black Psychologists*, New York, J. Wiley & Sons.

Wilkinson, S. (ed.) (1986) *Feminist Social Psychology*, Milton Keynes, Open University Press.

Williams, C. (1988) 'Gal ... you come from foreign', in S. Grewal, J. Kay, L. Landor, G. Lewis and P. Parmar (eds) *Charting the Journey: Writings by Black and Third World Women*, London, Sheba Feminist Publishers.

—— (1993) 'We are a natural part of many different struggles: black women organizing', in W. James and C. Harris (eds) *Inside Babylon: the Caribbean Diaspora in Britain*, London and New York, Verso.

Williams, E. (1964) *Capitalism and Slavery*, London, Deutsch.

Willie, C. V., Kramer, B. M. and Brown, B. S. (eds) (1973) *Racism and Mental Health: Essays*, Pittsburgh, Pa., University of Pittsburgh Press.

Wilson, A. N. (1978) *The Developmental Psychology of the Black Child*, New York, Africana Research Publications.

Wiredu, K. (1980) *Philosophy and an African Culture*, London, Cambridge University Press.

Wober, M. (1975) *Psychology in Africa*, London, International African Institute.

Yoloye, E. A. (1971) 'The effect of schooling on the performance of bilingual students in tests of intelligence', in *Research in Education* 5, pp. 25–34.

Index